BOOKS BY *Lawrence Wright*

Remembering Satan

Saints and Sinners

In the New World

City Children, Country Summer

Lawrence Wright

SAINTS AND SINNERS

Lawrence Wright is the author of *City Children, Country Summer; In the New World;* and *Remembering Satan.* His articles have appeared in *Texas Monthly, Rolling Stone,* and *The New York Times Magazine.* He is a staff writer for *The New Yorker* and currently lives in Austin, Texas, with his wife and two children.

SAINTS & SINNERS

Walker Railey • Jimmy Swaggart

Madalyn Murray O'Hair • Anton LaVey

Will Campbell • Matthew Fox

Lawrence Wright

Vintage Books

A Division of Random House, Inc.

New York

Portions of this work were originally published in *Texas Monthly* and
Rolling Stone.

Grateful acknowledgment is made to the following for
permission to reprint previously published material:
Warner Bros. Publications Inc.: Excerpt from "Mississippi Magic"
by Will Campbell. Copyright © 1969 by EMI U Catalog Inc.
All rights reserved. Made in USA. Used by permission of
Warner Bros. Publications Inc., Miami, FL 33014.

PolyGram Music Publishing Group: Excerpt from "Storms Never Last"
by Jessi Colter. Copyright © 1975 by Songs PolyGram
International, Inc. Excerpt from "Rednecks, White Socks and
Blue Ribbon Beer" by Chuck Neese, Bob McDill and
Wayland Holyfield. Copyright © 1973 by PolyGram
International Publishing, Inc. and Songs of PolyGram
International, Inc. Used by permission.
All rights reserved.

The Library of Congress has cataloged the Knopf edition as follows:
Wright, Lawrence.
Saints and sinners : Walker Railey, Jimmy Swaggert, Madalyn Murray
O'Hair, Anton LaVey, Will Campbell, and Matthew Fox / by Lawrence
Wright.—1st ed.
p. cm.
Includes bibliographical references.
ISBN 0-394-57924-0
1. Religious biography—United States. 2. United States—Religion—
1960– I. Title.
BL72.W75 1993
291'.092'273—dc20
[B] 92-54382
CIP
Vintage ISBN: 978-0-679-76163-1

146119709

For Roberta

My Partner in Life and Spirit

Contents

Acknowledgments

It's a pleasure to acknowledge the many debts I have incurred while writing this book. Gregory Curtis, the editor of *Texas Monthly*, and Jann S. Wenner, the editor of *Rolling Stone*, have been steady supporters over the years, and I thank them for giving me the opportunity to write about the subjects included in this work. I also wish to pay particular homage to Robert Vare and Eric Etheridge, two fine editors whose taste and sensitivity inform much of this book.

I've been fortunate to have the assistance of friends and colleagues who have examined these six stories with a caring and critical eye. Thanks to Jan Jarboe, William Martin, Jan McInroy, Betty Sue Flowers, and Lonnie Kliever, each of whom graciously contributed their own invaluable intelligence. In a special category, as usual, is my friend Stephen Harrigan, whose critical judgment is reflected on nearly every page.

I also wish to thank the often unrecognized fact checkers who devote themselves to the inglorious task of making a writer's words accurate. I salute Pat Booker, Valerie Wright, David Moorman, Amy Kaplan, and Tamar Lehrich.

While I was writing this book, I was a beneficiary of a grant from the National Endowment for the Arts. In this season of controversy surrounding federal support of the arts I want to say that this book, as well as my career as a writer, has been helped immensely by the financial assistance the grant provided. I hope other artists will continue to receive the support and recognition I enjoyed.

Finally, I thank my agent, Wendy Weil, and the editor of this book, Ann Close, for their encouragement, their insight, and their friendship.

Preface:
The Masks of Faith

Journalists have never known exactly what to do with religion. On the ladder of professional esteem, religious writing ranks between recipes and obituaries. We who write about what people do have a more difficult time with what they think or believe.

And yet spiritual matters are far more influential in people's lives than, for instance, politics, the mainstay of the journalist's craft. This is true even in this supposedly secular age in which we live. Yes, one can look at the evidence of the declining membership of traditional churches, at the loss of any sense of the sacred in public life, and at the corruption of television evangelists who accept MasterCard and Visa and holler the name of Jesus as their 800 numbers roll across the screen. It is easy to see the decay of the religious ideal in America.

That does not mean that religion is dead. We are—as usual in this country—in the middle of religious tumult. The growth of modern fundamentalism is one of the most significant social movements of American history, comparable to the "Great Awakenings" of our past. The continuing appearance of cults of various kinds testifies to the fact that the American hothouse still seems to be a suitable climate for the rise of freelance prophets and spiritual experimenters. Compared with the moribund, but state-supported, denominations of Europe, the religious life of the United States is continually refreshed by the schisms and improvisations of one new sect after another. Some are overnight fads; others will take hold and become the established congregations of the future. It is confounding to realize that the success of one belief over another has little to do with the apparent craziness of the doctrine.

The Gallup polls, which have been measuring religious trends and church attendance for more than half a century, show a remarkable stability over time. In 1991, 42 percent of Americans regularly attended church, which is almost exactly the same figure as the number of church-goers in the thirties (41 percent in 1939). More than half of all Americans said they believed in the existence of the Devil (up significantly from 39 percent in 1978). On Easter, 1991, 85 percent of Roman Catholics and 72 percent of Protestants attended services. Nine out of ten Americans prayed every week and said that they have never doubted the existence of God; eight out of ten said they believed in miracles and expected to answer for their sins on Judgment Day.

Compare those figures to the situation in Europe, where in France, for instance, about 12 percent of the population attends church, and in England, as a recent poll in the London *Sunday Express* discovered, 34 percent of Britons do not even know why Easter is celebrated. In the Western world, religion is an especially American phenomenon. And yet when a journalist unfolds his map of the spiritual terrain of America, he sees a patchwork of mysticism, hypocrisy, hucksterism, and violence, with an occasional dash of sexual perversity. Perhaps this is because religion tends to make the news only when it crosses into some other recognizable category where the journalist feels more at home. Sex crimes of clergy against children accounted for more than a hundred indictments in 1990 alone. A report to the 1991 Presbyterian General Assembly suggested that up to 23 percent of the Christian clergy nationwide has engaged in sexual behavior with parishioners, clients, or employees. My own files are stuffed with stories of blackmailed bishops, ritual murders, church-led real estate scams, apparitions of Jesus or the Virgin Mary, and feverish expressions of the millennium. Certainly in the last few years religious scandals have been a hallmark of our age—but they have been hallmarks of many ages in America. The religious scholar Lonnie Kliever speaks of religion as being the frontier between human creativity and lunacy. The truth of that statement is as apparent in our country as anywhere else in the world.

Thus the tendency of journalists to look upon religion as a marketplace of the weird and the absurd. I confess it is not easy to clear my head of this prejudice. I suppose that early on in my life I felt a need to choose between my allegiance to the worldview of reason, knowledge, and experience, on the one hand, and that of faith, on the other. The two perspectives seemed to cancel each other out. If one looks at life through the prism of faith, as I once did, then one is constantly having to reprogram the messages of reason, knowledge, and experience in order to make them conform to what one believes. And yet the person who commits himself to realism lives in a smaller dimension than someone whose life is animated by strong religious belief.

Many times in my career I have witnessed the transforming power of faith. I have seen it in prisons and ghettos as well as in boardrooms and chambers of power. I have often found myself admiring people who held views I strongly disagreed with—for instance, the Black Muslims, who believe that I am a devil because of my race but who have generated the moral power to bring order and dignity to prison life. Where addiction rules or where social values have collapsed, it is usually only those rare persons of faith who can survive and sometimes even transform their seemingly hopeless environments; I am thinking in particular about a foster mother I met once in the South Bronx, a Jehovah's Witness, who managed to overcome her own drug addiction and to save a number of abandoned or orphaned children. My wife and I spent a summer in Pennsylvania writing about Amish and Mennonite dairy farmers, and we were powerfully affected by the beauty of their simple ways, even though the intellectual confinement of that existence was as oppressive, in its way, as life in a totalitarian society. When I covered the waning days of the civil rights movement, I was moved again and again by stories of people whose faith in God led them to place their own lives in jeopardy. I have seen how faith enlarges a person, allowing him to transcend his circumstances and his own flawed nature. With all the advances of technology and psychology, there are some transformations that only faith can accomplish. I look upon such believers with a mixture of envy and pity. They live in a world that has meaning, which is comforting even if that meaning is delusory.

I sought to better understand why people believe what they believe. It was a question that only vaguely interested me a few years ago. I had the idea that one either was born into faith or else stumbled into it at a vulnerable moment, and that one might as well worship one thing as another. It didn't occur to me that the content of belief mattered, or that a person's faith might be a complex metaphor for the life he lived. Nor did it seem vitally important in my own life.

For most of that life, I realized, I had leaned on my father's faith. He was devout and comfortable with his beliefs, and I must have supposed that one day I would be as well—I was like him in so many other ways. He had been a religious leader on a small scale, as a Sunday school teacher;

but for me, of course, he was Belief itself, the personification of Christianity. At some point during my turning away from the church and the traditions I had grown up with, I had made a mental date with my father's religion. It was hard to imagine myself as a grown man without some firm conviction about the purpose of existence. I had expected that by the time I had children myself, I would have worked out my quarrels with religion and settled into some secure understanding about my place in the plan, and that I would be able to pass that sense of security—if not my actual beliefs—along to my children, as my father had done for me. But this expected rendezvous with faith never happened. Gradually I began to wonder if this was a failing on my part—or was it integrity? —that held me apart from religion. In any case, I still found some solace, even as a grown man, that my father was a believer.

Then, a few years ago, my father discovered that he had cancer. He faced it bravely, as I expected. The morning of his operation, after he had been given his injection and his hold on consciousness was beginning to fade, perhaps forever, he lay in his hospital bed and stared out at the whitish-blue winter sky. "I believe in God," he said thickly. "I believe within the limits of all rational understanding. But at the end it's not enough." His eyelids bobbed, and in a moment the orderly came and wheeled him away. Of course, my thoughts were on his operation and whether he would recover. I pushed aside those doubts that he had expressed. I had wanted then to reassure him, as he would have done for me, but I had only sat there feeling inadequate and awfully afraid. It was later, after he recovered and I could allow myself to think of something other than the possibility of his death, that I realized how angry I was at him, how betrayed I felt at his being nothing but a poor doubter like myself. If I couldn't rely on his faith any longer, then where could I turn?

He had done me a favor, I suppose, by showing me his doubt. But now I had the task of finding my own creed, even if that was atheism or some still unsettled form of agnosticism. I thought that by writing about people with various kinds of beliefs, I might find something worth believing, some anchor to secure the spiritual restlessness that was my constant shadow. Perhaps only a journalist, who lives so much of his life vicariously, would think this way. I imagined that I could test the value of a person's belief by seeing it manifested in his or her life. After all, this was what had put me off religion in the first place, seeing people believe one way and live another. Religion didn't have much value, in my opinion, unless it was transformative; otherwise it was lip service or a pointless guilt trip.

As a genre, then, this book presents itself as a travel adventure, in which the protagonist enters foreign territory in order to discover something valuable about himself; the only distinction here is that the traveler is moving through regions of belief rather than culture. For me, however, the experience of writing this book has called into question the whole notion of a "spiritual journey," as it is popularly called. If there is such a journey, then it is taken on rails. Imagine religious belief as a subway system in which there are many possible stops. Aboveground, people go about their business, perhaps unaware of the intricate commotion going on in the world below their feet. But should a person be drawn into this world, he will probably enter through a station in his neighborhood. He discovers that he is on a "line." Let us say it is my line—that is, mainline Protestant, which runs from fundamentalism to atheism with many intervening stops. If he looks at a map of the system, he will see the Jewish line, the Catholic, the Moslem, to name a few of the multiple possibilities, but they all pass through neighborhoods he is unlikely to visit except out of curiosity. As in other intricate systems, however, the lines intersect and parallel each other in various places. For instance, a number of different lines converge at the New Age station (formerly transcendentalism). The point of this analogy is that given who we are, we are constrained, if not actually destined, to arrive at the conclusions we eventually reach. That's not to say that a person cannot transfer from one faith to another, by taking another train, or that free will and intellectual striving and the lessons of experience and sudden mystical encounters have no effect. They do. But in the universe of possible beliefs, what one chooses to believe (or disbelieve) reflects the life one has led.

Not long after I began this quest I had dinner with the controversial British scientist Rupert Sheldrake, who is the originator of the intriguing theory of morphogenic fields, which supposes that there is a sort of species memory for all organic creation. Like me, Sheldrake is an ex-Methodist who had wandered away from his childhood faith to see if he could find some more acceptable system of belief. Unlike me, Sheldrake had found it. Over our meal we chatted about this proposed book, in which I would attach myself to various believers in order to try on their faiths and see what, if anything, fit me. Sheldrake's comment, ruthlessly appropriate, was "What a very Methodist thing to do."

My object then was to be able to reconcile the two worldviews I mentioned earlier. I might be willing to accept the possibility of faith in my life, but not at the expense of reason, knowledge, and experience. I would look at the phenomenon of belief with the same cold eye I would bring to any other story. Was there any faith that could survive such scrutiny? Because the people profiled in this book are not merely believers but religious leaders, they leave themselves open to having someone like me explore their lives to see how their faith operates on a day-to-day level. As a practical matter, this made them more interesting to me and therefore easier to write about. Looking past their homilies to see whether the values they preach have any relevance to the lives they lead was a way of bringing them down to earth.

I have to admit that part of what was powering this quest was my need to strip away masks and find the hidden truth. Of course, masks have always been a feature of religion. In primitive societies, which are useful mirrors of our own, masks are frequently associated with shamans and religious ceremonies. When a Zuni puts on a mask of a kachina spirit, he is thought to be transformed into the kachina itself. Similarly, among the Onondaga tribe of the Iroquois, there was a False Face Society, a shamanistic group that put on masks in order to acquire the power of the deities the masks were supposed to represent. They used these masks in their healing ceremonies. Each of the people whose lives are described in this book is a mask-wearer; indeed, one of the fascinating motifs I discovered is how much artifice goes into constructing the public personas of our religious leaders. The more recognizable the mask is to our subconscious—that is, the purer the archetype—the more power the mask-wearer will have. *Which* mask they choose to hold up is a result of the life they have led.

Walker Railey, the first of those religious leaders profiled in this book, in 1986 wrote an insightful article on Halloween trick-or-treaters in his church newspaper:

> In just a few short years, those same little people will grow up into big people. They will so mature in age and mind that they will no longer wear costumes on Halloween. Unfortunately, though, many of them will still be wearing masks. Instead of plastic masks that hide the face, they will wear emotional masks that hide the heart. They will learn to smile in public, even when they truly want to cry. They will develop a way of looking interested, even though they are bored to death. . . . Some folks are so good at wearing masks they never reveal their true identities to anyone—not their boss, not their spouse, not their children, not even themselves.

That certainly turned out to be an accurate description of Railey, but it also describes the situation of many people who try to hide human frailty behind the mask of holiness and spiritual certitude. Their faith is a portrayal of the life they would lead if they were something other than the all-too-human people they actually are.

Finally, a word about the title. When I began this book, the religious categories of saints and sinners seemed like an obvious way of looking at these figures on their own terms. I had become interested in the apparent paradox of people—like Walker Railey and Jimmy Swaggart—who struggled to be good but became victims of their own drive for perfection. Considering their fates, one could argue that the desire to be saintly is perilous, perhaps evil, perhaps even a form of mental illness. They tried to purge what they called the demons inside them; they tried to purify themselves and become as hallowed and sanctified as the masks they wore. Instead, their demons, their repressed needs, their disowned selves, whatever one might call them, took control. My own view is that these internal rebellions demonstrate the resistance of the human soul to being simplified and pigeonholed. I know that, by talking about the soul, I'm falling into the use of religious language, but that is the language we are speaking when we use such terms as good and evil, saints and sinners. The soul is the stage upon which this pageant is played out. In the real world, as we call the existential day-to-day, these words have no meaning. But in the masquerade of religious belief, words are symbols and symbols are power. One doesn't have to believe in the soul to acknowledge the meaningfulness of the drama.

I saw as well in the lives of Madalyn O'Hair and Anton LaVey a certain purity that one might otherwise ascribe to religious ascetics. Indeed, in spiritual terms they are heroes of their type, because they have chosen to embody the two most frightening manifestations of the religious urge, doubt and evil. They live in the chambers of despair. Those who condemn them should also consider the moral courage required to explore the dark, uncertain territories of the human spirit that we name atheism and Satanism. To my way of thinking, there is a certain saintliness involved in carrying so much hatred directed at them from people who are unwilling to accept these archetypal aspects of themselves. It is exactly this bewildering, perverse, and paradoxical mixture of the saint in the sinner and the sinner in the saint that I find so compelling and revelatory of the mysteriousness of the human predicament.

One can object that I have not included a *real* saint in this collection, someone like Mother Teresa (who, in fact, rejected my request to write about her). I am willing to believe that such a creature exists, although the testimony of saints is almost always obsessive on the subject of their own fallen natures. Also, as a journalist once again, I confess that perfection doesn't interest me. If I found a transcended personality who had achieved inner peace, I'm sure I wouldn't know what to do with him or her. Will Campbell and Matthew Fox come closer to our idea of saintly personalities, but neither will ever be canonized. That's because each has a hold on his humanity, what we might also call his flawed and sinful nature. What is truly saintly about them is the extent to which they resist the call to sainthood. Behind their masks, they remain themselves.

I discovered that each of these persons' beliefs was a metaphor for his or her life. Even Madalyn O'Hair, who claims to be free of religion, is waging a vendetta against God, and in that sense her life is a spiritual struggle as well as a symbolic continuation of her fight against her father. Look also at Railey's attempt to make the church his substitute family; at Swaggart's flight into perversion to escape his longing for his mother; at LaVey's embrace of the stigmatized, lonely child he had been; at Campbell's loathing for all institutions; at Fox's war with his father's Augustinian beliefs: it is easy to see the Oedipal drama that is being played out in these leaders' lives. For each of them, the individual mask of belief is a mythic way of expressing their emotional needs and their craving for love and acceptance.

It is no wonder that I would not find among these leaders a system of belief that I could accept. I have lived a different life. On the way to this discovery, however, I went on my own spiritual journey. My object was not just to see the sights but to change—to enlarge—myself. This is the chronicle of my search for faith.

SAINTS & SINNERS

Walker Railey's Demon

WIFE OF ANTI-RACIST CLERIC IS ATTACKED, I read in the *New York Times* as I flew home from Los Angeles a few days after Easter. Margaret Railey, the thirty-eight-year-old wife of the Reverend Walker L. Railey of Dallas, was beaten, choked, and left for dead on the floor of their garage. Her husband found her unconscious body when he returned from studying at the library shortly after midnight on April 22, 1987. The police had no leads in the case. "Dr. Railey, who is white, has been an outspoken critic of racial prejudice in this city," said the *Times.* According to the executive minister in Railey's church, Gordon D. Casad, Railey had received a series of threatening letters in the preceding weeks and had preached the Easter sermon wearing a bulletproof vest.

It took a moment for the realization to sink in that this bizarre episode had taken place in my very own church, First United Methodist on the corner of Ross and Harwood in downtown Dallas. This was the church I grew up in and angrily ran away from and retreated to on several guilty occasions. What I always had hated about my church was its instinctive fear of confronting society. But here was a minister who had spoken out against racial injustices and inequality in a city where such things are rarely said aloud. Here was a man threatened with death in that same sanctuary. And here was a man whose wife was strangled into what the doctors called a persistent vegetative state, for no other obvious reason than that someone wanted to punish Walker Railey for preaching love, tolerance, and truth.

Was this Dallas? I asked myself. Dallas is profoundly racist, but it is also subtle and complex. The open savagery of the Railey tragedy seemed oddly wrong in a city that cares little about justice but is deeply preoccupied with appearances. From the very beginning of the Railey story there was this vague but haunting discordance.

And yet I was willing to believe that perhaps Dallas had returned to the racial violence of the fifties. Apparently Dallas worried about that too, and for the next week the city was on its knees in prayer services and editorial self-reproach. It was a moment when people of various faiths and races stopped to pray for Walker and Peggy Railey and their two young children, Ryan and Megan. "Fight on, Railey family," cried the Reverend Daryll Coleman of the Kirkwood CME Temple Church in a rare gathering of the races at Thanks-Giving Square. "Fight on, soldiers of righteousness and truth. Thank God for today." The Baptists issued a statement that "the fact that a minister's clear stand against racial injustice and bigotry would jeopardize his life is an indicting commentary on our society." Rabbi Sheldon Zimmerman of Temple Emanu-El concluded that the Railey family had been "singled out because of his almost prophetic stance in regard to injustice in any form."

As Peggy lay in intensive care, hundreds of visitors came day after day to Presbyterian Hospital to pay homage to a woman few people knew well. The traffic was so great that volunteers from the church came to assist. Peggy's condition, at first critical, settled into an awful stasis. She was neither dead nor alive—it was as if she were waiting for some momentous resolution before she could either die or be released back into life. And as for her husband, his tragedy seemed unbearable. He had been "the shining star of Methodism," as some called him, a comet of belief and commitment in a dark season of spiritual despair. He had awakened the slumbering old church and infused it with his electric vitality. Now he was crushed by some unknown force too vast and heartless to be fended off by faith alone.

On the Sunday after the attack, the congregation of First Church returned to their sanctuary in a state of shock. There was an obvious show of security police, which added to the air of continuing menace. From the pulpit, Dr. Casad read a message from Railey, who remained in the hospital to be near his wife. "I do not know why senseless violence continues to pervade society, nor do I understand why the events of this past week took place," Railey's message said. "You have proven to me and all of Dallas that our church is a family. . . . I have been reminded once again that the breath of life is fragile but the fabric of life is eternal."

As gruesome as this episode was, I felt hope and pride in a city that was painfully examining itself—even though I had long since fled Dallas in dismay—and in a church that was nobly living its doctrine. It seemed to me that the attack on Peggy Railey might become another critical adjustment in the city's consciousness, just as the Kennedy assassination had been. Perhaps it was the special destiny of the citizens of Dallas to grow through tragedy and to know, as few others do, their own capacity for evil.

These were my thoughts until nine days after the attack, when Railey locked himself in his hospital suite and ingested three bottles of tranquilizers and antidepressants. He left a lengthy suicide note, explaining that there was a "demon" inside his soul and that he was tired of trying to be good. He called himself "the lowest of the low." By the time police broke down the door the following morning, Railey, too, had fallen into a coma.

◆

Although First Church is not even the largest Methodist church in Dallas, it has the reputation of being the mother church of Methodism. Eight men who stood in the pulpit before Railey went on to become bishops; indeed, Railey's own election to the episcopacy was regarded as a certainty, perhaps as early as 1988, when he would have become one of the youngest bishops in the history of Methodism. Even his appointment as senior pastor of First Church in 1980 at the age of thirty-three was an "astonishment," according to the eminent Methodist theologian and historian Albert Outler. "He leapfrogged over two dozen of his elders who thought they were his equal."

For ten years First Church had been losing members, as had many downtown churches all across the country, as had Methodism itself. But from the day of his very first sermon, when Railey stood in the pulpit and dramatically blew into the microphone, he seemed to breathe new life into the moribund church. Membership quickly increased, as did the budget, which more than doubled over the seven years of Railey's leadership. He was a vigorous, outspoken advocate of certain social issues endorsed by the yuppie element who had begun to make up the new, younger core of the congregation. He opposed capital punishment, supported equal rights for women and minorities, declared his ambivalence on the subject of abortion, and defended the rights of homosexuals. He preached an "open letter to President Reagan" calling for increased efforts at arms control. All of these stands, in the context of Dallas, seemed rather brave, although it is also true that other Methodist ministers in town had preached similar sermons, and Railey's right-thinking social liberalism was pretty much what Methodism had come to. As for the antiracism that was the supposed motive for the attack on his family, that reputation was based almost entirely on a single innocuous sermon Railey delivered on Martin Luther King's birthday, in which he made the statement that "there is more racial tension and polarization in Dallas, Texas, than many fine, upstanding citizens are willing to admit." One could scarcely call him a crusader.

Personal behavior—that is to say, morality and ethics—seldom rated a mention in Railey's church. He often inveighed against the disparity of great wealth and great deprivation that characterized the city, but he himself had grown comfortable with his $100,000 annual salary, his luxurious Lake Highlands home, and the many perks, favors, loans, and subsidies that come from being a high-steeple preacher in a wealthy Protestant congregation. For a young man who had grown up in the little western Kentucky farming community of Owensboro, the son of a sheet-metal worker, it had been quite a climb. "To a certain extent, he was an existential man," observed Dallas city councilman Craig Holcomb, who was one of those drawn to Railey's ministry. "He worked very hard and created who Walker Railey was going to be."

Because of the importance of First Church within the denomination, many of the congregation were ordained ministers who were either retired or working in other areas of the ministry. Among this group Railey was a highly divisive figure. Indeed, they were still wrangling over the Railey legacy when I returned to First Church to survey the chaos. "I've heard Harry Emerson Fosdick, Ralph Sockman, Ernest Fremont Tittle, and Norman Vincent Peale," a Railey confidant and former pastor told me, "and I still feel that Walker Railey was the greatest pulpiteer I ever heard." The Reverend Howard Grimes, who taught Christian education at Southern Methodist University's Perkins Theological Seminary for thirty-three years, claimed that Railey was "one of the greatest, if not the greatest, Protestant preachers in the latter half of the twentieth century. He had become God for a lot of people, and maybe me." The younger preachers in the congregation—Railey's contemporaries—tended to look at him with less awe and more than a little resentment. "His popularity at First Church was such for many people that they lost all sense that he had any imperfection," the Reverend Spurgeon Dunnam III told me bitterly. He and Railey had jostled for power in the corporation that is buried inside the denomination. Dunnam, the editor of the *United Methodist Reporter*, was himself sometimes mentioned as a potential bishop, and he recognized in Railey a tireless competitor: "The politics of the church are so subtle that only the most astute and discerning could understand what was going on. Walker was very analytical and perceptive; he took to that process very early. It became clear to me his primary agenda was to be elected to the episcopacy as soon as possible. He campaigned for it by accepting speaking engagements here, there, and everywhere. He seemed incapable of saying no to serving additional outside responsibilities. His ambition was so completely unchecked."

For four decades the most prominent churchman in town was the white-haired, white-suited eminence W. A. Criswell. His church, First Baptist, is a kind of Vatican inside downtown Dallas, occupying block after block of precious real estate. The pews of First Baptist are filled with the city's power brokers and by the conservative Southern Baptist hierarchy. Evangelist Billy Graham has been a longtime member of this congregation. When presidents came to town, they would call on Criswell. And of course, whenever there was news that required a comment from a religious authority, the press turned to the elder statesman at First Baptist.

Within a few years after Railey came to town, however, he began to rival even Criswell's great eminence. Railey became president of the Dallas Council of Churches. He served on the national board of United Methodist Global Ministries. In the press, Railey became a liberal counterweight to Criswell's fundamentalist, socially conservative views. Railey's greatest honor was being selected to preach the "Protestant Hour" sermons on a nationwide Christian radio network. Already his name was widely mentioned among Methodists who marked this gracious young pastor not just for the bishop's chair but for something more—for greatness, in whatever form that might assume.

Railey's professional model was that titan of the Protestant pulpit Harry Emerson Fosdick, the first of the "modernist" preachers, who railed against fundamentalism and pioneered the practice of pastoral counseling. John D. Rockefeller, Jr., built the magnificent Riverside Church in New York near Columbia University so that Fosdick could have a national forum for his progressive views. With a Bible in one hand and a newspaper in the other, Fosdick brought the weight of the church to bear upon the affairs of the world. For twenty years his voice was a familiar sound to Americans everywhere through his popular radio program, "National Vespers." Fosdick's gospel was broad and urbane and forgiving. Even a little backwoods community such as Owensboro, Kentucky, locked as it was in spiritual isolation, could hear a different message than the hard-shell fundamentalism of the country church. For countless Americans, Fosdick was a liberating force who bridged the secular world and the divine with his intelligence, wit, and moral passion.

For the past seven years, Railey had been working on a comprehensive Fosdick biography. Each summer First Church paid for his research trips to New York and Scotland. Naturally, many of Fosdick's preaching tricks showed up in Railey's own sermons—such as his habit of saying "Some-one out there needs to hear this" or "I know there's someone here today whose life is hanging by a thread." His staff called them "Walkerisms" because they added to the impression people often had that he was speak-ing directly to them. In fact these locutions were straight out of Fosdick. Later, some of the more knowing preachers in the congregation would wonder if Railey's real ambition was to succeed William Sloane Coffin, who was about to step down from the Riverside pulpit. That seemed too great a step for any Dallas preacher, however talented; but then no one had ever taken a full measure of Railey's ambition.

The extraordinary pressures of his job already were evident in Railey's personality. Several times he told Gordon Casad that the congregation at First Church could never forgive even a single bad sermon, so he slaved over his lessons, polished his delivery, choreographed his gestures, until each one was a characteristic Railey gem. Once, in the receiving line after the eleven o'clock service, an admiring seminary student asked what it took to preach a sermon like the one he had just heard, and Railey answered candidly, "About thirty-five hours."

In a church with a congregation of nearly six thousand members and a $2 million budget, a pastor spends a considerable amount of time visiting hospitals, preaching at funerals, counseling troubled youngsters, running administrative meetings, setting budget goals—it's a demanding occu-pation. Railey had a staff of sixty-five people to assist him, but just keeping them appeased was a full-time job. He insisted on knowing the name of every member of his congregation, even the tots in the nursery. He made a specific point of sending handwritten birthday greetings, and more than once he appeared at a high school play just to see a young member perform.

He had, it seemed, adopted the entire congregation as his family. The church came to represent the idealized loving family Railey had never known as the child of alcoholic and often neglectful parents. The soft-eyed choir director, John Yarrington, became "the older brother I never had." Howard Grimes was "a real father to me." It was typical of Railey to seek out "family" members, even at the expense of his real family, his wife and two children, who seldom saw him except on Mondays, his single day off. He wanted to be loved and esteemed; he also wanted to return to his congregation the steady, attentive care he had craved but not received as a young boy. Perhaps by pouring that kind of love on the thousands before him, he was ministering to the angry, untended child inside himself. He would not let them down, as he had been let down. When, in times of grief or trouble, a parishioner would stumble or his faith would fail, Railey was there to pick him up—strong, certain, unwavering. His faith was a compass point by which others in the church could steer their own fragile beliefs. In these ways Walker Railey became something larger than himself and, subtly, something other than himself.

For behind the public face of this caring, highly blessed young man, with his beautiful wife, his charming children, his prestigious job, his important future, there was another Walker Railey. This was a man so besieged by the doubts and worries he held aside during the day that he seldom enjoyed an untroubled night's sleep. This was a person seen only occasionally by people close to him—his staff, for instance, who idolized him and were sometimes crushed by a volcanic temper that slept and slept then suddenly savagely erupted, usually over some small point such as the lighting in the sanctuary or the presentation of the budget. Nor were these eruptions followed by periods of remorse, which would have made them easy to forgive; instead, a certain cold satisfaction took hold. He would not call back the rain of shattering insults that led to tears or angry resignations. In the recent past, when this uncaring, self-centered Walker Railey had gained ascendancy, friends had talked him into seeing a psychiatrist to help him cope with the stress of his position. Lately, however, when many of those closest to him advised him to slow down, take a sabbatical, and above all seek psychiatric help, he had coolly cut them off.

When word of another Railey outburst reached the congregation, it was usually seen as more evidence of his temperamental genius. How insidious that must have seemed to him! Whatever fault he confessed to, whatever awful behavior he committed, only brought him new credit.

Or perhaps—and this must be the worst thing that can happen to a preacher; it is where he crosses the line between serving the forces of good and those of evil—perhaps he had begun to believe in his own perfection. Some of the other ministers in the congregation suspected that Railey had become one of those preachers who see themselves as God's special messengers, one of those who "become so convinced that they are so holy that they are above the standards that they have to preach," as Spurgeon Dunnam observed. "The sin is to become as God, as one who would take God's place. Any time a human being reaches that level, he sets himself up for a fall."

◆

On Easter Sunday, three days before the attack on Peggy, Walker Railey preached what would be his last sermon in First Church. In the days to come, it would be reinterpreted in ways that no one in the congregation that morning could have imagined. On this holy day, which is set aside for hope, love, and rejoicing, the cast of characters who would figure in the tragedy was already in place in the sanctuary, about to begin a weird and—one could believe—demonic journey into a world of passion, violence, and madness.

Just before the eleven o'clock service someone slipped a note under Gordon Casad's door. It was the seventh in a series of threatening letters addressed to Walker Railey. "EASTER IS WHEN CHRIST AROSE, BUT YOU ARE GOING DOWN," the message said. There was already a police guard in the church, but the possibility that the author of those threats had walked unnoticed into the church offices left the staff and the police unnerved. They were even more surprised when an associate pastor, acting on a hunch, ran upstairs and typed out the same message on an IBM Selectric on the third floor. The typeface matched. Whoever was sending the notes was probably a member of the congregation—perhaps even a member of the staff.

Railey, a medium-size, balding man with intense blue eyes, was pale and thin-lipped but apparently determined to preach. He borrowed an ill-fitting bulletproof vest from a woman police officer, which he strapped on like a corset beneath his Easter vestments.

Few people in the congregation knew about the threats, but most sensed that something was wrong as soon as they entered the sanctuary. Councilman Holcomb observed that Railey did not join the procession behind the choir as he usually did. The pastoral staff entered through a side door—without Railey—and sat stony-faced behind the Easter lilies. Holcomb kept noticing two men standing beside the doors; he had seen them somewhere before, but not in the church—they were out of place here. Finally he realized that they were the same plainclothes officers who guard the city council. The congregation rose to sing the doxology, and when they sat down Railey abruptly appeared in the pulpit.

Looking out on his flock that Sunday morning, Railey saw three thousand parishioners in their Easter finery, filling the sanctuary and spilling out into the hallway, where uniformed policemen had just arrived to guard the exits. It was no longer the predominantly elderly congregation that had greeted him on his first sermon in this pulpit eight years before. Who could deny that Walker Railey had put his stamp on this church and invigorated it with the force of his personality? And yet, hovering over the sanctuary was a ghost that haunted Railey and would never let him feel entirely at home here. It was the spirit of Dr. Robert E. Goodrich, Jr., who had been minister of First Church when I was a child and whose legend overshadowed his successors. All the things Railey wanted, Goodrich had achieved. Goodrich had been elected bishop in 1972. He was followed at First Church by Ben Oliphint, who eight years later also became bishop. It was Goodrich with whom Railey was usually compared, however, and not always favorably. "In many ways I'll always consider that piece of wood in front of the sanctuary as Bob Goodrich's pulpit," Railey would later admit. Perhaps it was an act of charity or perhaps it was cleverness on Railey's part that he brought Bishop Goodrich back to Dallas in his final years when he was ill and doddering and placed him once again on the staff of his old church, where everyone could compare the frail old legend with his lively young successor.

In the congregation this morning was Goodrich's elegant widow, Thelma. (I should note that she continues to be a close friend of my parents.) Thelma was sitting with Lucy, the second of her four children, who was wearing a huge, floppy straw hat and a flower-print dress. Despite the mascara and frosted hair, one look at Lucy and you could see that she was Bob Goodrich's daughter. She had that knotted Goodrich chin, his thin, drawn smile, and the dark eyes that were his most distinctive feature—eyes that appeared removed but also searching and intelligent. It was a strong face, like her father's; and if in some lights it appeared hard, in others you could detect a vulnerable and even wounded soul who had lived past the point where life surprised her. When she was younger, Lucy played the piano in the Sunday school class that my father taught. Now Lucy was forty-five, with two teenaged children, but she was still slim and youthful, with the athletic carriage that was also a Goodrich legacy. She had been through two marriages before going off to California and becoming a clinical psychologist. Now she had come home to Dallas to set up a practice specializing in eating disorders. Along the way she acquired a new last name, one of her own invention: Papillon. The name, which means "butterfly" in French, suggested that she had spent her life in a cocoon, but now she had emerged and was ready to try her wings.

Mrs. Walker Railey sat in a pew halfway back, next to a woman police officer who happened to be a member of the congregation. It had become unusual to see Peggy in church. Over the last year she had withdrawn from the choir and the children's Sunday school class that she taught, then from the board suppers and picnics and retreats, and finally from the main Sunday service. Walker explained her absences as illness or as a need to be closer to five-year-old Ryan and two-year-old Megan. Although it was true that Peggy had suffered a bout of walking pneumonia in 1987, she had recovered from that; and as for the children, other mothers wondered why she couldn't leave them in the nursery, as they did. In any case Peggy always had seemed a fiercely private personality—as introverted as Walker was extroverted—so her retreat from church society was only partly noticed.

Later, while she lay in the hospital fighting for the marginal edge of life that had been left her, people would describe Peggy as cool and distant; but to those few whom she had allowed to know her well, she was a warm and devoted friend. The pictures that would appear in the newspapers did her no justice, because Peggy Railey was quite a beautiful woman. Where Lucy was strong and stylish and aggressively sexy, Peggy was frail and demure, but with a natural attractiveness, much like a fresh-faced milkmaid of her native Wisconsin. Peggy had a lovely singing voice—she was a second soprano—but her true talents were in her fingers. She had studied organ at SMU, obtaining a master's degree, and she might have pursued a career as a professional musician if she hadn't chosen to give herself over to the humbler role of being a minister's wife. In March, after she had recovered from her illness, she succumbed to friends' urgings and gave a small lunchtime harpsichord recital at the church, with John Yarrington joining her at the end of the program to sing a Bach cantata. In many respects Peggy had never been lovelier, although she appeared wan, and there was a new hollowness about her cheeks. What was most striking about this performance was Peggy's trancelike behavior. She played robotically, and when the audience applauded, she gave a sudden startled smile. Where was she? She seemed to be in some faraway, sad place. Later, people would remember that performance and wonder if Peggy had known then about Lucy.

Another of Peggy's talents was sewing. She had made many of the colorful seasonal stoles that the ministers wore over their robes—Walker was wearing one now, a white stole with the Greek letters alpha and omega appliquéd on either side. Beneath the stole was Walker's black robe, and under the robe was his suit jacket, and under the jacket was the bulletproof vest, so as Railey stood in the pulpit his first action was to mop his bulbous forehead with a handkerchief.

He began his sermon with a prayer for the memory of Bishop Underwood, who had once served as an associate pastor of First Church. "We're thankful, O God, for Bishop Underwood—for Walter—for the way he touched our hearts and lived within our lives," said Railey. Those in the congregation who had seen the flash of Railey's ambition wondered at the sincerity of prayer, since Walter Underwood's recent unexpected death had just doubled Railey's chances of being elected bishop: there were suddenly two vacancies to be filled in 1988.

By now most people had noticed the plainsclothes policemen behind the pulpit, scanning the faces of the worshipers, and the irregularities in the service. The tension in the sanctuary was so great that when a child in the balcony dropped his hymnal on the floor a gasp arose from the congregation. It had sounded like a gunshot. Railey started, then cast his eye ironically at the noise and took a deep steadying breath.

"Back in nineteen sixty-five Doctor Hugh J. Schonfield wrote a book entitled *The Passover Plot*," Railey said. "Its purpose was to put all the facts surrounding Jesus' crucifixion and resurrection in an understandable and explainable context. After proclaiming that Jesus perceived himself to be the Messiah from the very beginning of his earthly ministry, the book went on to suggest that Jesus actually orchestrated all the events during what we call Holy Week to live up to the Hebrews' expectation about how and when God's Anointed One would appear."

This was a provocative way to begin an Easter sermon—with the heresy that Christ's death had been faked. "The book speculated that Jesus' words from the cross, 'I thirst,' could have been a prearranged signal to a co-conspirator to give the Galilean a drug in a wine-soaked sponge in order to simulate death; that Jesus was only unconscious, not dead, when removed from the cross," Railey continued. "Finally the book concluded that, because of the intricate plans of Jesus, which were well orchestrated by his followers, the 'myth' of the resurrection was established in the minds of the early Christians even though Jesus himself never actually rose from the dead."

When he said these words, Railey could not have known that he would never again stand in this pulpit, that these were, in effect, among the last words of his ministry at First Church. He went on to dismiss *The Passover Plot*—"If there's ever a day you have nothing of substance to do, and you want nothing of substance to read, it would be a fine book to peruse"— but later people would note the macabre irony that the questions Railey was posing about Jesus were the same ones that so soon would be asked of him. Was he truly a martyr, the man now standing in Bob Goodrich's pulpit in a bulletproof vest, the man whose life for the next two weeks would be a march of catastrophe, beginning with the attack on Peggy, followed by Walker's evasive testimony to police, and culminating in his attempted suicide? Or was he orchestrating his own martyrdom, creating a myth for himself that would raise him higher and make the drama of his own small life into something grander, something divine? These are questions the members of his congregation, as well as the press and the police, would be asking as Walker Railey rose from his coma in Presbyterian Hospital.

◆

It was evident that there was something different about this story from others I had covered—at least in its effect on me. Ostensibly it was about a preacher who was suspected of trying to murder his wife in order to further his career. I proceeded to investigate it on that everyday, existential level. And yet it became hauntingly clear to me almost from the beginning that there was another plane of action upon which a larger, more significant story was being played out. This was the symbolic, or spiritual, level. Perhaps every story casts its shadow in another dimension, and I simply had never seen it, never even thought to look. But now I became conscious that while one part of me was doing my duty as a reporter, trying to ask the right questions and to understand the events as they must have unfolded, some rude creature inside me had been awakened. This unwelcome intruder was interested only in the saga that this isolated tragedy had opened in the spiritual realm—and in my own soul, if I could bring myself to use such a term.

Returning to that familiar sanctuary at a moment of such spiritual upheaval caused me to come face to face with old questions about faith that I thought I had long since left behind. I am distrustful of religious language, but during the months I spent investigating the events at First Church, I was also enduring a spiritual crisis, a dark night of the soul. I believed I was truly in the presence of evil, and evil was something I was unequipped to explain or even understand. I was thrown off balance and fell unexpectedly into despair. Nothing like this had ever happened to me; I was in a rage; my behavior was out of control. You can imagine how queer this seemed to the people I met; after all, I was a journalist, I was supposed to be neutral, and yet I was furious and on the edge of tears much of the time. I bullied my way into an interview with Railey's bishop, who said I was "beneath contempt." I told preachers who refused to speak to me about the case that they were sanctimonious hypocrites. I excoriated the staff of First Church for not confronting the evil that had taken place in their own sanctuary. My behavior was hard to excuse and hard to explain. What was going on? This was not *my* tragedy. Why couldn't I detach myself and become the sympathetic but uninvolved observer I was supposed to be?

Until now I had always enjoyed a comfortable relationship with the persona of the disinterested reporter, the friendly outsider who just wants to know. But the deeper I wandered into this story, the more frustrated and furious I became. I couldn't stop reacting personally to the events that had happened here—it was my old church, after all; I still knew many people in the congregation—but suddenly I seemed to be inside someone else's mentality. I wasn't thinking, I was merely reacting. I felt like I was playing out some ancient vendetta. Usually I am careful to make a good impression, but sharp words and judgments sprang out of my mouth without my seeming to have any control over them. It was as if they had been waiting to spit themselves out for years, and when the opportunity arrived, I—or the polite, inquisitive person I think of as "I"—was simply shoved aside and some angry, vengeful, emotionally volatile personality seized control.

Railey had spoken in his suicide note of there being a demon inside him: "My demon tries to lead me down paths I do not want to follow. At times that demon has lured me into doing things I did not want to do." I knew something about demons, although I did not call them that.

Certainly I understood what it was like to feel as if some other force had taken control of my life; indeed, that's what I was experiencing right now. Only, this new force did not feel demonic. Whatever it was, however, it was scaring me to death.

Where was all this anger coming from? In some part, I suppose, it was anger at Dallas, a city where pious public faces often hid secret dirty appetites. It is worth pausing to wonder at a city where a crime such as the assault on Peggy Railey can assume such metaphorical power. When I was a child in First Church, Dr. Goodrich used to speak about the "climate" of the city. It was one of his favorite sermons, one he turned to on that Sunday after John Kennedy came to town and became the 111th homicide of 1963. "Think back to September the first, nineteen sixty-two, the first day of fall football training in the Southwest Conference," Dr. Goodrich said in his consoling but high-pitched and occasionally pleading voice. He was referring to one of the most mysterious epidemics our state had ever experienced, one apparently caused by a freakish weather pattern. "It was a mild day—broken clouds, temperature in the high seventies or the low eighties—and before the day was over the SMU captain, an honor student, was dead. Several from the University of Texas were hospitalized at Austin, one of whom died within ten days. Seven were hospitalized at Texas A&M. Some were hospitalized in Fort Worth. Others were hospitalized at Rice University in Houston." What accounted for this fatal phenomenon? Dr. Goodrich said it was a "strange climate condition, never explained," which he believed had to do with a low barometric pressure combined with high humidity. "There's no question about a relationship between physical climate and life. How about the spiritual and cultural climate of a neighborhood, a city, a home?" In this allusive fashion Goodrich would imply that Dallas was not innocent of Kennedy's murder. Despite the city's air of progress and optimism, there was nonetheless something about the climate of Dallas that generated tragedy, that caused lightning to strike. Delicately expressed, that sermon nonetheless engendered a lot of resentment among members of the congregation—including my father, who counted Goodrich as his dear friend.

After the Railey tragedy, I wondered what Goodrich would say about the climate of the city today. It is a pious town, with more churches per capita than any other city and the highest-paid preachers in America. Many of the largest Protestant congregations in the world are in the Dallas–Fort Worth area, including seven of the top twenty churches in

United Methodism. Even the passing motorist would have to notice the exotic temples of fundamentalism along the interstate highways, the billboards hawking pompadoured evangelists, and the abundance of religious stations on the radio dial. But all this piety and bustle hide another Dallas. It is number one among large cities in the rate of overall crime: not Miami, with its mobster kingpins; not Detroit, where teenage gangs rule the streets with submachine guns; not Atlanta; not New York; but Dallas. And yet this is a city where the laws are sternly, frequently lethally, enforced. For many years Dallas prided itself on its relatively harmonious race relations, which depended largely on the high degree of demoralization among the minority populations. By 1988, however, the truce between the races had long since broken down; indeed, Dallas was getting a reputation as being one of the most racially divided cities in America. It also has the highest rate of divorce of any American city. "Dear Abby" surveyed her readers the previous summer and concluded that Dallas–Fort Worth had more unfaithful spouses than any other region. ("The wives say their husbands are too busy or indifferent. The husbands say their wives are cold and not exciting enough.") The rate of suicide in Dallas is 30 percent above the national norm. One out of every six murders in Texas occurs in Dallas County. These figures describe the climate of the city, and it is oddly true that in the attack on Peggy Railey all of these statistics—plus the small detail that Dallas leads the nation in the sale of cellular phones—have more than passing relevance.

But Dallas was an old war of mine, one that I had grown tired of fighting. The truth was that like any old contestant, I had begun to sentimentalize the battles of my youth and had become grateful to Dallas for helping me learn who I am. Beyond Dallas, in my angry mind, there was Methodism. I could not fairly hold my former religion responsible for the values of the city, because despite the fact that Dallas is a stronghold of United Methodism, only 7 percent of the population belongs to the denomination, a figure that represents less than half the number of Southern Baptists and is even behind the Catholics. This fact doesn't alter my opinion that Methodism is the state religion of corporate America, of which Dallas is the purest and most fervent example.

At that moment, the denomination was publicly exposing itself. The bishop of Houston, a secret homosexual, had just died of AIDS. Southern Methodist University, the Dallas rich kids' finishing school which is the centerpiece of the church's educational empire, had been cast out of the college football program because of institutional corruption and widespread payoffs to players. The governor of Texas, an SMU alumnus, admitted to being involved in the under-the-table payoffs, after lying about it previously. A 1986 survey of Methodist clergy found that the divorce rate among ministers was twice as high as the rate for lay people. In this polluted spiritual atmosphere, the Railey story seemed to be just another piece of evidence that Methodism had gone rotten.

And why should I be surprised? I have seen friends struggle to throw off the narrow-minded strictures of Southern Baptism or the ritualistic magic of Catholicism or the tribal creeds of Judaism. I have encountered religion in extreme forms, from Hare Krishnas and Amish farmers to snake-handling charismatics. And yet, with all my ambivalence about religion, what I feel about people who believe or disbelieve such stringent doctrines is a low-grade envy. At least a hard-shell Baptist has the literalism of the Bible to react against, a Catholic has the pomp and mystery of the liturgy, and so on; but a Methodist struggles in a fog, not really knowing what is to be believed or disbelieved but learning in a subliminal way what is to be avoided.

Methodism was born in the prisons and coal fields of Britain, where John Wesley began his ministry to the underclass. He preached more sermons against surplus capital than any other person in England and was rightly considered as radical a figure in his day as Karl Marx would be a century later. Wesley himself brought Methodism to America, on his ill-fated trip to the Georgia colony. He fled back to England under indictment for defaming a young woman he had foolishly pursued. But Methodism remained, and it advanced with the American frontier in the person of the lonely, tireless circuit rider. Thus it took root in an ambitious, immigrant, desperately poor but newly enfranchised pioneer people, and it grew with them, as their communities grew; as their generations prospered and changed, so too did their denomination, becoming essentially the very institution against which its founder had rebelled.

Now Methodism had turned away from Wesley's social activism and looked to the world of business for its model. Some people, even in First Church, were surprised to learn that Walker Railey was being paid a million dollars per decade for his services, but the church would defend its salary structure because Railey was making no more than a CEO of a major corporation. Methodist clergy instinctively compare themselves with IBM executives, not schoolteachers or parish priests. Never mind that the average salary of a Methodist minister in the Rio Grande Conference along the Mexican border was only $8,000 a year; the church could sanction such disparities because, like any vertically integrated corporation, it was competing for talent. It would tell you that it was in the business of saving souls, but a truer way of saying it was that it was in the business of selling salvation. Hot young salesmen like Walker Railey inevitably would be promoted out of the backwater churches of Kentucky and Oklahoma, where he had honestly labored as a pastor or assistant pastor since he was eighteen years old. He would be rewarded. He would be made a wealthy man, paid not only to endorse but also to represent the values of his congregation. He would speak to thousands. His voice would expand from the sanctuary and spread across airwaves. He would become a public figure, a man of stature in the community. Very quickly he would become a man with too much to lose.

Yes, I was angry at Methodism because I thought it had turned into Nothingism, and was only in business to stay in business. It was not surprising to me that the denomination was boarding up four churches every week. My particular quarrel with Methodism, however, began here in First Church, where for so much of my adolescence I had felt confused, overlooked, and more inclined toward depravity than anyone else in the sanctuary. It had seemed to me then that the special quality of my church was to float above the real world of lust, violence, cruelty, and greed, in a higher atmosphere of untroubled Christian behavior. Human failings were seldom addressed. I recall when our youth pastor left his family and ran off with a ski instructor. His name was never mentioned again. All that remained of him was some intoxicating vapor of sin and forbidden desire—an intimation of another world I was not supposed to know about. The church was like a timid old woman hiding behind shutters, shielding herself from confusion.

When the preacher came to call, we were always on eggshells. Now that I look back on Dr. Goodrich, I wonder if he was such a prude as my sisters and I made him out to be. He was one of those shy and introspective characters who is strangely more at home in front of an audience than with a single other person. He loved music, and while he was studying theology at SMU he started the renowned Mustang Band; he might have had a career as a bandleader if he hadn't been called to the ministry. He had played football during his undergraduate days at Centenary College in Louisiana, and he still had that big lineman's frame. Once Goodrich performed a skit during our summer Chautauqua services wearing a caveman outfit with a skimpy tiger skin draped across his shoulder. There was a gasp of astonishment. It was almost unbearably risqué—and therefore hilarious—because we had grown accustomed to seeing Dr. Goodrich as a bespectacled head floating above his robes, a sort of angelic intellect, and now we were shockingly reminded that he was also a big, physical man, with a man's body and presumably a man's needs.

When he came to our house for dinner, he wouldn't drink but he was a hungry smoker. This dependence surprised me, and perhaps him as well. He used to joke about a friend who told him that if he quit smoking they'd make him bishop—to which Goodrich had responded, "What if I quit and they don't?" That was his humor: gentle and self-deprecating. He was a likable, admirable man, although prim and too distant to be lovable. He seemed be partly transposed into heaven already. Of course, they were always going to make him bishop, although he stayed at First Church for twenty-seven years.

We sat at the dining table with our good manners on display. My parents adored Bob and Thelma; they had even thought of buying a vacation condo together. They seemed to be completely relaxed in their company. So why was I squirming? Was it my guilty conscience that made me so discomfited? There was something about Dr. Goodrich that made me feel less evolved. I was a teenager, roiling in a stew of emotions and hormones and desires. One might call them human desires, but in the preacher's presence they felt less than that, base and animalistic, not to be mentioned or noticed. I recall with horror the moment when our boxer dog came into the dining room triumphantly holding a used sanitary napkin in his mouth. No one said a word. We just continued eating while Beau nuzzled the Kotex on the carpet.

Perhaps Dr. Goodrich would have been grateful if I had laughed. In some respects it might have set him free. I think now that his spirit was larger than what we, his parishioners, allowed him to display. What a relief it might have been for him to be able to climb down from the pedestal—or, rather, the pulpit—that we kept him on and to laugh like an ordinary man!

My father had picked out First Church after leaving a hellfire-and-brimstone congregation in our neighborhood. That previous church had been damnation week after week. By contrast, Dr. Goodrich's sermons were optimistic and uplifting; I doubt he really believed in hell—the loss of the overpowering sense of God's love was enough of a hell for him. In our previous church, sin was always being thrown in our faces; but in Goodrich's church we were already redeemed by grace. And if it seemed sanctimonious at times, at least in First Church there was a worshipful sense of the glory of God's love and mercy and the miracle of redemption. I think that was what made Goodrich seem such a holy presence: he had come close enough to the miraculous to be radiated by it. He was still stunned, still in a state of shock somehow, so that when he delivered his sermons, one had the sense of a survivor groping to report the extraordinary news.

This high level of spiritual refinement left me behind. I didn't feel worthy of it—it was out of my grasp. Gradually I felt myself drifting farther away, like a child on an ice floe. I was beyond rescuing, because no one knew of my predicament and I was far too embarrassed to call attention to the fact that I was Not Saved. Instead, I hid behind a show of piety. I got involved with a Christian youth group in school. I attended Methodist Youth Fellowship and evening sermons; I even set pins in the afternoon at the church's two-lane bowling alley. Again and again I asked the Lord Jesus to come into my heart and begged for forgiveness; but the assurance I had once enjoyed of a benevolent, caring Father in Heaven began to lose authority, even while everyone around me seemed to be cloaked in holy bliss. I was reading my Bible and the Christian literature I had been assigned, but they were making less and less sense to me. I was slipping away, going backward. Instead of learning, I seemed to be unlearning. Where everything once had fit together, now it was all coming apart. The language itself was losing its attachment to meaning. It was all just sounds, just words, just marks on a page.

After Dr. Goodrich's daughter Lucy was revealed to be Walker Railey's mistress, I wondered whether it was even possible that Goodrich himself, saintly man though he was, had left a legacy that would somehow contribute to the disaster. Indeed, if there was a moral to be found in this wretched parable, it seemed to be that the pursuit of goodness is a treacherous path, and that what one may discover at the end of the journey is not enlightenment but the dark side of one's self.

✦

I saw Walker Railey preach on Christmas Eve, 1984, when I was back in Dallas to see my parents. It was a difficult time in my marriage, and I was in a raw state of mind. At eleven o'clock at night, the church was more crowded than I had ever seen it. We squeezed into the balcony, where my wife had to sit on my lap. That evening I experienced what so many would later speak of, the sensation that Railey was preaching to me, that those large and expressive blue eyes that swept across the sanctuary were searching for me. "We are parents and children who live in the same house but who sometimes cannot stand to be in the same room," Railey had said. "We are husbands and wives whose marriage hangs by a single thread, about the strength of the tinsel on the tree. . . . We are Christians in the church who sometimes, in our fervor to make Christmas happen, trample all over other disciples of Jesus who are seeking to do the same—like me two weeks ago this morning, when needlessly I blew my top toward a particular staff person about an issue that was important to me, but over against the ultimate redemption of the human family, was hardly worth mentioning at all.

"That is why this night is so holy. There is something about that infant, something about that child which disarms our aggressiveness and resentment and which saturates us with love. There is something about that Baby of Bethlehem that draws our attention to Him while at the same time pushing us back into each other's arms, as if to suggest that we cannot love Him without also embracing one another. There is something about that son of Mary and Joseph that destroys the barriers that separate us and which brings us together in love."

I was surprised by these words, and they registered deep inside me. They were comforting but also personal—and different in that respect from the sermons of Dr. Goodrich, who seldom revealed himself. It was odd, in this very sanctuary of First Church, where I had felt so unseen as a child, to feel so powerfully affirmed and forgiven. We were all struggling with our inner demons—even the pastor—and the fact that he was not elevating his own behavior made him seem all that more charming and authentic. His words awakened that old yearning inside me to surrender, to believe again in the healing power of the love of Jesus. My wife and I walked out of the church into Christmas morning, holding hands; the bells were pealing; we had both been touched, the love between us had been refreshed.

Now, nearly three years later, I was back inside the sanctuary of First Church once again, listening to another sermon that refused to acknowledge what had happened within the church's own family. Week after week had passed with only the most oblique reference from the pulpit about what was taking place in the world beyond the stained-glass windows. Nothing was said of Railey's attempted suicide. Nothing was said of the sensational revelations of Lucy Papillon's grand jury testimony, in which she talked about their affair, which had gone on for more than a year, their marriage plans, and their assignations "while he was out preaching." They had even arranged to meet in England when Railey returned from a World Methodist Council meeting in Nairobi. Nothing was said of Railey's refusal to cooperate with the police or his decision to plead the Fifth Amendment before the grand jury. The church was in a state of delirium. ("We're fine, the church is fine, everything's going to be fine," a board member assured me.) I fought an impulse to stand up and shout Walker Railey's name out loud.

I learned that Railey had become a sort of divinity in his church. People thought he was all good, that he was incapable of doing wrong. And yet he was a man, with a man's needs and flaws and appetites. I wondered at the effect of this adoration on him. It must be a gilded prison to be so idealized.

My anger at Railey was, I think, specifically Protestant in its origin. I had endured many years of Sunday homilies, those pointed morality tales that seem to mean something within the rarefied context of the sanctuary. Gradually I began to see those sermons for what they were, a sort of community lie. My own experience in the world told me that life rarely offers such clear moral lessons. I had thought that Railey might be one of those few spiritual leaders who could see past the homiletic half-truths to the taunting ambiguity that life really is. But I was wrong. For no matter what Railey's involvement was in the attack on his wife, in those weeks leading up to the Easter service he was obviously on a journey of the spirit that had taken him into the darker side of his nature. How hungry I was and had always been for news from that quarter! But he never addressed the sexual longing, the rage, the despair, the destructive stirrings of his own soul. Eventually he became, in the pulpit, something less than a complete human—a shell, a sham.

Of course it was all my old angers and prejudices that were rushing in on me—all my anger at Dallas, at Methodism, at First Church, at Railey, but also at God, at the whole tantalizing premise of the Christian faith I had once so fervently sought. If Christianity had the answer, then why couldn't it fearlessly address the leering tragedy in front of us? On the other hand, what could anyone have said? This was Walker Railey's church. It was his staff; he had handpicked many of them directly out of seminary; they had been utterly devoted to him. They were still fumbling, attempting to make sense of what had happened. And it was, after all, Railey's congregation, much of it made up of people like me, who had felt let down by the churches of their youth and who had been drawn back to faith by Railey's radiant ministry. They shared a common belief in the goodness of Walker Railey. Now they were having to consider whether what they had taken as good was actually evil—or, worse, that they would never really know the truth, and for the rest of their lives they would be bewildered, the truth would never be known, charges would never be filed, Peggy would neither die nor live again, and Walker Railey would never be revealed as either hero or villain but instead would haunt them forever, asking, "Who am I?"

◆

"I can hardly watch him without weeping," Howard Grimes said as he set me up in the First Church's well-equipped video room one autumn morning six months after Peggy's strangulation. "About the only way I can accept this without feeling bitterly betrayed is thinking he's a sick, sick man."

On the video screen, Railey was preaching about evil. He began by wondering how the good people of society relate to the evil ones in their midst. "The Roman Empire didn't fall because of the barbarians outside the gates," said Railey. "It fell because it couldn't deal with the beastly people within them."

"Gosh, that really is true," said Howard.

Railey was talking now about the "barbarians" inside the gates of our own society. "No, they don't look like barbarians. They wear suits, dresses, robes. They look civilized, but when you're around them, your blood pressure goes up. You end up saying things that surprise you but not them. The beast in you comes out. Something comes over you when they're with you that just makes you lose control. That's your barbarian.

"Who's the barbarian in your life this morning?" Railey asked, as he took a sip of water and scanned the congregation. I noticed the extra-wide wedding band on his finger. "Everyone has at least one. Who could it be? Your husband? Your wife? Your neighbor? Your pastor?"

Railey's sermons were filled with such suggestive allusions to his own failings. Looking back on them now, Howard Grimes wondered how he could have missed them. Perhaps it was because Railey had meant so much to him—too much. After Howard's son died, Walker had become a kind of substitute son for him. Railey had often said that Howard was more of a father to him than his own had been. "I would have done anything for him. He had power over me," Howard admitted as he loaded another videotape. Howard was a retired pastor and professor, thin as a fence post, who was fighting a battle of his own, with cancer. Their friendship had ended after Railey had chewed him out over a minor incident involving the sound system in the sanctuary.

"Barbarian" was an interesting term for Railey to use, neither religious nor psychological in nature. Here was a person who addressed the questions of good and evil every week of his life. If he was the kind of man police suspected him of being, then he must have spent a considerable period of time planning the murder of his wife. In that case, I wondered how he thought of himself, what words he used to describe his motivations. Perhaps, like me, he was frustrated by the inadequacy of language to deal with questions of human evil. The idiom of religion—of demons and possession—satisfies the question of where evil comes from, but at the expense of reason. The idiom of psychology—of psychopaths and childhood trauma—was more reasonable, but finally unsatisfying in terms of understanding the dark side of man's nature. Certainly violence and the thought of violence are not foreign to me, but it was not easy to imagine the kind of thinking that would have gone on in Railey's mind if he had decided to murder his wife. Once committed to this action, what would he have said to himself—"I'm insane"? "I'm possessed"?

In any case, the word Railey selected to describe evildoers in the sermon I was watching was "barbarians." It was a term that offered no explanations and no excuses. I thought it was bold. It was not a word one would expect from a liberal Methodist preacher. I could not help wondering if this was the way he secretly thought of himself, as a savage opponent of civilized behavior.

The next tape was a segment of "Faith Focus," Railey's Sunday-morning television interview show, which Howard produced. This particular show was from July 27, 1986. The subject, weirdly enough, was "Addicts of Love."

"It is possible to love for the wrong motives," Railey said as he opened the show, "to love simply for filling that sense of emptiness deep inside our souls. You can actually become addicted to love. Sound impossible? There's one person who believes it's not." Railey then presented his guest, Dr. Lucy Papillon.

Lucy was sitting forward in the chair, a bit stiff, with her hands folded demurely in her lap, wearing a stylish blue dress that flattered her figure and set off her frosted blond hair. "If we feel unloved and unlovable, we can't ever be really filled up," she said.

"So you become tied to this awful yearning," Walker replied.

"Yes, and that comes from—let's say, for example, you were a little girl and you really yearned to have your father's love and he was never around," said Bob Goodrich's daughter.

Railey asked her what causes love addiction.

Lucy began speaking about people who early in their lives "have the sense that they must take care of everyone else in order to get any of their own needs met. Perhaps their father is an alcoholic or dysfunctional in some way and their mother is depressed. These sorts of people give themselves up very early. They become pleasers. They develop a kind of attachment hunger."

She might well have been describing Railey's life. He was staring at her intently.

Walker and Lucy had met briefly several years before, when Lucy came to the church to see her father honored. Howard Grimes had introduced them. Then, in the fall of 1985, when Bishop Goodrich was on his deathbed, Railey spent time with the family at the hospital. Lucy had turned to him then, her father's successor, and in her grief they became friends. Later they would walk along Turtle Creek and just talk. One day they just kept walking, back to Lucy's house. "He didn't have intimate relations with his wife," Lucy later told police, "and didn't long for it before he met me—because he did not know what he did not have."

When they made this television tape, Walker and Lucy had been lovers for about a month. Lucy was speaking now about the pain of getting over an addiction. "I like to use the metaphor of the butterfly. The caterpillar's crawling around, feels like the world's okay, but if he wants to really fly he's got to go through the darkest thing he's ever seen, which is the cocoon."

◆

On the night of April 21, 1987, around six-thirty in the evening, Railey drove into the family garage. He would tell me that he had found his wife that evening working on a garage door latch with a bar of soap. The spring on the latch had been sticking lately, and Peggy was attempting to lubricate it. Because Railey never did anything mechanical, he simply sat on the hood of Peggy's Chrysler for a few minutes, talking to his wife. She and the children had already eaten dinner, and Walker wasn't hungry, so the two of them shared a glass of wine. He then left, still in his business suit, ostensibly to spend the evening at the SMU libraries.

At 6:38 Railey called the time from his car phone. Everyone knew that Railey did not wear a watch; he had given it up when he came to First Church, partially because of his habit of wearing French cuffs, which frayed when he kept pushing up his sleeve to check the time. The phone had just been installed that day, at church expense. It was another of the many security measures the church provided him, including a home alarm system and a second, unlisted telephone line. Railey says that he spent the next thirty minutes at Bridwell Library at SMU's theology school searching for a biography of Anne Sullivan, Helen Keller's teacher. At 7:26 he was back in his car, calling Janet Marshall, a family friend who was going to baby-sit for the Railey children while Walker and Peggy went to San Antonio for a badly needed weekend off. At 7:32 he called Lucy, then drove to her house, where he stayed for about forty minutes (the police say he was there for more than an hour). Railey would neglect to tell the police about this visit, or the several phone calls he made to Lucy that night. When confronted with these omissions, Railey would claim he went to Lucy's house to get some relaxation tapes to relieve his stress.

A librarian at Bridwell remembers seeing Railey some time after eight that evening, when the minister asked what time the library closed. At 8:30 the minister called his unlisted home number from a pay phone and Peggy told him she was just putting the children to bed. After that Peggy talked to her parents in Tyler, Texas, until 9:14. Meanwhile, Railey had left the library. He purchased gas at a Texaco station on Greenville Avenue at 8:53 and also bought a wine cooler, which he says accounts for the fact that the police would later report him as intoxicated when they came to his house four hours later. During this critical time, between the stop at the Texaco station and when he was seen again in the library, after eleven, Railey's whereabouts are unknown.

At 9:30 a jogger saw a man in a business suit running through a yard two streets away from the Raileys' house. Between 10:15 and 10:30 a neighbor heard rustling noises in the alley.

Railey says that he had gone to the Texaco station because he was thirsty. He contends that he then returned to his research in SMU's main library. A librarian noticed him there some time between eleven and midnight. Later Railey attempted to give his business card to the Nigerian student working at the checkout desk. On the back of the card was a message to the research librarian asking for help in finding the Sullivan biography. Railey had also written the time, which he noted to be 10:30. According to the Nigerian student, it was already midnight.

After leaving the library Railey phoned home from his car, but this time he called the listed line, which was connected to an answering machine and did not even ring in the house. "I don't have my watch on," said the man who never wore one, "but it's about ten-thirty or ten-forty-five." There was a clock built into the dashboard of his Honda. Telephone records show that the call actually was made at three minutes after midnight. "If you want to, go ahead and lock the door, and I'll park out front." At 12:29 a.m. he called the machine again, this time giving the correct time. "Hi, babe. It's twelve-twenty-nine and I'm on the way home from SMU," he said into the machine. "I had to leave my card with the reference librarian because there was one deal that I couldn't quite work out."

Eleven minutes later Railey drove into his driveway and found the garage door partly open. The garage was dark; mysteriously, the bulbs had been removed from the overhead light of the automatic garage door opener. Railey said he left his headlights on and got out of the car. He found Peggy lying behind her Chrysler, writhing in convulsions. Her face was hugely swollen and discolored, yet her hair was scarcely mussed and her glasses were in place. One of her shoes lay next to a tipped-over garbage can. At 12:43 a police dispatcher received a call from the Railey residence. "Uh . . . I just came into the house and my wife is in the k . . . garage. Somebody has done something to her, and my children are on the floor." The dispatcher inquired, "Has she been beat up or what?" "I don't know," Railey responded. "She's foaming at the mouth or something." (Later, detectives who reviewed the tape would conclude that Railey was about to say that Peggy was in the kitchen.)

Railey's next call was to Diane Yarrington, Peggy's closest friend and the wife of Railey's choir director. "Diane, something awful has happened to Peggy. Come quick, come right now." Diane and John raced over to the Raileys' house. By the time they got there the ambulance had already arrived. Walker was inside, holding his two-year-old daughter, Megan. His son, Ryan, who was five, was sitting by himself on the couch, looking dazed. Diane sized up the situation and announced that she was taking the children. She asked what they wanted to take with them, and each child grabbed a pillow and a stuffed animal.

"Don't leave me," Walker pleaded.

"I'll be here," John assured him. "I'm like your second skin."

The scene at the house was so confusing that John Yarrington was still uncertain what actually had happened to Peggy. When they arrived at the hospital and he had gotten Walker settled, he went to speak to the doctors. At that point the doctors thought that Peggy's neck might have been broken. "How in the world would that happen?" Yarrington asked, thinking it had been an accident of some sort. "Well, she was strangled," they told him.

Stunned and disbelieving, Yarrington went into the emergency room where Peggy Railey lay. It was a horrifying sight. Her face was the color of blue denim and was covered with blotchy purple spots. It didn't seem like a human color at all—but then, everything about this event seemed unnatural. Peggy—of all people for this to happen to! For most of the seven years the Yarringtons had known the Raileys, they had been the closest of friends. Diane and Peggy were like sisters. They spoke several times a day on the phone and sat next to each other in the choir. Peggy accompanied John's rehearsals every Sunday night. Walker had been John's boss but also his spiritual guide and soul mate. Walker once said that he felt closer to John than to any other man on earth, and John felt the same about him. Only a few months before, the couples had pledged that if anything were to happen, if one of the couples were to die in a plane wreck or some other tragedy should befall them, then the other couple would take care of their children. John had made the pledge in all sincerity, but who could have believed that so suddenly and so grotesquely it would come due?

◆

The day after the attack Railey went to the police station with a lawyer friend to talk to investigative officer Rick Silva. It was the only time Railey ever talked to the police about the case. His story then was that he had come home, spoken briefly to Peggy while she was working on the garage door latch, then spent the remainder of the evening in the library. He had no idea who might want to harm his wife, except for the still-unknown author of the threatening anonymous letters. Silva indicated that he would like to set up a polygraph examination, and Railey said he would be happy to oblige.

During the next week the police learned about the phone calls to Lucy, discovered the credit card slip from the Texaco station, and examined the garage door, which seemed to work fine. They found no evidence that the latch had been lubricated; in fact, they learned that the Raileys had complained to the manufacturer and that a new automatic door opener had been installed only a few days earlier.

In the meantime Railey stayed in his hospital suite, meeting friends and going through his voluminous mail. "If this had been some kind of accident, I think I could accept my wife being in coma," he tearfully told his friends, "but I can't—I can't accept the violence of this." One day he received telegrams from both Jesse Jackson and Billy Graham, and he went in to tell Peggy that she had made "ecclesiastical history." She looked at him with open, unseeing eyes. What she comprehended, no one could even guess. Friends played videos of her harpsichord concert for her and papered her room with pictures drawn by Ryan and Megan. There was some hope, in those early days, that something in Peggy would stir to life.

"Peggy, it's Diane." Peggy's face was still puffy and discolored the first morning Diane Yarrington got to see her. "The children are with me. It's just fine. It's all right." A tear rolled out of one of Peggy's eyes. Later others would see her crying—Walker did, even Detective Silva—and they would wonder what she knew or felt. The truth was locked inside her and could not be expressed, but that did not mean that it could not be experienced. What an unendurable tragedy that must be, to be alone with the truth.

One afternoon Lucy came to visit Walker, carrying a single red rose. She later testified that once they were alone, she kissed him, then told him she was going to San Francisco to see another man. Many people suspected that this was the reason that Railey tried to kill himself, not out of guilt but out of jealousy.

Meanwhile, the inconsistencies and omissions in Railey's story had accumulated to the point that Silva finally telephoned the hospital and told the officers guarding Railey's room that he wanted to question the minister. When the guards went to the room, they found the door locked, and no one would answer. They broke the door down. Inside they found Railey's unconscious body and his suicide note.

Once again John Yarrington would find himself standing in the same emergency room, this time over Walker's body as doctors pumped the drugs out of his stomach. Fortunately, Walker had not taken all the pills that were on his bedside table. Like Peggy, Walker had fallen onto that ledge of deep unconsciousness between life and death. Unlike her, he had not suffered a loss of oxygen and glucose to the brain, which doctors said probably would prevent her from recovering. Peggy was wrapped in a cocoon from which few ever emerge.

For the next five days Walker lay in intensive care in a room opposite Peggy's. It was a bizarre experience for their friends. On the left was

Walker and on the right was Peggy, and they looked much the same, not lifeless but suspended, as if they had been stopped in mid-sentence and placed on pause, and all one had to do was to push a button and motion would return.

On Wednesday after the Friday he had attempted suicide, Walker awakened. The first thing he remembers seeing is John Yarrington standing vigil at his bedside. Railey had absolutely no recall of anything since he swallowed the pills; for him, at least, the coma experience had been utterly blank. It was two more days before he fully surfaced, and when he did there was only one question on his mind. He wanted to know if he could regain the pulpit. Yarrington was startled. "I think it's very iffy," he said delicately. Walker seemed surprised and wanted to know why. "Well, number one, you tried to commit suicide," Yarrington reminded him. "And number two, a lot of people think you strangled Peggy."

✦

Most people read the suicide note as a confession, which it seemed to be, although it was too elusive to be used as such in court. "My demon has finally gotten the upper hand," Railey had written, and then he went on to describe the person Walker Railey really was: "All of my life people have seen me as strong. The truth is just the opposite. I am the weakest of the weak. People have seen me as good. The truth is just the opposite. I am the badest [*sic*] of the bad. People have seen me as virtuous. The truth is just the opposite. I am the lowest of the low."

Why couldn't he have said these words from the pulpit? Why couldn't he have turned to the three thousand Christians sitting in the sanctuary each Sunday morning and asked for their help or their forgiveness? The intimacy with his congregation that Railey had affected in the past was shown to be a sham, part of his preacherly guile. He would admit to small sins in order to hide his lustful, and perhaps murderous, heart. And yet again and again he had dropped hints in his sermons that he was not the man they idolized, that there was another, darker side to him. Was he teasing—or did he long to expose to the light this dark blossom that was opening inside him? Apparently no one would hear him. He would not be allowed to be an ordinary man. His congregation had turned him into an angel of the Lord.

"I have received more in this world than I have been able to give, but for some reason it just has not been enough to defeat the demon inside my soul," Railey's death note stated. "I have not given up on God; I have just given up on me. This is still God's world and God's Will still triumphs. It is simply time for me to get out of God's way."

I realized that these were the words of a despairing man, possibly of a guilt-ridden criminal who could not face the judgment of his friends or his own better nature. But this note filled me with questions. If Railey was willing to give up his life, why wasn't he also willing to face the police? What did he have to lose, if his life meant so little to him? Was there still something worth protecting—Lucy, perhaps? And after admitting so much, how could Railey then awaken from his nearly fatal sleep expecting to return to the pulpit?

I was posing these questions as a reporter, but as a former member of this congregation I had my own guilty queries. Preachers often say that after a few years in a church a pastor fashions the congregation into his image, and it was true that First Church had become Walker Railey's church: dynamic, yuppified, liberal, involved. But was the reverse also true? Perhaps Railey was just another victim in this tragedy—a victim of the expectations people had placed upon him. His congregation had worshiped him; they had exulted in his power and goodness and virtue. Was it possible for a congregation to—in some sense—drive a preacher to the Devil by worshiping him as a saint?

Lucy was still in town, trying to maintain her practice, but staying unavailable. I finally reached her by phone, but as soon as I explained who I was, I found myself listening to a dial tone.

Peggy's tormented spirit hung over the city, filling everyone with a sense of impatience and helpless frustration. Small details of her anguish kept appearing in the press. On the morning after the attack, police had found her private prayer journals wrapped in a blanket and buried under the linens in her bedroom closet. Presumably she had been hiding them from Walker. They revealed a frightened and bitter woman who was sometimes incoherent with rage. Even her closest friends had not seen this side of her. She wrote about feeling like an "appendage" at First Church: "When Walker not there I don't belong," she wrote in a telegraphic spurt. She was furious with her husband and prayed that the Lord would release her from her "emotional knots." "Be with Walker," she prayed, then continued in a blithering burst: "I am afraid. Dream: WLR—accusation—Why weren't you here at 2:00 p.m.!!! I feel guilt but ANGER—have tantrum. I hate him!—sorry revealed such! He: returns to insensitive, accusative, closed. Return: anger, frustration, violence in return. Father, there is great violence in my response, great anger in my being, great fear in my soul."

Peggy—or the comatose body that Peggy once occupied—was eventually transferred from the hospital to a nursing home in Tyler, where she could be attended all day every day by her elderly parents, who fed her and read to her and massaged her cramped limbs. As the months passed, Peggy would fade from public consciousness, except as a burden. In my conversation with Railey's bishop, John Russell, I had asked him whether the North Texas Conference of the United Methodist Church would continue to provide for Peggy's care. He assured me that it would, either through an extended insurance policy or through a private fund. I had been suspicious of what looked like an apparent deal between Bishop Russell and Railey. Various members of the Methodist clergy had been pressing the bishop to initiate a church inquiry into Railey's relationship with Lucy. Russell had then entered into a prolonged negotiation with Railey, which ended on September 2, 1987, when Railey surrendered his credentials. That action voided the church's jurisdiction over him and meant that there would be no embarrassing church trial. It also meant that Peggy's insurance would lapse after twelve months. Despite the bishop's assurances, the conference eventually dropped Peggy's premiums. Her friends at First Church held a rummage sale and raised over $100,000 for her care. Since then she has been on Medicaid. Her parents, Bill and Billie Jo Nicolai, brought a civil action against Walker to help provide support. The suit, which Railey did not contest, baldly asserts that Walker attempted to murder his wife. He was ordered to pay $17.9 million, but that is a judgment even the Nicolais never expect to collect.

Walker visited Peggy only three or four times. It was an almost unbearable sight: Peggy gaping at him with her wide-open mouth, phlegm draining from the hole in her trachea that refused to heal long after her feeding tube was removed, her feet clad in huge plastic orthopedic boots to keep her legs from turning in, her hands curled into rigid claws against her chest. Those fingers, which had been so loose and fluid, which had moved with their own separate intelligence on the keyboard, were now gnarled and cramped as if recoiling in fright. It was all her parents could do to keep her body from balling up into a fetus. Whenever Walker visited, he would only stand there and cry. Peggy's parents would look at him uncomprehendingly. Did he do this to their daughter? If not, why didn't he ever tell Peggy that he loved her?

If she were dead, one might feel at least that her spirit was at rest, that she was released. Instead she was imprisoned in this institutional limbo, alive, but so grotesquely muzzled. One couldn't escape the sense that she was waiting.

But that is to animate her with human qualities that she no longer possessed. The term the doctors used, "vegetative," was a more accurate way of understanding what Peggy was now. Most of her brain cells were dead; it was doubtful that she was thinking or even feeling, and the occasional tear that rolled from her open, incurious eyes was probably an autonomic response to some physical irritation. She had become, at least in my mind, a mockery of the whole notion of the afterlife. Even though her body was alive, the spirit that people had thought of as Peggy was dead; and that was what was so appalling—there was nothing there, nothing.

Where was God in all this? If there was a God such as the one Railey believed in, what kind of deity would play such tricks on its subjects— that, for instance, from the pursuit of goodness, evil would result? And was this God's will: that of the two comatose people lying in Presbyterian Hospital, the one known to be innocent would continue to suffer and shrivel, while the other would rise up and run off to California with his lover?

◆

The police had enough evidence to disbelieve Railey's story but not enough to charge him. Perhaps if he had not been the prestigious pastor of such a powerful congregation, the police might have been more aggressive from the very beginning; but by now the case had settled into a standoff that it would never break free from.

After he got out of the hospital, Railey checked in to Timberlawn Psychiatric Center. His attorney, Doug Mulder, a ferocious former prosecutor in Dallas County, arranged for him to take a privately administered polygraph. The test indicated that Railey did not attack his wife and did not know who did. The next day at the police department Railey took another polygraph, which proved inconclusive, although Railey "showed deception" about the threatening letters. Mulder and Railey arranged for another private polygraph, in Utah, but they never made the results public. Norm Kinne, the frustrated chief criminal prosecutor of the district attorney's office, convened a grand jury investigation and warned Railey in front of television cameras to either come before the grand jury or leave the country—an odd injunction to be directed at the only suspect in the case. When Railey finally did appear before the grand jury, he employed the Fifth Amendment forty-three times. No indictments came forth, but so much of the testimony spilled into the press that it appeared that the grand jury had been called for no other purpose than a public shaming of Walker Railey.

I expected that I would meet with Railey eventually. Periodically he emerged from seclusion to proclaim his innocence to reporters and to give his own version of the tragic events. These meetings were highly circumscribed, and when Railey finally answered one of my messages, he issued the following ground rules: we would not talk about the case and we would not talk about Lucy. "Are you a coffee drinker?" Railey asked cheerfully on the phone. He said he would have a pot waiting for me the following morning at his Lake Highlands home.

There was no For Sale sign in front of the white brick house on Trail Hill Drive, although the house was on the market for $279,000. The sole business that was keeping Railey in Dallas was the need to dispose of his property. He had already gone through the police, the grand jury, the bishop, and the local reporters, and there remained only me. Then he would be off to California and another life.

Railey opened the door and greeted me. How peculiar it suddenly felt to meet someone I had hunted for months and studied so intently! Railey wore khaki pants and a blue pullover sweater; though he was casually dressed, there still hung around him that heavy ministerial air. But perhaps this was my own projection, for wasn't he disgraced and fallen, a virtual fugitive—if not exactly from the law, then from the truth? In any case, the moment he opened the door and stared directly into my eyes, I felt reduced to a confused adolescent. I had to struggle to regain my composure.

The house was comfortable and spacious, with the sun glinting off the pool in the backyard and making wrinkled shadows on the living room ceiling. Outside, it was warm, but the house was unaccountably chilly— "like a mausoleum," Railey observed as we moved into the kitchen for coffee, but to me it felt submerged.

Perhaps it was simply the absence of family detritus, toys and books and newspapers, that made the house seem so impersonal. Of course, it was on the market and had on its best face; also, one supposes that the police had dusted every surface, turned over every cushion, combed through every strand of carpet, and that after such an intensive going-over there was bound to be some loss of personal imprint. My immediate sensation, however, was that no one had ever lived here at all; it was like a model home, a simulacrum of an existence.

As promised, Railey had the coffee ready, and we sat at the kitchen table to talk. In this room, at least, there was still some evidence of Peggy's life: the duck things she collected, plates and figurines. No doubt Peggy had sat many hours at this same table. I wondered where were the grocery lists or the scribbled phone messages or the bank statements to be balanced. Everything was disturbingly sanitized.

Railey had been monitoring my presence ever since I arrived in Dallas two weeks before. "I know that you have a couple of layers of subjectivity that are influencing your writing of this story, one having to do with me and one having to do with your inner quarrels with the institutional church," he told me, quite accurately. I realized that we had been stalking each other with a growing sense of recognition and mission. His mission, old and by now habitual, was to get me to believe in the church—and in him. Mine was to tear away the many veils of caution and evasion and get to the truth, whatever that was.

He already knew who I was. But did anyone, even Walker Railey, know who he was? "I get depressed," he admitted. "I see my psychiatrist twice a week and have been doing that since May, and he helps me look inside myself." Railey was spending his days now reading the Psalms and playing golf, "trying to let my soul and my body get together." A few days before, he had enjoyed "kind of a joyous highlight" because he had played golf with former district attorney Henry Wade. "It was a fun time. And I thought he showed personal sensitivity to me." Railey was obviously worried about the future, about his prospects for a job. "For the first time in my life, at forty, I have no earthly idea what, where, when, how, or anything else. So there's an element of fear."

He spoke of his ambition. "Most of the reports have written that I was drooling on my tie waiting to become a bishop, but that's not entirely true." Bishops are elected for life, he pointed out, and "you can only bless the opening of Sunday school units so many times until you get tired." He said his secret ambition was to stay at First Church another decade, then take early retirement and go to law school, so that he could set up practice in South Dallas defending underprivileged minorities. I regarded that statement as gratuitous and unlikely; on the other hand, I never did understand the appeal of being bishop.

"I had three books coming out in 'eighty-eight," Railey was boasting. "I was speaking all over the nation. I had been the 'Protestant Hour' preacher—I'd just finished taping the sermons." Everything that he was working for had been coming to fruition. "So you know, I was beginning to feel that my future was okay, but I was trying to get out of the future and more into the present, maybe for the first time in my life."

"And now, all that is lost to you," I observed. "You've resigned from the church, the books have been put on hold, your family has broken apart, and your future is in serious doubt. You're a man who has suffered tremendous losses. Why do you think this has happened to you?"

This question had been given to me by psychologists I had consulted, on the premise that Railey might be insane. If he was, he had done enough psychological consultation of his own to dodge the paranoic response. "I've always tried to avoid asking 'why' questions, because I don't think 'why' questions get you anywhere," he said, giving me his most defiantly honest stare. "If I'm asking myself any question, it's how can I feel the presence of God's healing power right now, when, for the first time in my life, I can't even tell you where I'll be tomorrow."

There was something wrong with this conversation, some dissonant note that, even in this weird setting, troubled me and set off some inner siren of alarm. Up to this point I hadn't thought he was lying; I had expected him to be guarded, but he seemed sincere nonetheless, and actually eager to help me fathom who he was.

He began to recount the events of Tuesday, April 21, leading up to the discovery of his wife's attack. He had lunch with Rabbi Zimmerman of Temple Emanu-El, then went to the FBI to drop off a couple of the threatening letters he had received before Easter. About five-thirty in the afternoon he picked up his car, with its newly installed cellular phone, from AT&T. First he called Peggy to see if it worked; then he called Lucy. He stopped by his house for about twenty minutes and talked to Peggy about their planned weekend trip to San Antonio. Then he went to SMU to do some checking on footnotes for his book of sermons. "I went to the library and started at Bridwell down on the south part of the campus," he said. When he finished there, he "walked up to Fondren," the main library. "On the way to Fondren I stopped by Lucy's house" —which is directly behind the campus—"for about forty minutes and back to Fondren after getting a Coke at the Texaco station and filling up the car. Worked at Fondren until a little after midnight—about twelve-fifteen or so. I had called Peggy to let her know that I was on the way. And I got home about twelve-thirty. I came into the garage and found her."

He had been telling the story in a rapid, shorthand manner, so fast that I completely missed the contradiction between his "walking" to Fondren and filling up his car with gas. He had said that he would not talk about the case, and obviously he wanted to skate past this portion.

"The police said you had been drinking that night," I said.

"Peggy and I had a glass of wine," he said.

"At what time?"

"Quarter of seven. And I had a wine cooler when I stopped at the Texaco station."

"I thought you said you had a Coke at the Texaco station."

"I said 'Coke,' but that was just a Coke break, a coffee break," he replied. "I went up there to get something. I refer to that as 'getting a Coke.' "

He would not be trapped. He started to talk about finding Peggy. "Come here—I want to show you." We walked through the den into the garage, which was large and empty of cars. Against the back wall were several storage closets. "I want you to understand that there's a freezer, there's a refrigerator, and there are toys that the children use, like the tricycle," Railey said, pointing to the clutter. "In the evening it was not uncommon—six, seven, or eight times at night—for one of us to come out here." He showed me the latch that he said Peggy had been working on early in the evening of her attack. "How it got bent I don't know." Railey's voice, even though it was nearly a whisper, reverberated in the vacancy of the garage. "Anyway, when I pulled in, the door was about up to here"—he indicated the height of his knee—"and Peggy was right here."

She would have been just behind her Chrysler, between the tool closet and the door that led into the house. As Railey explained how Peggy's body was oriented—"heels here, head here"—I thought what an intimate crime strangulation is, a gruesome and prolonged dance. Peggy had been garroted with a cord, which the police have not been able to find. "I was actually horrified," Railey was saying. "I have never seen such a thing—let alone my wife. Her face was purple and bloated, and her body was heaving from the waist up. Those were reflex actions, seizures, I later came to realize. I tried to shake her, tried to get some kind of response . . . and I couldn't get anything and ran in and checked on the children."

We walked back into the house. "Megan was lying down in front of the television," Railey said, pointing to the carpet. The family TV sat beside the picture window that looked out on the pool. "The TV was on and muted and she was on the floor. My first impression was that she was dead. I picked her up and she said, 'Daddy.' She had her little fingers in her mouth, and she was okay. She had evidently gotten up, looking for Mommy, and the TV was on and she laid down in front of the television."

"Had she found her mother?" I asked.

"I don't think so, but I don't know." We went through the house to the children's rooms. "This is Ryan's room," Railey said. It was still filled with Ryan's dolls and toys. "His bed's been moved over to the Yarrington's," Railey explained, "but his bed was here, and he was three-fourths of the way asleep but kind of in a fog." (Several months after my conversation with Railey, the police would release information that Ryan had been partially strangled as well. There were bruises on his cheeks and upper neck. Ryan has repeatedly told a story of seeing his mother throwing up while being strangled in the kitchen with a blue cord. Several times he has implicated his father in the attack, although he has also hinted that it was a playmate, the playmate's father, and a masked robber.)

The attack had happened well after midnight, when the children ordinarily would be sound asleep. Perhaps the assailant thought, as I did, that strangulation is a silent crime, but who knows how Peggy may have fought, what kind of racket she might have made. Did she wake the children? The awfulness of that scene played horribly in my mind, along with the growing suspicion that the person who caused this appalling tragedy was the same polite preacher who was giving me the Cook's tour of his home.

"So anyway," Railey continued, "I came in and called the police. I called the Yarringtons and I went across the yard and got my neighbor and he came over. He stayed with Peggy. I brought the children into the den, sat them down on the sofa with me, and just held them. Both were extremely quiet, 'cause they could obviously pick up on my panic. I was hyperventilating and scared to death."

We were interrupted by the doorbell ringing. Railey was not actually living in the house any longer, and he was taken by surprise. A highly apologetic property appraiser had come to price the house. Obviously, she hadn't expected Railey to be at home. "I can come back," she said pleadingly. "No, no," Railey said. "We'll just go to my study."

He and I went up to his special lair on the second floor. As a writer, I have a particular interest in the places people make for themselves to write in. Two walls were covered with floor-to-ceiling bookshelves. There was an imposing desk of the sort that would belong to a bank vice-president, and a more modest work area with a computer. One of Railey's manuscripts sat on the table. Under a dictionary stand was a copy of *The Plays of Eugene O'Neill*. It was a handsome office, but once again I noted an absence of personal effects. Two items in the room caught my eye. One was an SMU basketball on the ledge behind Railey's desk. He had bought the house from an SMU coach, it turns out, and had written into the contract that a basketball would come with the house. The other was a doll that resembled Big Bird. Railey said he had bought the doll for Ryan when he was in New York, and he recounted the spectacle of himself walking through the lobby of the Waldorf-Astoria with the doll under his arm. I laughed, but it struck me as curious that Railey, not Ryan, had the doll now. Railey sat in his easy chair, and I sat on a couch beside him.

"Tell me about your relationship with Peggy."

"Well, we'd been married sixteen years. Peggy was a lot quieter than me. We had respect for one another. We were not the kind of couple that held hands and watched television on the sofa. When we went on vacation and went to the beach, we'd both take a book and read and listen to the sea gulls and watch the waves.

"We were married eleven years before we had children, and once the children came, we became more and more committed to parenting. Peggy had a great love for the church, and the impression that she didn't enjoy being the pastor's spouse I think is unfair to her. She was a private person and didn't talk a lot about the inner parts of herself. I think her best friend on the face of the earth was her mother. I don't know how else to answer. We didn't have a lot of arguments."

"Did she know about your affair?"

"We . . . That never came up."

"She didn't know?"

"I can only say it never emerged."

"Did she suspect?"

Railey took a steadying breath. "I have no way of knowing, regarding that, that she suspected anything at all, about anything."

I knew I was crossing the line he had drawn. I started to press further, but he cut me off. "I've told you I won't talk about Lucy," he said.

"Do you plan to divorce Peggy?"

"That is not a question I will answer."

I observed that both the church, through the bishop, and the city, through the district attorney, had advised Railey to leave town to avoid being an embarrassment to them. "I guess you could interpret it like that," he said. "They don't really have to ask me to leave. I just feel like I got into a situation and it's time for me to go."

"Would Lucy join you?"

"I don't care to answer that."

"You're going to California?" Friends of his had said that was his plan.

"No, not necessarily. I'm looking for a place to work, Larry. You know, if somebody asked me to become a journalist, I'd give it a thought."

More than once, Railey asked me for information about my business, which was unsettling to me, because I already felt a greater sense of identification with him than I cared to feel. Railey must have felt that as well. Several times during the interview he had even urged me to "push harder," to do a better job, the job he might have done on me if our roles had been reversed. We were the same age. We were both ambitious. I had to admit that there was a moment in my religious youth in which I might have taken the same road Railey had, to the pulpit. I had swerved away from faith, but the longing for revelation was still a part of me. Now I could see that in many ways the difference between writing and preaching was not so great; nor, really, was the difference between belief and disbelief—it was the intensity of the struggle that mattered. The lesson I had drawn from Walker Railey's life so far was that good and evil are not so far apart either. They were both inside Railey, warring for control—as they were in me as well. Whether or not Railey was guilty, he had caused me to look into myself and see the lurking dangers of my own personality.

"I hope," he said at one point, "that you won't let this . . . ah . . . affair affect your own relationship with God."

"I don't have a relationship with God," I said.

Railey hesitated, but it was a challenge he chose not to pursue. "I'm surprised you haven't asked me about my suicide attempt," he said, once again presuming on my role. He talked about it and started to cry. I found myself oddly removed. I began to tabulate the times he had cried so far. He had cried when he talked about the death of Bishop Goodrich. "What I was aware of"—here is the point where he cried—"was the death of tradition." He had come close to crying when he spoke about having to leave this office we were in, which was dear to him. He had cried when I asked about his recent return to First Church for a memorial service for his baby-sitter, Janet Marshall, who had died suddenly of lupus. "When

I walked back into that sanctuary," he had said, "the first thing I saw was the pulpit, and at that point I just kinda lost consciousness of what was going on around me." Later in the day, when we were at lunch, he would cry when he remembered his neglected childhood. I didn't question the genuineness of these responses. These were real losses: of his tradition, his comfortable home, his profession, his childhood, and nearly his very life. But they seemed—what? Was it fair of me to compare his losses against Peggy's? Against his children's? Why didn't he cry for them?

What interested me about his suicide attempt was the note he left behind, in which he had spoken of a demon. In First Church there had been much speculation about what Railey's demons might have been: perhaps sex; certainly ambition. This is the usual Methodist metaphorical construction of biblical language. I asked Railey what demons meant to him.

" 'Demons,' " he said, "that's just not—that's not a word I use a lot. I've talked to you about depression—that's a demon. I've talked to you about low self-esteem—that's a demon. I've talked to you about a great fear over the uncertainty of the future—that's a demon. And there may be a lot more demons, but my point is that several things I've struggled with would fall under the category of demons."

"And yet your very first sermon was 'On Seeing Satan Fall,' " I reminded him. "I wonder what your opinion of Satan is. Is he a figurative creature or a real force?"

"Well, first of all, I preached 'On Seeing Satan Fall' because that was taken directly out of the text of the Scripture. It was a sermon on the church. I do not see Satan as some incarnated presence in my life, who's over against God and therefore the two are in a battle and we're kind of little pawns in the game. That makes me less responsible for my own actions. I think there is evil in the world and I think that both the inclination of good, which would be godliness, and the inclination to evil, which would be satanic, are inside us."

"But you don't think that you were controlled by forces you couldn't—"

"No, no, I don't," he said abruptly. "I think that's a theological and psychological cop-out."

Railey turned the conversation back to the church, to the moment when he had returned to the sanctuary after his resignation for Janet Marshall's service. Several years before, when Janet's illness flared up, she had summoned her pastor to her hospital room and demanded to know what he was going to preach when she died. She had him actually write out his sermon and read it to her. "Her death became the first occasion that I was not able to do something in an ordained way that I would have done," he remarked. Instead, he had slipped into the church at the last moment, hoping that no one would see him but knowing that everyone expected him to be there. "There were some people who, I think— I can't be sure of this—but there were some who went out of their way because they didn't know what to say. But there were a whole lot more people who did. They just squeezed, hugged, kissed, slapped me on the back. They could feel my pain," he said, crying again. "I wasn't able to conceal it; I wasn't trying to. I think everybody knew that I was there under a great price, just emotionally, to walk into that sanctuary. So there was a great combination of pain but also a sense of joy that the community was there, and I felt its love."

"Did you feel a sense of shame?" I asked.

Railey looked at me sharply. He was, of course, alert to insinuation. "I felt, probably, every emotion you could feel."

"But did you feel ashamed?"

"I felt a great need to be forgiven, if that's what you're talking about."

When he said this, it seemed to me as great a concession as I was likely to get. We were still talking in generalities and metaphors—Methodistically, as it were—but I had the feeling that we were nearing the truth, as much as I was likely to see of it. On the other hand, perhaps I was merely twisting his words, finding more meaning than was actually there.

"I felt a great need to . . . to . . . to be reaccepted," Railey offered.

"As who you really are?"

"As who I really am," he agreed. "As someone who never wants to lose being part of the community that the church represents."

"And having had that experience, do you feel now that if you"— here I searched for another word, but none would come—"I'm going to use the word 'confess,' to whatever you are not talking about now, that they would forgive you?"

"That's a pretty leading question."

"It's a hard question to ask."

"That . . . that really . . . you—I wish you would ask it another way," Railey said, "because I'm not going to answer it like that. It's too much of a setup."

I tried to think of another way to ask, but he cut me off. "Let me just make a statement," he said. "I was aware that night of the love that permeated the sanctuary, God's love, in their lives. God's love is both a judging love and a forgiving love; it's both a healing and a haunting love. And I experienced God's love in all four ways that night. Okay? And I think that's about the way I would say it."

Before I left, Railey wanted to know what I thought of him. "I don't know what your impression is, and you don't have to give it to me, but I've been real honest with you today."

"I think you're guilty," I said.

There was a pause, and I recounted his misleading testimony to the police, his avoidance of the grand jury, his inexplicable actions on the night of Peggy's attack, his affair with Lucy, and so on. "I can't construct an innocent man out of that behavior," I said.

"I hear what you're saying," he responded.

I didn't know what to think. Here he was, reflecting my feelings, while I was accusing him of trying to murder his wife.

"I appreciate your even responding to that," Railey continued. "I'm aware that nobody can sit down with all the facts that are supposedly known and make it all fit. That's a frustration that everyone has felt, including me."

"Confess," I said, "or it will haunt you forever, it will drive you crazy."

"I don't know if that's a word of advice, a backhanded comfort, or what," Railey said. "I am not guilty. I didn't do it. I don't feel tormented by the guilt of what I didn't do."

◆

It would be days before I understood some of what disturbed me about my conversation with Walker Railey. There was, of course, the possibility of his innocence. If he was guilty of no more than infidelity, then what an awful fate for him to bear. How cruel of me to disbelieve him. But if he strangled Peggy and was going free, then what kind of person was he? I still didn't know.

I had been struck, in a literary way, by the metaphorical parallels between Peggy's condition and that of her children, who were in a custody limbo, and that of the congregation, which was still stunned and bewildered, and that of the crime, which continued to be unsolved, and that of Walker, who was, as I pointed out to him, suspended between one life and another. "Yes, yes!" he said with an eagerness that surprised me. "Somebody asked me three or four months ago, 'How've you been?' And

I said I felt like I'm in an emotional coma. In that I'm breathing, existing, and living, but at that point—this is while I was still in the hospital—like anybody in a coma, like Peggy and others, I hear people around me talking and making decisions that affect my life, and at this point I don't seem to have control over those decisions. So I'm in a kind of fixed state. I guess you could say the same thing now."

Perhaps it was the very eagerness with which he accepted this observation that chilled me, because of course there was no real equivalence between Walker Railey's tragedy and Peggy's. Soon after our interview he left his children to start a new life in California with Lucy. Eventually, in 1992, Railey would be indicted and he would return to Texas to face trial (which had not begun when this book was completed). Peggy's life would never start again, however; at best, it would continue only blankly. For Walker there was a future, but for Peggy there is only an unending present, until she finds the death her assailant did not provide. And I have the feeling that she is waiting—waiting for justice, waiting for salvation, waiting for the truth to set her free.

Jimmy Swaggart:
False Messiah

A friend of mine, a psychologist and university professor, undertook a study of fundamentalist Christians in a small town in West Texas. Once a month he would drive from Austin to spend several days observing church services and interviewing informants. Like me, he was interested in the phenomenon of the growth of primitivism. There has always been, in America, a profound and curious duality between the impulse toward progress and modernity, on the one hand, and a yearning for the restoration of an earlier, ideal time, on the other. The Puritans, the Quakers, the Baptists, the early Episcopalians and Methodists, the Amish and the Mennonites, the Mormons, the Churches of Christ, and the modern-day Pentecostals are all expressions of this latter sentiment. Perhaps because we are verging on the millennium, there has been an explosion of growth in primitivist churches, which seek a return to the simpler and holier days of the first church. But what was the nature of the primitivist appeal? And what kind of people are drawn to these Holy Roller–type churches? Those were the questions my friend sought to address through his scholarly study.

He is a gracious and intelligent man, and he quickly made himself welcome in the congregations of this small community. Most of the churchgoers were farm families and country people; they couldn't be more different from this learned professor who brought his tape recorder to their services. They were, in his eyes, fanatics. They represented another America, a country that until now he knew about only vaguely, through television documentaries and the occasional monograph. He himself was not a believer; like me, he was more a student of belief. Now that he was getting to know them, however, he saw that they were not fools. He came to appreciate the genuineness of their faith; he may even have felt a little envious (after all, what had motivated this study in the first place?). After two years of weekly visitations, certain barriers inside him that held him apart from the people he was studying began to dissolve.

And then it happened. One Sunday morning at a church service, when the congregation was singing and waving their arms overhead, praising God and shouting hallelujahs, a terrifying impulse came over the professor. He was seized with an urge to throw up his hands and run to the altar. He wanted to surrender, to give over his soul. But how could he? His panicked mind reminded him of his position in his own community, the esteem of his colleagues, his intellectual signposts of Freudianism and skepticism, and his whole ironic way of being in the world. Everything, everything he valued in life—or thought he valued—was at risk. He could not be a hand-waving, hallelujah-shouting Christian and still be the man his friends and family thought he was. Shaken, trembling, he stumbled out of the church and found his Volvo among the pickups in the parking lot and sped back to Austin, to his home and his job and the person he had grown into being.

He might have been me, I thought when he told me this story. I would have done the same—I would have fled from transformation. I too was drawn to the edge of what I think of as the wilderness, the place where sophistication and learning and the defenses of civilization become moot and silly. The wilderness is a savage democracy; perhaps that's why the poor and the unlettered go into it more readily—they have less to lose. The legend is that deep in the heart of this howling wild place there is ecstasy and holiness itself. There is no sign posted INTELLECTUALS NOT ALLOWED, but clearly one cannot think oneself into the wilderness; the entire point is spiritual abandon and unthinking acceptance of the absurd and the miraculous. It's no wonder that intellectuals stand on the perimeter, jeering and fretful.

I think this fear of the irrational accounts for the particular glee in certain quarters that accompanied the downfall of Jimmy Swaggart. No voice expressed the primitive urge more persuasively than his. Anyone who has come across his wide, fleshy face filling the television screen and heard his syrupy but nonetheless quite musical voice may have felt the gravity of this man and his apparently genuine sense of transport, which he expresses by dancing and crying and speaking in tongues. His is a voice from out of the wilderness, calling us—I could even say luring us

—deeper into the places where the mind doesn't wish to travel. He was more than a threat to my identity; he asked me to leave my identity behind. Follow him, follow Jesus, into the dizzying labyrinth; hearken to the sounds of jubilation that come from the mysterious, irrational center.

On several occasions I had chanced upon Swaggart by skimming the cable channels. My memory is that I would click on past him, but even in this split second of exposure he had already made an impression of vitality and super-assurance. It was a sort of tug at my sleeve. If there was not some more attractive offering ahead, I would retrace my steps and settle on the honey-haired preacher with the Louisiana drawl who seemed to be speaking directly from his unconscious, spewing himself into the audience and into the unseen, peeping eyes like mine on the other side of the television set. Even then, before the scandals began to break, I might have described his style as ejaculatory.

I told myself that it was curiosity that kept me from switching him off, but there was another emotion, which I hesitate to admit. It was fear. The basis of my fear was that Swaggart and the rest of his ilk were right—that the whole point of life was to plunge into the wilderness, joyfully throw aside the resistance and anxiety that characterize the skeptic, and become like Swaggart himself, bursting with spiritual power. If I failed in this, then I had missed everything.

I resented this (what seemed to me) emotional blackmail. But what if he was on to something? I didn't like to think that there was a right answer in life and a wrong one, but there was enough uncertainty and longing in my life that I was willing to believe that I was on a path to nowhere. Here was Swaggart saying that his way was a better way, the *only* way. Therefore his abrupt, spectacular self-destruction came as a relief, and I happily absorbed the details of his fall. At some levels, it was the Railey story redux: an overreaching preacher undone by his carnal nature. This is a morality play that repeats itself again and again in the scandal sheets and the daytime talk shows. Sex is the great leveler, the shadowy companion of the transcendent spirit. But there was a mystery to Swaggart's disgrace that I couldn't grasp. Why had he brought himself down?

◆

To understand clearly that Jimmy Swaggart plotted his own destruction, you must stand here in the courtyard of the Travel Inn, that squalid rendezvous on Airline Highway just across the parish line from New Orleans. A few hundred yards away looms the vacant brick building that formerly housed the largest congregation in the entire state, the First Assembly of God, which was pastored by the Reverend Marvin Gorman until the avenging finger of Jimmy Swaggart brought him to ruin. About an equal distance in the opposite direction is the Jefferson Parish sheriff's office. It was here, between his bitterest enemy and the law, that Jimmy Swaggart, dressed in jogging clothes, would cruise Airline Highway in his Lincoln, searching for cheap women and his own inevitable downfall.

Why? Why would the most popular television evangelist in the world, a man who once claimed a worldwide viewing audience of more than 500 million, whose weekly telecast was carried on more than thirty-two hundred stations (not counting cable outlets), whose show was seen in 145 foreign countries and "available," he could boast, "to more than half the homes on this planet"—a man, moreover, who saw himself as God's messenger, the only real hope for the evangelization of the world and the salvation of America—why would such a man sabotage his reputation and his career and perhaps his very soul for the guilty pleasure of watching women masturbate?

Hold that question in mind as we move seventy-five miles north, to Baton Rouge, to the 279-acre empire of Jimmy Swaggart Ministries, passing the immense headquarters building on World Ministry Avenue, framed by flags of the 195 nations reached by Swaggart's missions, passing the vast complex of his partly finished Bible college, his $10-million teleproduction center, his printing plant, his private Christian school for grades kindergarten through twelve, until we come to the eight-sided Family Worship Center, where off-duty policemen are waving traffic into the acres of parking lots. It's Easter Sunday, 1988. The azaleas are blooming. Inside the lobby of the church there are world maps on opposing walls, one indicating the countries receiving the Jimmy Swaggart telecasts and the other showing missions, churches, hospitals, and schools supported by his ministry. Both maps are clotted with dots. There is a concentration of missions in Central America, the Caribbean, and the west coast of Africa. The television broadcasts blanket the United States, Canada, most of South America, and extend into the unlikeliest places— Mongolia, according to a red dot in Ulan Bator, and several atolls in the remotest stretches of the Pacific Ocean. All of this has come to pass since New Year's Day, 1969, when Jimmy Swaggart made his first radio broadcast.

He had erupted from the poor hamlets and lonely whistle-stops of the rural South. Uneducated and unexposed to the larger world, he was propelled nonetheless by an inner certainty that he called God's anointing. He had stormed the dirt-road churches and Holy Roller tent revivals in the piney woods, gathering force, learning how to sway the multitudes with his muscular voice and his boxer's body, dancing, crying, damning, beseeching the brokenhearted and despairing souls to come forth and be saved. He had known since childhood that God would lift him above all others. And God did. He led him out of the tents and backwoods churches and into city auditoriums, and onto radio, and then onto his ultimate instrument, television.

It was an unparalleled rise to power and prominence, beginning in 1973, when Swaggart taped his first television program in the "Hee Haw" studios in Nashville. His invasion of the airwaves started with UHF stations and spread to independent cable and Christian networks. And it was not just his Sunday sermons that went out to the world; at one time, Swaggart had seventeen different programs on the PTL ("People That Love" or "Praise The Lord") Network and a similar number running day and night on other stations. The casual cable viewer scanning the offerings of this flea market of American culture was perhaps more likely to see Jimmy Swaggart's face than any other.

"Monday morning, July the first, nineteen eighty-five, at about nine-thirty, God spoke to my heart that we should put the telecast on every station throughout the world," Swaggart has said on many occasions. "He said, 'Do this immediately, and do not fail!'" Later, Swaggart revealed other messages God desired his servant to deliver. "What he said was so strong I fell! I fell on my face! I said, 'God, I cannot say it—it's too hard!' And God replied, 'I will give you a face as flint! I will give you a head like steel! I will give you a tongue, I will give you a mouth, but you will say what I tell you to say!'"

What Swaggart has said includes statements that Catholicism is a "monstrosity of heresy" and a "complete contradiction of the word of God"; that all dancing, including aerobic dancing, is "sinful and harmful"; that "AIDS can be contracted by eating at a restaurant where food is prepared by homosexuals"; and that "all rock music . . . being aired today is demonically inspired." According to Swaggart, "The main problem in the free world today is that *there is no punishment for crime*!" He offers an answer for this uncurbed lawlessness: "In all honesty, I have two answers for it—the side-by-side answers of a double-barreled shotgun!" He has called homosexuality "the worst sin in the world" and has said, "I'm sick to death of words like *gay* being used to amass respect for people who don't deserve respect. Why don't we use words descriptive of their chosen lifestyle—such as *pervert, queer*, or *faggot*?" He is opposed to public education and has said that the "Newnighted" States Supreme Court and the Congress are "institutions damned by God." He resents the media for advocating "a system of atheistic socialism where all decisions are imposed by this small, elite, superior intellectual class who do the thinking for all common people." He has told reporters, "You can write your poor little old pitiful pukish pulp in your papers if you want to, but you can stop what I'm preaching about like you can stop a Louisiana hurricane with a palm branch."

These wild tirades are delivered as Swaggart waves his Bible overhead, his baritone voice rising into shrieks or falling into breathless whispers but always demanding, insinuating, taunting—an untamed, irresistible performance. He kneels, he struts, he dances, he sings, he bursts into tears; then he abruptly rains laughter on the thousands of worshipers waving their arms before him. Suddenly he breaks into the incantatory language of the Holy Spirit: "*Hun da sheek kulaba sone do roshay ketab do rotundai!*" he cries. "I speak in tongues every day of my life."

In the evangelical community, Swaggart was an object of wonder and dread. "He was preaching on the edge," the Reverend Glen Berteau told me when I arrived in Baton Rouge. Berteau had spent four years as director of Swaggart's youth ministry. "There is something glamorous about being on the edge of anything. You always had the feeling with Jimmy Swaggart that he was going to the limit every time."

"Is it Jimmy's masculinity, his macho? What is it that makes him what he is?" asked Richard Dortch, past president of the PTL Network, who was once a close friend of Swaggart's but became one of the many people ruined by Swaggart's purge of his television competitors. "What is it that makes him what he is? His music has a lot to do with it, and his abandonment to the Holy Spirit. When he would preach, he would just kinda go into overdrive." "He's got a style that's perfected in terms of the words, the body language," added University of Virginia sociologist Dr. Jeffrey K. Hadden, co-author of the book *Televangelism*. "It's the dynamism of a Billy Sunday and the populism of a Huey Long."

That is a powerful combination. Indeed, until February 21, 1988, there seemed to be no brakes at all on the expansion of the Swaggart empire. His Baton Rouge office, which has its own ZIP code, handled more mail than any other entity in the state of Louisiana. Most of the fifty thousand letters received each week at 70810 contained money, an average donation of forty-five dollars, amounting to nearly half a million dollars a day in 1986.

Although Swaggart's ostensible goal was to evangelize the world in the last days before Armageddon—he claimed to be saving 100,000 souls per week—he also had allied himself with the Christian right and was vigorously pressing its political and social agenda. No other single person had ever assembled such a global television audience, and it was difficult to foretell what the consequences of such a supranational phenomenon might be. Already his telecast was being translated into sixteen languages, including Russian, Mandarin, Icelandic, Persian, and Swahili.

But now, suddenly, this soaring preacher was falling, falling, and no one could say for certain where he would land. He had been revealed as a sinner, and he had bravely admitted his sinfulness to the world, bawling as the translators rendered his remarks into the tongues of men, humbling himself before his wife, his congregation, his God, even the news media. "And to the hundreds of millions that I have stood before in over one hundred countries in the world," he cried, becoming almost incomprehensible, "I've looked into the cameras, and so many of you with a heart of loneliness that reached out to the minister of the gospel. You that are nameless—most I will never be able to see you except in faith—I sinned against you. I beg you to forgive me."

The fifty-three-year-old Swaggart delivered his confession on February 21, 1988, the first Sunday of Lent. In the six weeks that followed, Swaggart's fate became a matter of church politics. Here he would seem to have had an advantage. The state council of his denomination, the Assemblies of God, was controlled by Swaggart's close associates and relatives and by members of the board of Jimmy Swaggart Ministries. They met and announced that their repentant brother would be removed from the pulpit for three months of rehabilitation, not the usual full year. A more severe punishment threatened to put an end to the entire Swaggart ministry—not just the television show but the Bible college, the private school, the missions, and the one million dollars a month that Swaggart contributed to the national Assemblies of God. At once, the switchboard of the Assemblies' national headquarters in Springfield, Missouri, lit up with three hundred phone calls an hour, almost evenly divided between Swaggart supporters and those who wanted his punishment increased. The thirteen-man executive presbytery, which decides denominational matters, overruled the Louisiana district and imposed a two-year suspension that called for a complete absence from the television ministry for the first year and a probationary period thereafter. The next day Swaggart rejected the Springfield ruling and said that he intended to abide by the original three-month ban. Two days later, however, even the Louisiana district reversed itself and called upon its most famous minister to remove himself from the television screen for a full year.

And so this Easter Sunday, April 3, was a crucial moment in the life of Jimmy Swaggart. Would he return to the pulpit and be defrocked? Or would he stand aside and watch the satellite bookings and time slots that he had spent so many years putting in place be lost to reruns of "I Dream of Jeannie" and "The Dukes of Hazzard," not to mention the highly competitive sulfurous evangelists behind him, who were waiting for just such an opportunity? And isn't this the predicament he had sought, even longed for, on those Saturday afternoons when he was supposed to be off rehearsing his sermons and talking to God but instead was sneaking down to New Orleans to pay women to take off their clothes?

The seventy-five-hundred-seat Family Worship Center was only partly full at 10:00 a.m. as the bass drum sounded and the curtain rose on the crumbling Swaggart empire. The choir, which formerly spanned the bleachers across the rear of the auditorium, was reduced by at least a third. The brass section of the Swaggart band was down to two horns and five empty chairs. The amen corner, where the fifty-four associate pastors usually sat, was also missing some notable faces—including, at this moment, Jimmy Swaggart and his wife, Frances.

There was a sullen air in the Worship Center, which on any previous Easter Sunday would have been overflowing with ecstatic worshipers singing the praises of God and his beloved deputy in Baton Rouge. Many here today had come only to gawk, and even the faithful rose grudgingly from their seats when the hymns began. We had all heard about the graduating seniors of the Jimmy Swaggart Bible College who were trying to get their diplomas changed, and about the defecting undergraduates, some of whom had just learned that the college was never accredited by the Assemblies of God, and about the hundred employees who had received their pink slips. The band and the choir were belting out a rollicking gospel number, but the faces of the mostly middle-class congregation registered No Sale. Indeed, the entire production had the atmosphere of a Las Vegas revue on its closing night. It had come to the end of its run.

During the second chorus, Jimmy and Frances slipped in from the rear of the stage—she in one of her sensational designer outfits, which have always been the talk of the Pentecostal world. This time it was a turquoise skirt with a sort of Joseph's-coat serape. Frances Anderson Swaggart has been a dominating force not only in Jimmy's life but also in his ministry, which has numerous members of her family in key positions. "If you can imagine a bull's-eye," a former aide said to me when he was describing the Swaggart hierarchy, "the inside circle is Jimmy, Frances, and Donnie [their then thirty-three-year-old son]. The next circle is the rest of her family, some thirty people." Her brother, Robert Anderson, treasurer of Jimmy Swaggart Ministries, was the subject of several exposés by Baton Rouge TV reporter John Camp, who has accused him of financial improprieties. In the past, when Frances suspected that staff members were talking to the press, she made them take lie-detector tests. A fit and stylish woman herself, Frances also supervised an effort to slim down the employees, requiring them to be weighed once every quarter to see if they were meeting the guidelines posted by the personnel department. Reporters and even scholars who have questioned Jimmy's ethics or theology often had to answer to a ferocious Frances angrily demanding a retraction. Until February, however, the Swaggart empire had never really been in peril. Now everything was on the line—not only the fortunes of Jimmy Swaggart Ministries but also the future of the entire Anderson clan.

Swaggart's suspension prohibited him from preaching—from appearing *at all*—so his mere presence on the stage this Easter Sunday was a technical violation. He and Frances took their places at the head of the amen corner, Jimmy fiddling with the microphone in his lap, into which he occasionally sang counterpoint to the choir. Indeed, it was that gentle, Elvisy baritone in the background that alerted most of the worshipers in the congregation that the Founder, as he designated himself, was onstage.

The Reverend Jim Rentz, official pastor of the Family Worship Center since February, preached the service while the smoldering Swaggart shifted restlessly in his seat, like a bull in a rodeo pen. Bridled as he was, his energy seemed to expand and feed on itself. At last, after the choir had sung "I See a Crimson Stream of Blood," Swaggart could contain himself no longer. He leaped up and rampaged across the stage, imploring the choir to sing another chorus. "Satan says it's over!" he cried ecstatically. "Jesus says, 'Look at the blood!' The angels say, 'Look at the blood!'" It's this sort of passionate Swaggart riff that usually gets the audience to its feet, but today the response was leaden, the cheers hollow, and some in the audience appeared shocked by the Founder's shameless defiance.

"*Brother Swaggart!*" came the voice of a teenaged boy from the balcony. "*Brother Swaggart!*" The church grew quiet. Swaggart did not turn around. "Your hypocrisy is scornful of the government of God! Liar! Hypocrite!" Swaggart's plowboy shoulders hunched around him. Rentz asked the congregation to stand and "just praise the Lord" to drown out the rain of accusations as the ushers raced toward the youth and dragged him out of the sanctuary. In an instant he was gone; but his indictment hung in the air, a weird and penetrating moment of truth. Swaggart made a characteristic jutting gesture with his chin like a boxer shaking off a punch.

A few minutes later he was up again to sing with the choir, this time a tune of his own request. "I'll rise again," he boldly sang on this resurrection morning. "Ain't no power on earth can keep me down."

◆

Some of the reasons Jimmy Swaggart would destroy himself may be found in Ferriday, Louisiana—"my beleaguered little town," he would call the place of his birth, ten miles from Natchez across the Mississippi River Bridge. It has been rather routinely described by passing journalists as a "typical" southern crossroads town—an adjective weighed by the natives with a sense of disbelief, for even in the Deep South, Ferriday has the reputation of being one of the darker and more gothic pockets of humanity.

Here Swaggart grew up with his cousins Jerry Lee Lewis and Mickey Gilley; the three were born within a year of one another in the mid-1930s. Back then the town was run by their uncle Lee Calhoun, a "vile, vulgar, profane old man," as Jimmy later described him, whose name was carried forward by both Jerry Lee and Jimmy Lee. Although Uncle Lee made his fortune from bootlegging and cattle rustling, he seemed to float eerily above the world of law and consequence. "He was well respected in the community," Jimmy writes in his autobiography, *To Cross a River* (co-written by Robert Paul Lamb). "He never seemed to have the problems all my other relatives had. His house was constantly full of people looking for money, politicians asking for favors, and preachers hoping for some kind of contribution."

Uncle Lee's main moonshine still was busted by revenuers in January 1935. One of the men captured in that raid was W. L. "Sun" Swaggart, a fur trapper, pecan picker, and occasional fiddle player. As the revenuers were leaving with a truckful of arrested men, they passed a heavily pregnant woman walking on the side of the dirt road. "Who's she?" one of the agents asked Sun Swaggart. "That's my wife," he said. "The agent paused, then shrugged," Jimmy writes. " 'Well, you get her out of here,' he said to daddy. 'And if I see you around here a minute longer, you're going to jail.'

"Daddy grabbed mama and took off down the road, but all the other relatives, including five of my uncles, wound up behind bars.

"Two months later I was born."

Jimmy's aunt Mamie Lewis was also pregnant when the revenuers took her husband, Elmo, but she was not as fortunate. Elmo, however, soon escaped from prison and was back home when his son Jerry Lee was born, eight months later.

The following year, 1936, a woman called Mother Sumrall and her daughter Leona, from Laurel, Mississippi, wandered into Concordia Parish and began knocking on doors. They were inviting people to attend their "church"—an overgrown vacant lot with benches and chairs set among the weeds. Eventually they erected a tent.

As it happened, Mother Sumrall's lot was across the street from the Ferriday Community Hall, where Sun Swaggart and his wife, Minnie Bell, would play community dances, he on the fiddle and she on the rhythm guitar. In that same hall, Sun's amateur boxing career had come to a sudden halt one night when a professional slugger rudely separated him from consciousness. By then he had raised enough money to purchase a small gas station a block away, on the main highway. Sun had been to church only one time in his life, for a Catholic funeral; but as he sat in his gas station, the music from Mother Sumrall's gospel tent came tugging at his sleeve. One evening Sun and Minnie Bell picked up their instruments, and the Swaggart family entered the Assemblies of God.

That night they became a part of a religious movement that already was profoundly changing the country and much of the world. The great Pentecost revival began on New Year's Eve, 1900, in Topeka, Kansas, when a young Bible student named Agnes Ozman prayed aloud in a language she had never heard before. Some syllables were later identified as Chinese, and for the next three days she was unable to communicate in any other language. Soon other students began speaking in tongues; their words were variously identified as French, German, Swedish, Czech, Japanese, Hungarian—twenty-one languages were counted in total.

Glossolalia, or speaking in tongues, was already known to anthropologists, who have cited accounts of American Indians who talked to animals or spoke in languages they never could have learned, and even of Tibetan monks who quoted Shakespeare in English. Ecstatic religious utterances similar to glossolalia are mentioned in early Egyptian accounts as well as by Plutarch and Virgil. In the nineteenth century, spiritual mediums often claimed to speak in foreign or unknown tongues, such as the famous case of Hélène Smith, reputed to speak and write in Martian.

Until Agnes Ozman spoke Chinese, however, glossolalia was practically unknown in the major denominations of the Christian faith. Ozman's vocalizations were performed during a prayer experiment, the object of which was to see if the students at Bethel Bible College might receive the baptism of the Holy Spirit as it is described by Saint Paul in his epistles. For the believers who would later be known as Pentecostals, the significant passage is the second chapter of the Acts of the Apostles, which recounts the day of Pentecost, fifty days after Easter. The apostles were gathered in an upper room in a Jerusalem inn when "suddenly there came a sound from heaven as of a rushing mighty wind." The apostles were filled with the Holy Spirit "and began to speak with other tongues, as the Spirit gave them utterance." Charles Fox Parham, Agnes Ozman's teacher, also received the gift of speaking in tongues, as did a dozen other preachers of various denominations. They planned a coast-to-coast evangelical tour to spread the message of the "full gospel"—a message that the powers of the early church fathers, which included healing and prophecy and other "gifts of the Spirit," were available to modern-day Christians. To Parham it was a signal that the end times were coming. He called it the Covenant of the Latter Rain, a reference to the passages in Deuteronomy 11:14, Joel 2:23, and James 5:7, which speak of God's bounty being provided in an early rain, which prepares the crops, and a latter rain, which brings them to fulfillment. For Pentecostals, the reappearance of these gifts of the Holy Spirit means that the human harvest of Apocalypse is near.

Parham's tour fell apart on its very first stop, in Kansas City, where the preachers were met by the incomprehension and derision that would always accompany the Pentecostal movement and mark it as a refuge for the credulous and the ignorant. Broke and dispirited, Parham drifted away and began preaching on street corners. Eventually he established another school in Houston, Texas.

One of his students in Houston was William J. Seymour, a black minister who carried Parham's message to Los Angeles. Seymour arrived in

April 1906 and set up a church in an old livery stable on Azusa Street. What followed was one of the great revivals of American history. It went on day and night for more than three years. People of all races and classes passed through, shouting hallelujahs and singing gospel music and speaking in tongues. Indeed, it was this radical fusion, especially of the races, that would give Pentecostalism its particular primitive fire. It was born of the same mixed marriage that later produced rock and roll.

And because Pentecostalism was an interracial phenomenon, even in the Deep South, there has hung about it the taint of broken taboos. Of course, this has always been a feature of ecstatic religions. It is a legend of those early camp meetings and tent revivals that a population boom would follow nine months later. In the twenties, the first voice of Pentecostalism to capture the national airwaves was that of radio evangelist Aimee Semple McPherson, who scandalized the country by staging her own kidnapping, which appears to have been a cover-up for a five-week sexual escapade.

Derided as Holy Rollers, the Pentecostals nonetheless represented a powerful and growing counterforce to the ascendancy of scientific thinking and the belief in social progress that had taken over the cities and universities. The Pentecostals lived instead in a world of miracles. They longed for a return to the primitivism of the early church; indeed, the gift of speaking in tongues was proof enough that modern science had been turned on its head by the triumph of primitive faith.

Science, for its part, looked upon Pentecostalism as a kind of mass psychosis—although research seems to indicate no personality differences between glossolalics and nonglossolalics. Linguists who studied these prayer languages easily demonstrated that they were not French or Japanese, as a speaker might claim, but a linguistic façade, like Sid Caesar's French or John Belushi's samurai Japanese. On the other hand, these sounds were not mere gibberish; they had the shape and form and sound of languages and could readily be distinguished from arbitrary noises. Oftentimes the speaker himself assumes no knowledge of the meaning of his utterance, although other Pentecostals who hear the sounds can interpret them and agree on their meanings. Perhaps more important from the speaker's point of view is that once he gives voice to such noises, he crosses a social barrier. It is a "bridge-burning experience," as social scientists would say; the speaker has left the world of accepted values and entered a separate community. He has been born again in the Holy Spirit.

The legacy of the Azusa Street revival is manifested today in more than three hundred Pentecostal denominations in the United States, with 10 million adherents. By far the largest of these is the Assemblies of God. Founded in Hot Springs, Arkansas, in 1914, the Assemblies has become the fastest-growing denomination in America. The church has seen its population swell from 300,000 members in 1950 to approximately 4 million by 1990, outstripping such established groups as the Presbyterians and the Episcopalians. (The Assemblies also claims 14 million believers outside the United States, most of them in Brazil.) Moreover, the number of mainline Protestants and even Catholics who claim to be charismatic Christians—who have received the *charis*, or gift of the Spirit—has grown steadily, even as the overall population of many of those denominations has declined. Swaggart estimates the true number of "Spirit-filled" Christians in the United States to be closer to 30 million. And although today many of the more than 11,000 Assemblies churches are glistening suburban tabernacles, radiating prosperity and respectability, the roots of the denomination are in the rural congregations like the little white church in Ferriday that was built on Mother Sumrall's lot and paid for by the old reprobate Lee Calhoun.

In the Pentecostal world, that little church on Texas Street in Ferriday has become a kind of shrine to the movement's most famous preacher. Here the Swaggarts, the Lewises, and the Gilleys came to find God. The women were particularly fervent. Eventually Mamie Lewis and Irene Gilley and Jimmy's grandmother Ada Swaggart would all become evangelists, as would Jimmy's own father. The cousins, Jimmy, Jerry, and Mickey, were in the same Sunday school class, which was taught by Sun Swaggart, and they each carved their names into the pew in the back of the church. Jimmy was quiet in church, but he enjoyed the Bible stories. "David and Goliath were my favorite," he would later recount. "Many times I sat pretending it was me hitting the giant with the rock."

Minnie Bell Swaggart had been saved for about a year when she began praying for her son. Jimmy preferred to spend his time with Jerry and Mickey, going to see Hopalong Cassidy or Johnny Mack Brown movies at the Arcade Theatre. "You really shouldn't go," Minnie Bell pleaded. She herself had given up going to movies when she became a Christian. Jimmy went anyway, defying his mother and the will of God. But his mother's prayers would affect him nonetheless. As Jimmy stood in line to buy a ticket, "an entreating voice suddenly spoke to me. 'Do not go in this place. Give your heart to me. I have chosen you a vessel to be used in my service.'" Jimmy began to weep. He was eight years old.

Still, he resisted the call. Once during a revival, both Irene Gilley and Mamie Lewis fell to the ground and began speaking in tongues. These demonstrations offended Minnie Bell. "This shouting and hollering is ridiculous. I'll never do it." But the Spirit seized her during that same revival. One morning when the young evangelist J. M. Cason was playing his accordion and singing "By and By When the Morning Comes," Mamie suddenly leaped out of her pew and began rolling in the aisle, speaking once again in tongues. Irene, who had been praying at the altar, was also slain in the Spirit. And then it hit Minnie Bell. She began to dance and shout, and soon the sounds that came from her lips were strange to her, but eerily natural.

Jimmy had not gone to the meeting that day; he was playing with Jerry Lee and some other boys several blocks from the church when they all heard someone shouting at the top of her lungs. "A dread swept over my heart," Jimmy writes. "I knew it was my mother." He ran home in shame.

But that summer the Spirit found him as well. A woman named Thelma Wiggins came from Houston to preach. "The last night of the services something finally released within me," Swaggart records. "Kneeling at the altar, praying as usual, I became aware of what seemed to be a brilliant shaft of light descending from heaven and focusing on me. Moments later I was speaking in tongues.

"For days afterwards, I spoke very little English."

◆

The little church where Jimmy met the Holy Spirit still stands on Texas Street among the pecan trees. When I arrived in Ferriday, however, the family of a visiting evangelist was packing up and leaving the parsonage under a cloud much darker than the one hanging over Jimmy Swaggart. "We call it the Crime of the Century," said Frankie Jean Lewis Terrell, Jerry Lee's sister. "This poor little Assemblies of God man was arrested over here. He raped his four children and the animals that he had there—two sons, two daughters, two dogs, and they're lookin' at the parakeet."

On Frankie's dining table was a copy of the Concordia *Sentinel*, with a photo of the forlorn pastor on the front page.

"But the real tragedy," Frankie Jean continued, "is that he sent his last five dollars to Jimmy Swaggart."

Frankie Jean is a female photocopy of her famous older brother, with his small, delicate mouth, sharp chin, and high Indian cheekbones. She lives in the five-bedroom brick house that once belonged to Lee Calhoun and then to Elmo and Mamie Lewis. It has been carefully preserved, at her brother's insistence. "Jerry didn't even want me to put a microwave in the kitchen," she says. "He won't let me vacuum in her old bedroom because it's got Mama's heel prints in the carpet." Both Jimmy and Jerry were born in this house.

They were closer than brothers—more like twins, Jimmy would say—and indeed, the lives of Jerry Lee Lewis and Jimmy Lee Swaggart were destined to be intertwined in complex ways. It was almost as if they were opposing halves of a single person, neither of them complete without the other. Jimmy was serious and fiercely shy; Jerry was hilariously boisterous. Jimmy was afraid of girls; Jerry was a teenaged Casanova. Jimmy was a frugal, sanctimonious teacher's pet; Jerry was a profligate, untamed hellion. Anyone in Ferriday could assemble a list of such personality traits, marking Jimmy at one extreme and Jerry at the other. The only characteristics they had in common were an intense competitiveness with each other, a boiling need to get out of Ferriday, and a tendency, as the world would see later, to lead symbolic lives.

Each was fanatically devoted to his mother, and this would affect the twisted relationships with women that awaited the boys when they became men. "These boys were mama's babies," Frankie Jean told me, as she sat at her baronial dining-room table with a rack of ironed shirts behind her and a police scanner crackling in the background. Frankie Jean "may or may not" be an occasional correspondent for the *National Enquirer,* and she tends to speak in that publication's exclamatory style. "I loved my mother, and I loved my aunt Minnie Bell," she says. "They didn't mean any harm. These were two wonderful ladies! But they had a way of just pulling you in. They would sit around and talk about what they were going to say to Jimmy and Jerry—'He must do this,' 'He must do that'—you see? Their little cult! They brainwashed the hell out of 'em! All of a sudden this religious thing came over them. They just became so righteous. I mean, these were moonshiners! It was just church, church, church! Jimmy's been programmed! Jerry's been programmed! Mother would tell Jerry that every hair on his arm was perfect. Aunt Minnie Bell would tell Jimmy, 'You're going to be completely perfect.' Jerry was the bad one. Jimmy was going to walk with God. Well, look at 'em! These boys were robots!"

Catty-corner from Frankie Jean's house in Ferriday is the forty-five-foot trailer where Jimmy's father lives with his fourth wife. Sun Swaggart was seventy-three years old when I visited him, and despite his thick plastic bifocals and a nervous cough, he still carried the frame of an amateur heavyweight. Although he lives poor, Sun is a wealthy man, according to his relatives—"a millionaire several times over," says one of his nephews. His frugality is a matter of legend. "He still gives me his leftover tea bags," says Frankie Jean.

There has existed between the Swaggarts and the Lewises an ancient antagonism over how the children were raised. "Jerry has a good heart," Sun says of his nephew, "but it would take a miracle to save him. Jerry's mother and dad—they was Christian maybe for a few months, and then they'd go cold on God, y'see. So naturally he didn't have the rearing most Christians have." Frankie Jean says of her uncle Sun, "This is a very domineering man. Uncle Sun had the only word in his house, and I think this has made Jimmy very insecure. Everything was so damn tight. Sure, I know Jimmy has giggled a bit and had a tiny bit of fun, but Jimmy has not been allowed to think, act, or breathe like a normal human being. Jimmy's been held—I'm gonna cut the namby-pamby—Jimmy's been held down. He's been so deeply suppressed—this guy has never been allowed to be anything. No talking at the table. 'Yes sir' and 'no sir.' This kid has had a difficult time. If he challenged his father, Uncle Sun would put on boxing gloves and just deck him. Now we would call it child abuse."

In their tenth year, the lives of both boys would be forever changed. During Christmas, Jerry Lee sat at the piano in Lee Calhoun's parlor and picked out "Silent Night," mostly on the black keys. Jimmy and Mickey would also play their first notes on that piano—a small historical oddity, since the three cousins would one day rise to separate peaks of musical prominence in rock and roll, gospel, and country music. Jerry Lee must have made an impression, because three months later his father mortgaged his house for nine hundred dollars and bought his son a used Stark upright. Eventually the bank foreclosed on the house, but Jerry Lee kept the piano. By then he had worn the ivory off the keys.

Jerry's formal musical training ended after four lessons when his teacher slapped him across his face. The rest of his education came from Haney's Big House, a black nightclub in Ferriday's "Chocolate Quarter." Jerry and Jimmy would slip in on Friday and Saturday nights to hear the Devil's music. Later, Jimmy would claim that "my family started rock and roll," but the roots of the music were already there in Haney's Big House, in the driving blues of B. B. King and Muddy Waters and a local piano player named Old Sam. "We'd go down there and sell newspapers and shine shoes and everything, and we'd keep on doin' it till nobody was lookin'," Jerry told an interviewer many years later. "And man, we'd sneak in there and old Haney, he'd catch us. He'd say, 'Boy, yo' Uncle Lee come down heah and *kill* me and you both!' And he'd throw us out. But I sure heard a lot of good piano playin' down there. Man, these old black cats come through in them old buses, feet stickin' out the windows, eatin' sardines. But I tell you, they could really play some music—that's a guaranteed fact."

Jimmy was drawn to the piano as well. He had been moved by the performance of Brother Cecil Janway, a traveling evangelist who came through Ferriday and lifted the roof off the little frame church with his righteous piano style. Jimmy sat as close as he could to Brother Janway, and while he watched, he prayed aloud. "Lord, I want you to give me the gift of playing the piano," he said over and over, sometimes so loudly that his father punched him. "If you give me this talent, I will never use it for the world. . . . I will always use the talent for your glory. If I ever go back on my promise, you can paralyze my fingers!" As soon as Brother Janway stepped away, Jimmy boldly approached the piano and began to pick out simple chords.

"Jimmy wasn't very talented," Frankie Jean says, "but he prayed all day and night for that talent, and it came to him. I was about as shocked as the rest of them. I thought the days of miracles were behind us."

On the contrary, miracles were abundant during that summer of 1944. Mickey's mother held prayer meetings in her home above the pool hall. The war raging in Europe and the Pacific seemed far, far away, but it grew suddenly closer when little Jimmy Swaggart began to prophesy in tongues. Jimmy spoke for five days in German and Japanese (the languages were verified, says Sun Swaggart, by war veterans who were drawn to the meetings) and then gave his own interpretations in English. "It would make cool chills run up and down your spine, because he's speakin' in the supernatural, he wasn't speakin' like just an ordinary person," his father recalls. "He was a child in the third grade, y'see, and yet he spoke as a college graduate."

It's a small detail, but I think a relevant one, that the languages in which little Jimmy Swaggart expressed himself were the tongues of the enemy. Moreover, if one were to examine the incident strictly through the lens of psychology, what a clever coup this was on the part of this "deeply suppressed" child, who had been so mortified by his parents' conversion. Now this child who was scarcely allowed to speak in his own house was preaching to the multitudes while his amazed parents stood aside.

"I didn't know what was happening," Jimmy writes in his autobiography. "I felt like I was standing outside my body. Then I began to describe exactly what I saw '. . . a powerful bomb destroying an entire city . . . tall buildings crumbling . . . people screaming.' " Each day more prophecies poured forth. The crowds that gathered to hear this entranced, flaxen-haired child grew large and forced the meetings to be held in the church. Word spread across northern Louisiana as far as Alexandria and Monroe. "Many outsiders, wandering into the little church on Texas Street, were saved after hearing the prophecies," Swaggart writes. "Some dismissed the whole matter because I was only nine years old. But a year later, when the two Japanese cities of Hiroshima and Nagasaki were destroyed, nobody thought the prophecies were childish anymore."

There were other prophecies issued that week that were not recorded in Jimmy's memoirs. Sun Swaggart says there were ten divinations altogether, of which nine already have come to pass. "Of a hydrogen bomb, of a cobalt bomb, of an atomic bomb—they're all here, y'see. And many other things that were stated about the affairs of nations and the entire universe." More than that he won't tell, especially about the unfulfilled tenth prophecy.

"The last one's water," Frankie Jean says. "Something about water covering this town. It's never clear. Something about Ferriday being wiped out."

After the prophecies, Jimmy's future seemed sealed. God had claimed him. Jimmy resisted the call, however; instead, he turned to crime. He and Jerry began to break into local stores. "It was a lark to us," Jimmy writes. "We even stole some scrap iron from Uncle Lee's own backyard and sold it back to him." Jimmy's only interests then were playing the piano and boxing—his ambition was to become the heavyweight champion of the world. His big frame was filling out. Already he sensed the power inside himself, the raw force that could dominate the world of men, both physically and spiritually. The only opponent he couldn't conquer was God.

"I no longer considered myself a Christian," he has said of this period, despite the fact that everyone in his community saw him as a spiritual prodigy. He and Jerry worked up a stage act, where Jimmy played the bass line on the piano and Jerry played the treble, and together they swept talent contests around the state. One night they played separately, and Jimmy began a romping version of "Drinkin' Wine Spo-dee-o-dee," one of Old Sam's numbers at Haney's Big House. "A strange feeling came over me," Jimmy writes. "I was able to do runs on the piano I hadn't been able to do before. My fingers literally flew over the keys." The frenzied crowd in the school auditorium stomped and cheered. "For the first time in my life, I sensed what it felt like to be anointed by the Devil." Remembering his promise to the Lord never to play for the world, Jimmy felt a sudden rush of fear.

At this juncture in their lives, in their early teens, the future careers of Jimmy and Jerry might have changed places. Each saw the choices of life as being all good or all bad. The roads out of Ferriday led only toward good or evil, toward God or Satan, and each boy was standing at the crossroads. At the age of fifteen, Jerry got a job playing piano in the notorious Blue Cat Club in Natchez, "the meanest, lowest-down, fightin'-and-killingest place in the world," he said later; but on Sundays he was preaching in Ferriday. When he was sixteen, he married the first of his six wives, a preacher's daughter named Dorothy Barton, and dropped out of school. Uncle Lee paid to send Jerry to a Pentecostal Bible college in Waxahachie, Texas, but he lasted only three months. He was booted out for playing a boogie version of "My God Is Real" during chapel. He came home and started preaching at the church on Texas Street.

Jimmy would remember this period as the darkest time of his life. God had called him to preach, he believed, but Jimmy wanted less and less to obey him. One day, to Jimmy's horror, his father declared that he was giving up his successful grocery business to go into the ministry full time, along with Minnie Bell. Jimmy began to cry and plead for them not to do it. For the first time in the history of the Swaggart family, they had become financially comfortable. Now all that was being thrown away in the pursuit of a pulpit in a little Holy Roller church in the dismal neighboring town of Wisner. Jimmy was profoundly ashamed. "For years after that," he writes, "when I had to fill out a school form listing my parents' occupation, I left it blank." Whenever his father and mother and sister, Jeanette, went to preach revivals in the little towns around Ferriday, Sun would ask Jimmy to come along. "We need you on the piano," his father said, but Jimmy refused. Jerry went instead.

There is a pattern here, isn't there? God calls, Jimmy resists. As why should he not? God wanted his soul, but Jimmy wanted his identity. His mother had told him repeatedly that he was going to "walk with God," that he would be "perfect." His cousins thought he was close to perfection already. "He wouldn't put on a bathing suit and go swimming in public," Mickey Gilley would recall years later, after the scandal broke. "Jimmy to us was like Jesus walking on the face of the earth again." To be perfect, to be Jesus, was a role Jimmy wasn't quite ready to play. Later, when he was a middle-aged man trapped inside this holy persona and God was making one dramatic demand upon him after another, what was left of the real Jimmy would conspire to break free. It was no accident that the route of his escape was through women.

Women became spiritual metaphors for his relationship with God. They were holy vessels of God's love, and the holiest vessel of all was Minnie Bell Swaggart. It was she who had led Jimmy to Jesus, and Jimmy's estrangement from his mother made him feel his separation from God most acutely. Minnie Bell and Sun would be off preaching out of town and would come home late at night; then she would slip into Jimmy's room. "I would not open my eyes when she kissed me on the cheek," Jimmy writes, "but after she left, I would remember the prayer she whispered over me. Many nights I would lay awake for hours, crying." Other nights this haunted child would awaken "in the wee, still hours of the morning. The house would be quiet, and I would not hear a sound. I would suddenly be assailed with a terrifying thought: 'Jesus has come, everyone is gone, *and I'm left*!' "

Where had everyone gone? They had been raptured. They had risen to meet Christ in the clouds of heaven. Those who were left behind, the unsaved, would, according to the Book of Revelation, endure the seven years of the Great Tribulation, a period marked by the appearance of that dark figure of prophecy the Antichrist. This was the very core of Jimmy's belief. "When I was a boy," he writes, "every other sermon that was preached from behind our pulpits was based on the rapture. We were continually cautioned to be *ready*. Jesus was coming at any minute." Had he come and left Jimmy behind? "More than once, I slipped out of bed and crept to my parents' bedroom door. There I would kneel and put my ear to their door in the hope that I would hear my mother breathing or, as she would so often do in her sleep, say the name of Jesus out loud. . . . I knew if I could hear them, the rapture had not as yet taken place —and there would still be a chance for me."

At the age of seventeen, Jimmy followed Jerry's lead and dropped out of high school, then married Frances Anderson, a pretty girl with dark hair and a crafty face who sang in the choir in Sun's church. "She was fourteen," Frankie Jean says. ("She was fifteen," Swaggart contends, "and not pregnant.")

"I couldn't believe Jimmy made the fatal step," says Frankie Jean. "He got married for sex. We were all laughing about it. Of course, I had gotten married myself when I was twelve. We're all kind of earthy, to say the least."

Until he met Frances, Jimmy had never expressed interest in girls. Thirty-five years later he was still describing her as "the only woman I ever kissed." Given the nature of his relations with other women, that sad boast might actually be true.

Through Frances, Jimmy found the Spirit once again. He began preaching on street corners around the state. Once when he was sermonizing in Ferriday, he spotted Mickey and Jerry standing in the back of the crowd. Tears were streaming down their faces. "I wish I had the guts to do that," Mickey told him. Jerry Lee said, "Jim, I just want you to know, me and Mickey are going out and hit the big time—and help support you in the ministry."

That prophecy would soon come to pass. In 1954 another young communicant of the Assemblies of God, a nineteen-year-old truck driver from East Tupelo, Mississippi, named Elvis Presley, cut a record titled "That's All Right," and the age of rock and roll was born. Soon after that, Jerry's dad drove him to Memphis to audition for Sam Phillips, who had produced not only Elvis but also Roy Orbison, Carl Perkins, and Johnny Cash at the suddenly legendary Sun Records. Jerry sang "Crazy Arms" on a demonstration record. Two months later the song had sold 300,000 copies.

Jimmy was digging ditches at the time. He was eating lunch in a diner when he first heard his cousin's voice come over the jukebox. He thought about all the times he and Jerry had played piano together and the plans they had made to leave Ferriday and hit the big time. For Jerry Lee Lewis, those dreams were coming true.

Why weren't they coming true for Jimmy Swaggart? Despite his talents and his prayers, he seemed paralyzed, unable to get out of the ditch he had dug for himself. Years later, he would learn that his mother and her sisters were spending hours of their time asking God to block his path. The women in his life were praying that the Lord instead would permit Jimmy to preach to thousands, "just like Billy Graham."

Although it wasn't evident at the time, the lives of Jimmy Swaggart and Jerry Lee Lewis were already linked in a curious seesaw in which the fortunes of one would rise as the other's fell.

While he was in Memphis, Jerry prayed to God for "one hit record." With the profits he pledged to establish a church and spend the rest of his life preaching the word. God granted his wish. By 1957, Jerry had sold 21 million records. When "Whole Lotta Shakin' Going On" came out, two more record-pressing plants were built to handle the demand. He was becoming a coast-to-coast sensation. Sam Phillips had a new song he wanted Jerry to record, titled "Great Balls of Fire." For Jerry, the Bible student and part-time preacher, that phrase could mean only one thing. It occasioned a weird and passionate argument between him and Phillips, which the sound engineer inadvertently recorded. Phillips was contending that a person could play rock and roll and still save souls. "How can the devil save souls?" Jerry cried out. "Man, I got the devil in me—if I didn't I'd be a Christian." When Phillips tried to reassure Jerry that the song's title did not refer to the Devil, Jerry replied, "It ain't what you believe, it's what's written in the Bible!" "Then how do you interpret the Bible?" asked Phillips. "H-E-L-L," Jerry said dismally, then struck the opening four notes of the song that would become his trademark, which would make him an international superstar, and which would, he devoutly believed, doom the "Ferriday Fireball" to eternal perdition.

Back in Louisiana, Jimmy was still draining swamps. He was a father now, preaching the backroads churches, living in a house trailer with Frances and the baby, and driving a crummy old Plymouth with faulty valves that he claimed to have "healed" with an anointing of oil on the hood ornament. What a contrast it was when, one Sunday in early December 1957, Jerry wheeled into Ferriday driving a new Cadillac. He seemed to be on top of the world; but that night in church he held the pew so tightly his knuckles turned white. "I preached that morning to be factual with you," Jimmy later told an interviewer, "and God dealt with the boy [Jerry]. I mean dealt with him to such an extent that he sat there and wept as if though his heart was shattered. . . . Of course, then there was nothing but the roses, nothing but the grandeur, nothing but the glory. There was no bitter pill to swallow then."

After the service, the cousins stood in front of the church, and Jerry began to boast about how much money he was making, how many cars he owned, how he was going to be "the biggest thing in the world." "I said, 'Yes, Jerry, but what about your soul?' " Jimmy recalled. "He never answered me. He dropped his head, his eyes once again filled with tears, and he got in his car and drove away."

Soon Jerry would taste that bitter pill. A crowd in Boston rioted following one of Jerry's performances. Police arrested the concert promoter and charged him with inciting anarchy. The reaction against rock and roll was just beginning. A few weeks before the Boston concert, Jerry had married his third wife, his thirteen-year-old second cousin, Myra Gale Brown, a wide-eyed seventh-grader who still believed in Santa Claus. The following spring Mr. and Mrs. Lewis flew to London for a series of performances, but when the British press uncovered his "child bride" and the fact that he had never been divorced from his previous wives, he was chased out of England as a bigamist and cradle robber. He got home to find his bookings canceled. Disc jockeys had dropped his songs from their play lists. Barred from television and most concert halls, he was reduced to one-night stands in the beer halls and ballparks of Waycross and Sulphur Dell.

In the meantime, Jimmy's career as an evangelist was picking up—thanks to Jerry's notoriety. He had posters made up saying, COME HEAR THE FIRST COUSIN OF JERRY LEE LEWIS. Despite his burgeoning popularity, Jimmy was still driving his rattletrap Plymouth. He had begun to pray that God should instruct Jerry to give him an Oldsmobile. Eventually Jerry did, bowing to the pressure his mother brought on him to share his bounty with God's anointed one in Ferriday.

With the gift of the Oldsmobile 88, the jinn of success passed out of Jerry Lee's hands and into Jimmy Lee's. Jerry would never again know the wild popular acclaim that had once been his. He watched Mickey Gilley, whom he would deride forever as "an imitator," become a popular country singer, with three number-one records in a single year (a feat Jerry never accomplished), and the owner of a colossal nightclub in Houston that was the setting of the movie *Urban Cowboy*. Jimmy, too, was becoming a recording star. To date he has issued forty-six albums and claims to have sold 15 million copies. (Since most of them have been sold through his mail-order business, the Recording Industry Association of America has no figures to support the claim.) "I have sold more long-play albums than any gospel singer on the face of the earth," Swaggart liked to brag, as he pointed to the walls of his office, which were lined with gold and platinum records that he had printed and awarded to himself.

As the decades passed, Jerry's success continued to pale. He seemed to be trapped in a horror-house ride. He would see two of his children die, one in a car accident, possibly under the influence of drugs, and the other by drowning in Jerry's own backyard pool. Jerry was drinking steadily, taking pills by the gross, wrecking cars, going through women. The turbulence inside him was impossible to contain. One night he shot his bass player in the chest with a .357 magnum. (The man survived.) In 1973 he got arrested outside Elvis Presley's mansion with a gun in his hand. The IRS seized his property for unpaid taxes. (He was acquitted of charges of tax evasion because the jury ruled that he was too ignorant to do his own taxes.) In 1981 his stomach burst open and he was rushed to the hospital. It was as if some demon inside him were trying to break free. Doctors didn't expect him to survive, but Jerry's hold on life was prodigious. He returned meaner than ever.

Jerry had a history of beating his wives, and many people would suspect him of murdering his fifth wife, a bouncy twenty-five-year-old blonde named Shawn, who was found dead in Jerry's guest bedroom in 1983, with blood in her hair and bruises on her body. (After a quick inquest, the authorities in DeSoto County, Mississippi, where Jerry lives, attributed her death to a drug overdose; Jerry denies any involvement in her death.)

All this time he would watch Jimmy Swaggart grow mightier and more censorious, until he appeared as some volcanic prophet from the Old Testament. Jerry might be sitting in another anonymous hotel room in another dimly perceived city, and he would see Jimmy on television thundering like a new Isaiah, clothed with the garments of salvation and covered with the robe of righteousness, proclaiming the coming day of vengeance. Where had he gotten this terrible authority? Jimmy's faith had seemed, until now, somehow unearned. He did not have to seek belief. From the time he began speaking in tongues and delivering prophecies, faith had been thrust upon him. He resisted, but he never doubted. There had been moments of struggle in his life, moments when he had fallen into the abyss of despair—without ever sinking very far. Faith kept him afloat.

By contrast, the story of Jerry Lee Lewis was one of endless doubt, anguish, and struggle. Indeed, there seemed to be no bottom; there was only this endless fall. His life was a form of living damnation, but he endured it with a certain integrity. It was as if he were paying the price for Jimmy's belief.

They had each discovered the power of the erotic. Jerry's life and music was a trail of broken sexual and social taboos, possibly even to the point of murder, the most forbidden of the erotic appetites. He was a hero of the libido. From the beginning of his career he had been ringmaster of a wild generational urge toward chaos, destruction, sexual excess—in a word, ecstasy—no matter what the cost. He stood defiantly outside the borders of convention; the lyrics of his anthem were "I am what I am, not what you want me to be." Would they also form his epitaph? Who could say that he would stop short of the grave, for, after all, wasn't he imprisoned in the metaphor of his own life? He was a fallen angel, falling from salvation, falling from the Jerry who once had preached and spoken in tongues himself, falling from the Jimmy who had called to him so many times to repent, to come home.

This dissolute life had taken its customary toll. Although Jerry was a few months younger than his cousin, he had aged in such a way that a stranger would no longer have placed them within a decade of each other. Jerry had always been loose and wiry, until his belly blew open, and after that he became hunched and brittle. His hair, once so blond and flowing, had thinned and turned the color of a tobacco stain. And although in his middle fifties he was still a hellcat, there was a new note of uncertainty in his performances. The anger was still there, but it was coated now with caution, and perhaps with a sense of boredom, even of duty.

Jimmy, on the other hand, had stayed unnaturally young and vigorous; in fact, he appeared to grow in vitality year after year. Despite the bifocals he sometimes wore, he remained eerily baby-faced. His entire being testified to good health and good living. But there was something else as well. When he was younger there had been a kind of gelded prissiness about him; he had been so cloaked in goodness and denatured sanctity, despite his powerful frame, that one could not help thinking of the mama's boy, the teacher's pet. Gradually, however, that soft layer gave way. As his empire magnified, so did Jimmy's confidence. His preaching took on an edge, a razor edge. Now, when he stood in his "poolpit," he seemed to lose awareness of who and where he was. Gradually the hands of restraint would let go; he would sink deeper and deeper into his subconscious; he would journey past reason and conscious meaning into the slashing emotions and buried fears and unnamed desires that bubble below. His voice would rise and tremble, his grammar would fall away, but still he stumbled toward that cowering raw nerve of longing. He knew where it was. One watched him with both dread and desire, because this is the nerve that is attached to faith. Longing to be loved, longing to be saved—it is when he finally touches this nerve that the tears flow and the audience stands with its hands upraised, laughing, wailing, praising the Lord, speaking in unknown languages and quivering with the pain and pleasure of this thrilling public exposure.

At the peak of his success, Jimmy Swaggart had become the erotic phenomenon that Jerry had been thirty years before. To see him strut and dance on the stage, full of juice, his voice rippling with insinuation, was to be reminded of the young Jerry Lee, his wavy locks flying, as he gave himself up to ecstasy.

Now, in his middle years, despite the confusion of narcotics, Jerry trembled in the sight of his cousin's judgment. He was constantly tortured by the idea that he was playing Satan's music. "A man can't serve two masters," he would often say. "Satan has power next to God. You ain't loyal to God, you must be loyal to Satan. There ain't no in-between. Can't serve two gods. I'm a sinner; I know it. Soon I'm gonna have to reckon with the chillin' hands of death."

In February 1982, Jimmy preached a sermon at the graveside of Mickey's father. Jerry was there, a bitter man. At the end of the sermon, Jimmy asked of the mourners, "Whosoever among you believes you wouldn't go to heaven with Uncle Arthur if you died today, come forward." Jerry walked up and stood right in Jimmy's face. "Will you accept Christ as your savior?" Jimmy asked. Jerry just stared at him, then turned away.

Their paths would cross again in Dayton, Ohio. Jimmy was there on a crusade. He had forgotten that Jerry was going to be there as well and was surprised when Jerry's fourth wife called him. She was sobbing and hysterical. Jerry was in serious shape, she said. "You've got to do something," she cried. "There's nobody else that can."

After his service, Jimmy went over to the auditorium where his cousin was performing. When he came in, Jerry was playing "Meat Man," a dirty honky-tonk ditty, but his words were scarcely intelligible; he might as well have been speaking in tongues. Jimmy walked onstage and took the mike out of his hands. Jerry was astonished—flabbergasted—but he didn't resist. Jimmy had always been more than a match for him physically. The crowd sat stunned, and the music drifted to a confused halt. "Jerry Lee's my cousin, and I've come to get him," Jimmy announced. When the promoter protested, Jimmy pulled out a wad of cash and paid him off on the spot.

He flew Jerry to Baton Rouge in his private plane and fed him malted milk and shrimp for the next seven days. Jerry left there sober, for the first time in decades, but it didn't take. Nor did Jimmy's plea to join him in the ministry. By now the cousins had been absorbed by forces much larger than themselves.

One summer night in Los Angeles, high again, Jerry was mumbling through a radio interview about serving Satan. "He got power next to God," Jerry said. "He'll drag you . . . to the . . . depths of . . . of agony."

"How does Satan benefit from your entertaining people?" asked the puzzled interviewer.

" 'Cause I'm draggin' the audience to hell with me."

In the meantime, God was courting Jimmy. He came to him in a dream. There was an enormous field of cotton below a gloomy sky. God told Jimmy that the field needed harvesting before the storm came. Then he said, "If you fail, there is no one else to do it. I have many laborers, but none to reach the masses, and *you must not fail!*"

No one else! This was the stark commandment that Jimmy lived with. He had become the new Messiah. "I must do it," he writes. "God has called me to do it. He has laid His hand on my life to do it. . . . If you think there are many others out there—or even one other person—who can do it, you are so sadly mistaken. . . . So if I do not do it, it will not be done. I know that to be the truth."

It was this awesome responsibility, the very fate of the world itself, the salvation of humankind, that would lead Jimmy Swaggart to ruin himself on Airline Highway.

◆

> *Therefore thus saith the Lord of hosts concerning the proph-*
> *ets; Behold, I will feed them with wormwood and make*
> *them drink the water of gall: for from the Prophets of*
> *Jerusalem is profaneness gone forth into all the land.*
>
> JEREMIAH 23:15

"May I help you?" the receptionist asked the ragged blond man who had just wandered into the lobby of WBRZ-TV in Baton Rouge.

"I am a prophet of God," the man informed her.

"And what do you want me to do about it?"

"I've seen visions," said the prophet. "I want to talk to a reporter."

The receptionist pressed a buzzer. In a moment a security guard appeared and, without a word, grasped the man under the arm and steered him outside.

"I don't like that sort of thing," the receptionist confided when the lobby was cleared. "I hate having those weirdos breathing down my neck."

"Does it happen a lot?" I asked her.

"You'd be surprised. All the time."

In a moment the door opened again and John Camp, WBRZ's award-winning investigative reporter, greeted me. For years, Camp had been following the Swaggart Ministries; indeed, during Swaggart's confessional sermon, he had singled out Camp, "my old nemesis," for a particular apology.

Until the recent scandal, Camp had spent a considerable amount of time inquiring into the finances of the Swaggart Ministries. He exposed the "children's fund," one of Swaggart's most successful fund-raising appeals, which purported to provide food, education, and shelter to needy children around the globe, although in fact there was no such designated fund for children until Camp asked for an accounting. Even then, says Camp, only four cents on the dollar actually went to children's projects.

He told me a story he had heard from a disaffected Swaggart employee who had been in charge of spiritual counseling. Two elderly sisters had contributed everything they had to support Swaggart's ministry. They wrote a letter asking if it would be a sin for them to commit suicide and give the insurance money to Jimmy Swaggart. This was at a time when Swaggart was adding on to his million-dollar, nine-thousand-plus-square-foot mansion, with its floors of Italian marble. He and Frances also enjoyed a vacation retreat in Palm Springs, new Lincolns every year, diamonds and Rolex watches, a personal jet, and a two-story, air-conditioned playhouse for the grandchildren. At one point Frances decided that she didn't like the shape of the pool and had it entirely reconfigured. All this while Swaggart was making one desperate claim after another that the ministry was failing and more dollars were urgently needed.

"We're talking about people who I believe are inherently evil—particularly Frances and her son, Donnie," said Camp. "They've developed an opulent lifestyle based on the hopes and dreams of people like those little old ladies who offered to commit suicide. We all have to answer for ourselves, either here or in the hereafter. I think that Jimmy, at least, realizes this—and that is the conflict that underlies his personality."

Camp set a spool of tape on the editing machine. It was an interview with one of the prostitutes who claims to have had sexual relations with Jimmy Swaggart, a redhead who calls herself Peggy Carriere. (She would later fail a lie-detector test administered by a Swaggart employee.) The raw version of this tape had become a sort of underground classic in the newsrooms of Louisiana. "I was in the washroom of the Texas Motel with another girl," Carriere's story begins. She is a thin woman with a sharp face and small eyes. She said she had noticed a tan Lincoln Town Car pulling up by the dumpster in the back of the motel. "I looked and I looked and I said, 'Girl, that's Jimmy Swaggart. Maybe he needs some directions or whatever.' So I walked over to him and said, 'Hello, Jimmy Swaggart. How are you doin'? What do you think about this Jim and Tammy Bakker stuff goin' on?' . . . And he said, 'I'm not Jimmy Swaggart.' And I laughed and I said, 'Yes you are.' And then he started doin' like this with his pants, and I realized he had an erection when he drove up. . . . He was tryin' to get it to go back down, and I kept talkin' about Jim and Tammy Bakker and how was he makin' out with his own congregation and all that. He kept insistin' he wasn't Jimmy Swaggart, that he was just there to meet a man and two little boys, that he was supposed to help this man adopt these little boys. The back of the Texas Motel is an empty lot and a garbage dump. So I jus' tol' him, 'Yeah, all right,' and he drove off."

Several days later she saw the same tan Lincoln parked in the back of the motel. She looked inside to make sure. "He had the telephone in there, the same color seats, plush-velvet brown seats." Then she saw the man she claims was Jimmy Swaggart coming downstairs. "He had on red joggin' shorts with a white V-neck shirt and the white sweatband and the tennis shoes and white socks." As he left, Carriere said to a man standing downstairs, "You know, that's Jimmy Swaggart." And the man replied, "He just gave my old lady twenty dollars for a head job."

At this point the reporter asks Carriere what sort of sex Swaggart had had with her. "He watched me play with my pussy while he jacked off," she said. "He was slumming. That's what he wanted, ten- and twenty-dollar tricks. It was like he wanted to see how low he could go."

◆

The secret that burned inside Jimmy Swaggart was that he had been a slave of sexual perversion since the age of ten. This he confessed in February to the elders in Springfield and to a small group of his own aides. And yet God had lifted him above all others. This was the terrible paradox of Swaggart's life: he had been chosen by God to evangelize the world in the last days, but his own soul was losing ground in a desperate battle with Satan. "Once the individual indulges in pornography, bondage is sure to follow," Swaggart has preached. "He must now wallow deeper in perversion to satisfy the demands of a mind that is rapidly becoming warped by this disease of hell." According to Frankie Jean, Swaggart told his father, "There were demons hovering over me; they came from every direction. . . . It was in my every thought, my every thought was this lust."

Does this account for his rage in the pulpit? For his savagery in bringing down the ministries of his competitors and his feverish jeremiads over the sexual transgressions of other preachers in his denomination? He began by attacking the ministry of the elderly radio evangelist Herbert W. Armstrong, who had proclaimed that his Worldwide Church of God was the only source of salvation in the world. "This is always the first mark of a cult," Swaggart wrote in his denunciation of Armstrong, although Swaggart himself would soon be making similar claims. He quoted I John 4:1: "Beloved, believe not every spirit, but try the spirits whether they are of God: because many false prophets are gone out into the world." Next he turned to Oral Roberts, his main rival among the Pentecostals, who had claimed to raise the dead in his revivals, and who was now begging his supporters to send him $8 million or else "God is going to call me home." "It's abominable," said Swaggart, "and tragically, all in the name of God." He called Roberts a false prophet as well. "Somehow," the wounded Roberts replied, "Satan has put something in your heart, that you're better than anybody else."

And then Swaggart brought down Marvin Gorman.

Gorman, like Swaggart, was ordained by the Assemblies of God. He had risen in the denomination to become the assistant superintendent of the national presbytery. In many respects, the Marvin Gorman Ministries was deliberately modeled on the Jimmy Swaggart Ministries—all too successfully. Recently Gorman's church, the First Assembly of God in New Orleans, surpassed five thousand members, becoming the largest church in Louisiana and eclipsing Swaggart's Family Worship Center congregation of forty-three hundred. Although still a small-time televangelist by Swaggart's standards, Gorman was rising fast. He was a regular guest on Jim and Tammy Bakker's "PTL Club." His own show, "Marvin Gorman Live," was broadcast over thirty-seven independent stations. He operated two television stations of his own and was in the process of purchasing a third, but the big news for Gorman's ministry was that he had just secured a satellite uplink, which would make his program available internationally.

On July 15, 1986, a fellow Assemblies minister confronted Gorman with the charge that Gorman had been carrying on an affair with the other man's wife. Late that evening Gorman drove to Baton Rouge to confront the aggrieved husband in Swaggart's home. Swaggart's lawyer and two other Assemblies preachers were present. After hearing the complaint, Swaggart handed his Bible to Gorman and asked him to read from the fifth chapter of 1 Timothy, where Saint Paul prescribes the conduct of the Christian ministry. "Against an elder receive not an accusation, but before two or three witnesses," Gorman read. "Then that sin rebuke before all, that others may also fear."

"Rebuke before all"—that was the text of the sermon Jimmy Swaggart preached in his home that night before Marvin Gorman and his witnesses. According to Gorman's $90 million defamation suit, Swaggart demanded that Gorman confess his sins, step down from his ministry, and seek rehabilitation (the same procedure Swaggart himself would refuse to follow). Gorman refused, claiming he was innocent, but by the time he arrived back in New Orleans, well after midnight, Frances Swaggart had already called Gorman's associate pastor and several prominent members of his congregation to tell them of the allegations. The next day Gorman resigned from the Assemblies of God. That Sunday a statement prepared by Jimmy Swaggart and several others was read aloud to the stunned parishioners in Gorman's church. In it, Swaggart accused Gorman of having had numerous adulterous affairs. Although Jim Bakker took Gorman's side and actually pleaded for his forgiveness, Swaggart muscled Gorman's show off the PTL Network. The Gorman empire, such as it was, quickly collapsed. His church, his television stations, and especially his reputation were lost to him. He was reduced to preaching in a drafty warehouse in Metairie to a congregation of folding chairs. There he began to consider his revenge.

By now Swaggart had turned his attention to Jim Bakker, the boyish host of the "PTL Club" and president of the PTL Network. Bakker was the darling—as Swaggart had never been—of the Assemblies of God hierarchy. With his amusement park and talk show, his four Mercedes-Benzes and two antique Rolls-Royces, his several mansions, his prosperity gospel and psychological counseling, Bakker represented the status and acceptance and air of sophistication that the Pentecostal movement had longed for since its founding.

Swaggart lived splendidly too, but not so garishly. Moreover, there still hung about Swaggart the taint of Mother Sumrall's weedy lot. There was still something hungry and deprived about Swaggart, something resentful and savage, some blind urge toward chaos. "I don't fit in with anybody, I really don't," Swaggart concluded. "I don't even fit in with the Pentecostals anymore. Because, you see, most Pentecostals have 'grown up.' We've gotten on the right side of the tracks now, and that's what's ruined us. They used to throw rotten eggs at us and laugh at us, but now, you know, we can go to those old movies and we can drink . . . our wine with our meals, just like the Baptists and the Methodists and the Presbyterians can. Am I *bothering* you? Am I *offending* you? Somebody said, 'Don't rock the boat'—I'm trying to turn a rotten thing over."

Like many Assemblies preachers, Swaggart had heard rumors that Bakker was bisexual, and lately Swaggart had been tipped by a defrocked evangelist named John Wesley Fletcher about a tryst he had arranged between Bakker and a then-unnamed young church secretary. Swaggart aired his suspicions before the executive presbyters, but they ignored him. It would be nearly a year before Swaggart would have the proof he needed of Bakker's involvement with Jessica Hahn, but when he had the information, he knew what to do with it. "Jimmy took on Jim Bakker like a pit bulldog taking on a French poodle," one of Swaggart's former aides told me. "Just ripped him to shreds, destroyed the man."

Swaggart was now the scourge of television evangelism. Who could tell what was in his mind as he drove to New Orleans to preach in Marvin Gorman's vacated pulpit on Airline Highway? It was there that he told the congregation about his dream, how *no one else* could harvest the fields of the Lord. Neither the demons nor "all the corrupt preachers they could get on their side" would stop Jimmy Swaggart from doing God's bidding.

And yet it may have been about this time, Palm Sunday, 1987, with Jim Bakker in exile and Gorman destroyed, that Swaggart began to consort with prostitutes. Marvin Gorman received the first of several anonymous calls claiming that his nemesis was cruising his neighborhood. After a while the police began getting similar reports.

Why? Why would Swaggart return again and again to Airline Highway, where he was well known and easily recognized? Consider the thoughts that must have been in his mind. God had commissioned Jimmy Swaggart to blanket the globe with his message. The minister's power continued to multiply. He was on his way to becoming the most visible man in the world. Whether he was walking on the beach in Africa or through slums in the Philippines, he would be recognized. Rulers hailed him, as well as the drifting masses. Such power could only come from God's hand. But at the same time, Satan had gained control of Swaggart's soul. The seed of sexual perversion, which he said had sprouted at the age of ten, had now grown and matured and was terribly ripe. Compared with that of the men he had brought down, the men he had publicly excoriated as false prophets, Swaggart's behavior was even more obsessive and bizarre. So who was he really serving—God or Satan? Was he a false prophet as well? Or had his power grown so great that he was swelling into the mighty Prince of Darkness, of whom Jesus had warned, who would be received as the Messiah but would be revealed in the Great Tribulation as the Antichrist?

The Travel Inn is one of several deteriorated motels along Airline Highway that rent rooms by the hour. NO REFUNDS AFTER THE FIRST 15 MINUTES, reads a sign in the manager's office. Outside their narrow rooms, facing the muddy courtyard, women sit in molded fiberglass chairs waiting for customers. Many of them kill time by watching evangelists on television. Across Airline Highway, poking above the privacy fence, a large billboard proclaims, JESUS SAID UNLESS A MAN IS BORN AGAIN HE CANNOT SEE THE KINGDOM OF GOD: JOHN 3:3. YOUR ETERNITY IS AT STAKE. Perhaps it is not surprising that Jimmy Swaggart would chose this spot to give himself up to his enemies. Here, in this highly charged battleground between God and Satan, he found a twenty-six-year-old mother of three with a crucifix tattooed on her right arm. Her name was Debra Murphree.

"Sometimes I would see him drive down the street every week, and he wouldn't stop unless he knew I was there," says Murphree. (Like Carriere, Murphree failed a lie-detector test, although she was identified in a photo taken with Swaggart. She believes the polygraph results were affected by her heavy drug use.) "He told me to get naked and maybe lay on the bed and pose for him. . . . To me, I think he's kind of perverted, or, you know, talking about some of the things that we talked about in the rooms, you know, I wouldn't want him around my children." Several times Murphree commented that he reminded her of the famous Baton Rouge evangelist. "A lot of people tell me that," she says Swaggart replied. He told her his name was Billy and that he lived in St. Louis.

Despite reports of his frequent sightings on Airline Highway, Swaggart admits to only a single instance of what he called moral failure. So what are we to make of the detailed descriptions Murphree gave to *Penthouse* (for a sum reported to be in six figures) about their multiple encounters?

Swaggart had been a leading figure in the attack by the Christian right against newsstand sales of teen and rock and especially men's magazines. *Penthouse* alone was losing $1.6 million a month in lowered sales after such major outlets as 7-Eleven stores removed the magazines from their shelves. No doubt this accounts for the sanctimonious pleasure with which *Playboy* and *Penthouse* and *Gallery* and the like chronicled the fall of Swaggart and the Bakkers. To underline the seediness of Swaggart's trysts, *Penthouse* assigned a news photographer to shoot Murphree in the various postures she supposedly assumed for Swaggart—in stark black and white, without the customary airbrushing that their more "wholesome" models receive.

Swaggart has admitted a lifelong obsession with pornography, so one can assume that there is more to his story than he has told. One might say that this entire battle for Swaggart's soul, outwardly manifested by his verbal war against harlots and dirty magazines, inwardly by his struggle against his own yearning for the same, is a particularly Christian phenomenon. Pornography and Christianity are necessary opposites, and it is not surprising that, for instance, the vilest publisher of them all, *Hustler*'s Larry Flynt, would become a Christian convert—no more than that Jessica Hahn, the church secretary who slept with Jim Bakker, would wind up living in the Playboy mansion. The same gravitational pull that would cause Debra Murphree to tattoo a cross on her arm and watch Jimmy Swaggart on television brought Jimmy Swaggart to Airline Highway to watch Debra Murphree.

If we accept Murphree's account, Swaggart visited her twenty or twenty-five times—often enough to set off alarms in Marvin Gorman's neighborhood. Eventually he was bound to be discovered. His enemies would have their day. Gorman and the pornographers would triumph. But there was another inevitable consequence of Swaggart's self-destruction. That was the fact that others who had cared nothing about his ministry until now would suddenly be drawn into the drama of his life. It's a small matter, and probably it never occurred to Swaggart when he entered room 7 of the Travel Inn, that people like me would eventually follow him here, even to this same room, to pick up the miserable details of his ruination.

I thought about this as I sat on the slumping double bed and stared at the orange carpet and the nubby green chenille drapes, the purple walls, the vaulted ceiling with a pink crossbeam, the pale yellow tiles of the bathroom. There was a television, of course, and a telephone ("He was so cheap he would call and try to get me to get him off over the phone").

The coffee table was illuminated by a suspended lamp on a gold chain—the characteristic "classy" touch that filled the room with despair. Above the bed was a mock-Picasso-blue-period print of mandolins and a typewriter.

The moment Swaggart entered this gloomy little compartment, he made a date with me in his future. I am not trying to inflate my importance; he had made the same date with dozens of other reporters who were at this moment filling up the bar at the Sheraton in Baton Rouge or chasing the increasingly reticent whores up and down Airline Highway. I was merely a part of the press mob that was prying into the catastrophe he had made of his life.

I felt an unhappy kinship with this man. In his church, I had experienced that familiar longing for transcendence; yes, even in his disgrace he had managed to touch me. He had built that giant structure as a theater to contain his belief; and although it was crass and showy, it was also thrilling and defiantly emotional. It seemed to me a more spiritual place in many respects than the arid intellectual refinements of the church I had grown up in, precisely because it was so untamed. At least in Swaggart's church, one could sense the raw and sometimes dangerous expansiveness of the human spirit. His was not a religion I could believe in—but then, mere belief was not what he was after: it was surrender, total, abject surrender of the spirit. And of course a part of me longed for exactly that, the ecstatic abandonment of my own busy, judgmental, ironic mentality.

Room 7 was another sort of theater. Here Swaggart sought ecstasy of another kind, that of degradation. After all, it was not sex he was seeking, exactly, but obscenity. "He'd always try to talk me into pulling my pants off and facing him sideways with my legs spread apart," Murphree says. Sometimes he would ask her to undress in his car and run outside, which she wouldn't do, because she didn't trust that he would not drive off and leave her. When they were here in her room at the Travel Inn he would get her to use a dildo while he sat in the green fiberglass chair and masturbated. Several times he asked if she would let her nine-year-old daughter watch them, but she refused.

If her story is true, then again I could only stand in awe of Swaggart's willingness to go to extremes. Only once, she says, did Swaggart ever enter her. "I was on my knees, doggie-style, with my feet hanging off the bed." Let us stop here, for a moment, and consider this scene. There is a woman stripped of everything—not merely her clothes and her dignity and her personality but also, one might say, her humanity. She has been reduced—"doggie-style"—to animal status. But isn't there, in her subjugation, in the very lewdness of this scene, something sacred? Her utter surrender is perversely like the surrender of the *penitentes* who abase themselves before the majesty of the Lord. The shame, the submission, the degradation of the ego, are the same, and in this sense we can see how obscenity both mocks and mirrors the divine.

Jimmy Swaggart stands behind her, pants down, staring at her ass. No doubt he thinks he is staring into hell itself. Perhaps he sees a vision of himself, humiliated before his enemies and his loved ones and indeed before the entire electronic world. There is a power inside him—he thinks it's a demon—that has dragged him to this low place and now draws him closer. But there is also the noble urge to destroy himself. This immensely public man, this almost universal symbol of righteousness, has repeatedly brought himself to a place where his discovery and disgrace are so likely that one could say he was playing Russian roulette with his reputation. It is a game no one plays for very long. Swaggart himself had been the agent of destruction for other men just like him, priestly men brought to ruin by their animal desires—one of whom was searching for him right here on Airline Highway with revenge in mind. "He stuck it in and pumped a couple of times and pulled it out," says Murphree. Then he cried out, "Oh, God, I don't want to come yet, but it's coming already!"

On October 17, 1987, Gorman would have his revenge. His son Randy worked part-time for the Jefferson Parish sheriff's office and had spent some time with Debra Murphree himself. Both the father and the son had been waiting for Swaggart to reappear, and they were ready. While Randy snapped photos from behind a curtain in another room in the motel, Swaggart went into room 7 in the company of a woman who, according to church officials who have seen the photograph, resembles Murphree. Shortly after that, Marvin Gorman drove into the courtyard and found Swaggart changing his tire. Someone had cut the valve stem. The two evangelists spent the next two hours talking in Gorman's car. Gorman says that Swaggart asked repeatedly, "What do you want, Marvin?" and that he replied, "Jimmy, I want you to just get your life straight and to love me."

The following day Gorman met with Jimmy, Frances, and their son, Donnie, at a Sheraton in the New Orleans area. Gorman gave Swaggart a grace period of four months to "clean up his act." What that meant, according to a friend of Gorman's, was a public confession and apology from Jimmy Swaggart. Some people in the Swaggart camp suspect that the bankrupt Gorman was actually angling for a significant settlement in his defamation suit against Swaggart.

But four months passed with an eerie silence from Baton Rouge. Swaggart continued his telecasts and his crusades, traveling to the Ivory Coast and Liberia and then swinging through Central America. At times his despair would break through, and he would ridicule himself as a "poor, pitiful preacher," even comparing himself to Judas. "Let me tell you this," he cried out in a Thanksgiving camp meeting. "Demon powers, fallen angels, work more in religion than they work anyplace else. I pray constantly: 'God, don't let spirits get in Jimmy Swaggart.'"

It was, no doubt, an awkward time in his marriage.

In January of 1988, nearly at the end of Gorman's four-month deadline, Jimmy and Frances went out to dinner with several of their top aides, including Jack Pruitt, who was director of financial development. Pruitt and Frances were both serious joggers, and at dinner they were talking about their training regimens. "Something I've been using lately that has helped me is bee pollen," Pruitt said. "I have some candy bars with bee pollen in them and they're a great energy boost. They help your endurance; they even say they will increase your sex drive." Everyone laughed, especially when Pruitt produced a candy bar from his pocket and tossed it to Swaggart. "You eat that, Jimmy, and Frances will thank you for it," Pruitt joked.

Swaggart sat quietly, staring at the candy bar, as the laughter subsided into confused silence. "Well, Jack, I'm trying to think of a gentlemanly way of answering you," Swaggart finally said. "I don't need something to speed me up. I need something to slow me down."

That same month of January, according to Peggy Carriere, Swaggart returned to New Orleans. She says she saw him "cruising, looking for ladies," once again dressed in his tennis clothes but this time driving a white Lincoln. (Swaggart owned a tan Lincoln, his wife a white one.)

In February, the deadline passed. Gorman sent a note to Swaggart, reminding him of his terms. Again he received no response. Instead, Swaggart traveled to Managua to preach to forty thousand Nicaraguans in the Plaza de la Revolución. Gorman flew to Springfield with his package of photographs. Jimmy Swaggart had accomplished his sad task. He had brought himself down.

◆

SWAGGART: HE THREATENS DIVORCE AS MARRIAGE CRUMBLES, read the headline in the *National Enquirer* in the supermarkets and convenience stores in Baton Rouge. "She treated him like a little boy, and like a little boy he rebelled," an unnamed family member told the *Enquirer*. The actor Dennis Quaid had just checked out of the Sheraton on Interstate 10, where he was staying while working on a movie, to go on to his next role, that of Jerry Lee Lewis in *Great Balls of Fire*. Jerry's career seemed about to rise out of the rock and roll archives, an ominous development for his cousin on the other end of destiny's seesaw. One wondered if there was not a sense of relief—perhaps on both the cousins' parts—that Jimmy had fallen from his throne. After all, how exhausting these roles must have become for them, good boy and bad boy, what a tiresome pair of roles to have to play day after day, night after night—two lifetimes spent in the service of opposing mythologies, now suddenly rendered counterfeit by Jimmy's spectacular self-destruction.

And here came the reporters. For it was Pentecost Sunday, May 22, 1988, the day Swaggart chose to return to the pulpit. A month earlier he had been officially defrocked by the Assemblies of God. In the course of his self-imposed three-month suspension, Swaggart had to lay off about five hundred workers; he had been booted off the two major Christian television networks; his worldwide television coverage had been reduced, according to church officials, to only four or five countries; missions had been closed down; students had deserted his Bible college; every minister on his staff was forced to choose between working for Swaggart and keeping his Assemblies credentials; IRS agents were poring over his books; and Marvin Gorman's defamation suit was marching toward trial. "Maybe there is no other man in history more humiliated than me," Swaggart cried out, with his usual breathtaking perspective on his own importance.

The death knell was sounding for Jimmy Swaggart, or at least for what Jimmy Swaggart could have been. He promised to come back more contrite and less accusing than he had been in the past. "I believe my message will reflect a deeper compassion and love," he wrote in his monthly column in the *Evangelist*. But it was unclear if that was the message his audience wanted to hear.

"I preached to some of the largest crowds in the world, but I guess that I stand today with more fear and more trembling than I ever stood before in all my life," he said as he surveyed a crowd of about five thousand. He spoke of two dreams. In one he was "in a church. The church was empty—it was not this one—and I was tied or held down to the floor flat against the far wall. I remember wanting to get to the platform, to the pulpit, but I could not." In the other dream he fought a serpent with a sword or club. . . .

"Halabi man ni kasaba man!" A middle-aged black woman interrupted with a chant in tongues.

"Sister, give your utterance just a few moments from now," Swaggart requested. Two ushers led the woman out while Swaggart continued.

"I fought this thing, fighting with all the strength I had, and I finally subdued and killed it. . . . I was standing exhausted with this club in my hand," Swaggart continued, unself-consciously relating this marvelously revealing masturbatory dream. "Then I looked to my right. I thought at first it was a huge concrete pillar standing a hundred or so feet high, but it moved, and I saw it was another serpent. . . . And I remember my knees buckled. I awakened from the dream and said, 'God, do I have to fight this, and I don't know how to do it?' " But God showed him. He did not have to fight the serpent. Jesus had already slain the leviathan.

"I have suffered the fire of the eternal Lord!" Swaggart cried, suddenly breaking into a jig. "CNN is going to be taking a picture. . . . CBS and ABC and NBC! I want to serve notice on all the demons and devils and hell itself: the best is yet to come!" The crowd stood and praised him. Some of them were sobbing. It seemed obvious that Swaggart would never be reduced to "sweeping out a little mission house across the tracks," as he put it; he would always have an audience. And yet he said God had told him, "You'll be a cripple the rest of your life."

"Malala mani goboso maniki!" The black woman was back in the sanctuary. This time her voice was louder and more insistent. As she gave her utterance, she rocked back and forth, and her hands shook in front of her face. When she finished, Swaggart asked if anyone in the audience was moved to interpret the message. Abruptly a slender white woman rose and in a quaking banshee voice related the following: "Yea, I am a God of purpose. . . . Yea, I say unto thee, go forth in my name for I am with thee, I shall never leave thee or forsake thee. . . . I will flow like a river through you, and I will preach to the Holy Ghost's fire . . . and they will not be able to deny my power and my spirit!"

At the end of the service, the worshipers came to the altar to hug Swaggart and, as they often do, stick love offerings in the pockets of his suit. I got in line. Swaggart had refused to see me, or any other reporter, during this time. I knew I couldn't change his mind; I didn't really know why I even felt the need to speak to him. Perhaps, like everyone else here, I just wanted to spend a moment in his embrace. When it finally came my turn, he put his arms around me and whispered "God bless you" into my ear.

When I identified myself, he jumped back as if he had touched a snake. He said he was sorry but he didn't want to be interviewed.

"I just want you to know that I'm not your enemy," I blurted out.

"Why—why—I can see that," he sputtered. "Yes, there's a good spirit on you."

That felt oddly like a benediction. I accepted it gratefully, with no clear idea why I had sought his forgiveness. Swaggart was still smiling at me when the next person in line, Marvin Gorman's private investigator, stuck a subpoena in his pocket.

Outside the Family Worship Center, summer had returned to Baton Rouge with a damp embrace of its own. The drama that was playing out in the soul of Jimmy Swaggart was coming to a close. He had defeated his demons, for the moment, at least, by crippling himself forever—and for that we must be grateful. No one else could have done it. Yet it would not be long before the public catastrophe of his life would open another chapter. (He would be caught with another prostitute in California two years later.) One has the sense that it is not damnation but obscurity that causes Swaggart's knees to knock. In the meantime, he will still be waiting for us, on the Airline Highways of cable TV, asking us to pay him for his precious love.

Madalyn O'Hair and God Almighty

"You have been sued," the citation said. I stood in my doorway looking dumbly at the constable who had just handed me the document. "Wait a minute," I heard my wife say in the background. "Let me get the camera."

Cause number 475,798 in the state of Texas, in the district court of Travis County, was Madalyn O'Hair, plaintiff (described as "the leading proponent, educator and spokesperson for Atheism in the World"), vs. Texas Monthly, Inc.; Gregory Curtis, editor; and Lawrence Wright, writer. Often I had thumbed through complaints that looked exactly like this one, but there were always other people's names attached, not my own. Now, as I tried to read the legal language, the words wouldn't penetrate; they seemed to have lost all meaning. It was like trying to hold mercury in my hands. I turned to the end to see the amount of damages she was asking. Nine million dollars.

The constable put her arm around me and looked into the camera. "Smile," said my wife.

It was already in the newspaper. People were calling. They weren't exactly sympathetic; they seemed oddly excited. It was as if I had stepped into the gladiators' arena and was about to entertain them by being eaten in public. "It's a very curious case," a lawyer friend of mine told me, as if I should be happy to have aroused his professional interest. "It's not libel, it's not a true invasion-of-privacy, it's really on the edge of a lot of interesting law." He was regarding me, I could see, as a potentially historic figure in legal annals, the defendant in *O'Hair* v. *Wright*.

"I thought it was a nuisance suit," I said dismally.

"Oh, it is," he said. "But you never know."

A Jungian scholar suggested that this was an eruption of my unconscious. "But this is really happening!" I said. "I'm not *imagining* it—it's on the docket!" "No, no—of course it's real, but it's also a force you've summoned. I mean, it's really a tribute to you. Madalyn O'Hair is your shadow! That's very powerful."

When my mind was finally settled enough to read the suit, I realized that O'Hair's principal complaint was that I had portrayed her in a magazine article in a "false light" and that my "co-conspirators" had used the plaintiff's "INTERNATIONALLY FAMOUS PERSONA" to sell magazines. Her fame, O'Hair contended, was a property right, which we had used without her permission. That was the part that had the lawyers interested. There is a muddy margin of opinion that surrounds the issue of whether a well-known personality should derive benefits from the use of his or her image for commercial gain. One cannot, for instance, use Madonna's face in an advertisement without her permission. Madonna owns the commercial use of her face. But what about putting her face on the cover of a magazine (or just her name, as in the case of O'Hair)? Is selling magazines different from selling soap? Well, yes, say the advocates of the First Amendment. Magazines sell information, and Madonna's face on a magazine is a form of free speech. That's different from commercial speech. But how, exactly? If a magazine makes money by using Madonna's image, why can't Procter & Gamble?

This was a collision of interests that I didn't wish to be caught in. I suspected, and hoped, that O'Hair was suing me and *Texas Monthly* in order to save face with her followers, and perhaps to cause me discomfort. If that was so, the suit would probably sit on the docket for a year or two until it was purged for nonaction (in fact, that is exactly what did occur). In the meantime, I would simply have to wait to see what happened.

It seemed odd—more than odd; bizarre—that this woman whom I had admired for decades as a champion of free speech would be suing me for writing about her—for even having the *right* to write about her. But then, one thing I had learned about Madalyn O'Hair was that she was never what she pretended to be.

◆

"Madalyn is napping," my guide told me that summer day in 1988. "Would you like to take a look?" We wove through offices filled with visitors from around the country who had come to Austin, Texas, on June 17 to attend the dedication of the handsomely appointed new headquarters of the American Atheist Center and to mark the twenty-fifth anniversary of the Supreme Court decision that removed prayer and Bible reading from public schools. Madalyn Murray O'Hair, the woman usually credited with instigating that famous lawsuit, was sixty-nine years old now and in frail health. As usual at this hour in the afternoon, she was taking a snooze on her couch. Several visitors were peeking through the glass wall into her office. They gave way reluctantly as we approached. There before us lay the first lady of atheism, as she calls herself, in a flower-print dress. "It's a little like Lenin's tomb," my guide observed.

Did she hear us? Suddenly O'Hair started awake and swung her bare feet to the floor. She ran a hand through her vivid, abruptly cropped white hair. A heavy woman, she appeared even in this half-awakened state like a bowling ball looking for new pins to scatter. Before I could gracefully escape, O'Hair turned to look at the peering faces in her office glass, and I was caught by her stare. There was no surprise in her face, only resignation and a look I would see several times again in those brief, unguarded moments when O'Hair stepped out of the spotlight and her mask of anger dropped aside—revealing the anxiety, the fear underneath.

I slipped away in embarrassment, realizing I had started badly with her. As with most Americans my age, my life had already been given a good shaking by Madalyn Murray O'Hair. For the first ten years of my schooling, I had listened to prayers and Scripture every morning following the announcements on the PA system. Sometimes I myself had had the honor of choosing and reading the morning devotional. I don't recall ever questioning the propriety of such action or wondering what my Jewish classmates, for instance, might think about hearing Christian prayers in public schools, or my Catholic classmates about listening to verses from the King James rather than the Douay version of the Bible. But in the fateful fall of 1963 we began classes amid the enormous hubbub that followed the Supreme Court decision. The absence of morning prayers was widely seen as a prelude to the fall of the West. And the woman who had toppled civilization as we knew it was some loudmouthed Baltimore housewife—that was my impression, but it was widely shared—who then proceeded to wage another legal campaign, to tax church property. She was the first person I had ever heard called a heretic. She jumped out of the front pages with one outrageous statement after another; indeed, the era of dissent in the sixties really began with Madalyn Murray, who styled herself as the "most hated woman in America."

Certainly she was the most provocative. Soon after the school prayer decision, Mrs. Murray, as she called herself then, was charged with assaulting five Baltimore policemen (she sometimes inflates the number of policemen to ten, fourteen, twenty-two, or twenty-six). She fled first to Hawaii, where she took refuge in a Unitarian church. When the governor of Hawaii granted an extradition request to the state of Maryland, Murray and her family left for Mexico, which summarily deported her to Texas. Her odyssey ended in Austin in 1965, where she successfully fought extradition, married an ex–FBI informer named Richard O'Hair, and has remained long after the Maryland charges were dropped.

Over the years I followed Madalyn O'Hair in the way one keeps up with celebrities, as she bantered with Johnny Carson, sued the pope, or burst into a church and turned over the bingo tables. When I was at college, she came to speak. By then she had achieved a kind of sainthood status with the undergraduate intelligentsia. True to her billing, she raked over capitalism and Christianity and especially Catholicism, unsettling if not actually insulting every person in the auditorium. Afterward she repaired to the student center and held forth in the lobby, giving an explicit and highly titillating seminar on the variations of sexual intercourse. I had never seen anyone with such a breathtaking willingness to endure public hatred. "I love a good fight," she boasted to the press. "I guess fighting God and God's spokesmen is sort of the ultimate, isn't it?"

It was, one had to admit, a lonely battle, not only against God and God's spokesmen but also against hypocrisy and the indignant defenders of the status quo. How revealing it was of the sanctimoniousness of American society that the voice of a single woman denying God would create such mob hysteria. "I am a walking, talking personification of their doubt," she once acutely observed. "The more they doubt, the more tenuous their hold, the more they're going to attack." For preachers and evangelists, she was a convenient bugaboo, apparent proof that the archenemy is real. When there was a rumor floated in 1975 that O'Hair was getting twenty-seven thousand signatures on a petition to stop prayers on the joint American-Soviet Apollo-Soyuz mission, more than a million pieces of mail flooded into NASA supporting prayer in space. A similar report that she was petitioning twenty-seven thousand signatures (a number that seems to have a magical connection with atheism) to eliminate religious broadcasting persisted for years, generating more than 25 million outraged letters to the Federal Communications Commission—"more mail than we have ever received on any [other] issue," a spokesman said. There was never any truth to either rumor, and yet such responses demonstrate that for millions of religious Americans Madalyn O'Hair is a symbol of the rising forces of immorality, social chaos, and spiritual despair—secularism, in a word.

"I am more than just an Atheist," she boasts. "I am, in fact, *the* Atheist." It is a bold and oddly theological claim, and it infuriates many of her fellow nonconformists. "Madalyn Murray has brought more discord to adherents of the freethought movement, more bad publicity in the press, more hatred by the public at large toward freethinkers, rationalists, secularists and humanists than have all the combined theologians from the beginning of man's fight for freedom from religion," an editorialist wrote in *The American Rationalist* in 1964. "As a public representative of atheism, Madalyn Murray's general abnormal behavior has branded all atheists in the eyes of their antagonists as extremists, vulgarists, opportunists and law breakers."

Neutrality is never present around O'Hair; she polarizes everyone. "The insults she stood, the beatings she suffered paved the way for more modern atheists," says her friend Frank Zindler. "She has done the consciousness-raising. It is accepted now that atheists have the right to exist in America, whereas when she started, that was not a given." Charles Dews, a political activist in Austin who used to work for the American Atheist Center, says, "She's really a freedom lover. Beneath everything else, Madalyn Murray O'Hair is about freedom." On the other hand, G. Richard Bozarth, another former employee, calls her a "petty, jealous little ex-bureaucrat who once shouted loud enough to gain attention and has continued shouting for lack of imagination to do anything else—and because it pays." Her former treasurer, Brian Lynch, says, "I really think she hates herself, and that hatred is projected onto everyone else she comes into contact with." Everyone has an opinion about Madalyn O'Hair, yet no one who knows her well claims to understand her.

Hungry all her life for money and power, she lives at last in a world of material comfort, surrounded by luxurious German cars and expensive artwork, yet the organization that she created to carry on her crusade is little more than a hollow shell, a sounding chamber for the roar of O'Hair's complaints. She has suffered the loss of her husband to cancer and the defection, in 1980, of her elder son, William Murray, to Christianity.

Perhaps those losses might account for the anxiety that one sometimes sees in O'Hair's eyes. More than once I had heard from some gloating Christian that even Mrs. O'Hair stood quaking at the prospect of death. That may be so; but the more I learned about her, the more I wondered whether it was not death but life that frightened her—life, and the contradictions, the lies, and the deceit that make up the furious existence of Madalyn Murray O'Hair.

◆

Awake and arguing, O'Hair was in the computer typesetting room trading opinions with Arthur Frederick Ide, who had identified himself to me as a former Lutheran minister and former Carmelite monk. He is also the author of *Unzipped: The Popes Bare All*, which was published by the American Atheist Press. O'Hair and Ide were talking about the government conspiracy to control the flow of information through the mails. A bony, white-haired visitor from Ohio was creeping forward in an office chair, and he ventured the opinion that it was a goddamn shame one couldn't buy stock in the post office monopoly.

"Oh, but you can," O'Hair said.

"No!" said the Ohioan, suddenly shooting backward in his chair. "But Madalyn, it's a government agency."

"The hell you say," O'Hair barked. "It's no more a government agency than General Motors."

"It says 'U.S. Postal Service,'" the man insisted, edging forward again. "It's like a department—"

"It's nothing of the sort," O'Hair replied. "It's—it's a . . ."

"It's an instrumentality," said Ide. "An instrumentality is an entity that serves the functions of government but is privately constituted."

"An *instrumentality*!" said the flabbergasted Ohioan.

"Just like the gawddamn Federal Reserve," O'Hair observed, in an accent that harks back to the broad vowels of Baltimore.

"The Federal Reserve!" the Ohioan cried. His chair flew back against the wall.

I walked past the typesetting room, following Robin Murray-O'Hair, who is both O'Hair's granddaughter and her adopted daughter. Robin edits the *American Atheist* magazine and presides over the forty thousand–volume Charles E. Stevens American Atheist Library. She is a redhead, with many of her grandmother's features, including freckles and a strong, round jaw. She also shares O'Hair's famous love of animals. At the moment, Robin was being towed along by a black spaniel named Princess, one of six dogs that sometimes occupy her office. "We have commissioned ten new books," Robin said as we passed through the art department on our way to the audiovisual room. "The latest is *I Bought My First Six-Pack When I Was 35,* which is about a Mormon who overcame religion." Robin smiled shyly. On the wall, among the many photographs of O'Hair, was a framed letter from Bertrand Russell protesting one of O'Hair's various arrests. "Mrs. O'Hair has been in jail eleven times," Robin said. "Many of the charges were, of course, trumped up. In Baltimore there was a law on the books that one can't tether a horse for twenty-four hours. Someone interpreted a horse to mean a car in modern times, so when Mrs. O'Hair left her car parked on the street for two days, she was arrested for abusing a horse."

Robin left me in the bookstore, where I browsed among T-shirts, coffee mugs, and the rather extensive selection of books and pamphlets for sale, most of which seemed to have been written by O'Hair. In addition to her weekly cable television show, her frequent public appearances, and her prolific interviews, O'Hair writes much of the monthly *American Atheist* magazine and an *Insider's Newsletter* for members.

"I feel that Madalyn Murray O'Hair doesn't belong to the public, only her public activities do," O'Hair told me when she finally invited me into her office for an interview. I had asked her to reflect on the twenty-five years since the school prayer decision. "My life is my own. It doesn't do anybody any good, anytime, anywhere, for anyone to look back and say, 'I'm going to re-evaluate.' What good does that do? The answer is not a gawddamn bit of good.

"I do think we're in a steady retreat. There's an absolute steady retreat into what I call neofascism—but it's really old-time fascism—into a robber-baron society and a religiously dominated society, and that's not cyclical, because they have new weapons at hand now, mainly communications technology with which they can rapidly disperse ideas. . . ."

She was off. Like most people who have been interviewed too many times, O'Hair has learned the art of avoiding questions; in her case, she bulldozed right through with her massive opinion machine. ("I am convinced that the pope should be arrested tomorrow for crimes against humanity—just for the fact that he goes out and tells women to breed indiscriminately, to be fruitful and multiply, to get one in the oven tonight. He should be put in a cage.") As she hammered home her points in this unsought, uncontested debate, I found myself losing focus. I absently studied the awards and plaques that have been given her by various free-thought societies. Next to the door was a framed law degree from the South Texas College of Law. The extent of O'Hair's education, like practically everything else in her background, is a matter of dispute. She likes to be called Dr. O'Hair and has claimed on occasion to have attended as many as twenty-three schools and eleven colleges. "Compared to most cud-chewing, small-talking, stupid American women, I'm a brain," she once told *Life.* "We might as well admit it, I'm a genius." "My degrees are primarily in history and law," she vaguely informed a student audience. Later she boasted of an "alphabet of degrees—B.A., M.A., LL.B., M.P.S.W., Ph.D., J.D." Her erudition is frequently remarked upon in the press. She has spent "more hours in college than many professors," said *Esquire,* which noted that she had a law degree from Ohio Northern University (according to the associate dean, O'Hair attended one year but did not graduate). "There is no woman in the United States," O'Hair claimed in 1980, "who has the education, the family, the background, or the IQ I have." However, except for the 1952 law degree from South Texas—an LL.B. that was later automatically converted to a Juris Doctor when the terminology changed—most of the other degrees appear to be imaginary, although that is a subject Madalyn foreclosed with her vigorous refusal to discuss anything personal. Her Ph.D. in divinity comes from a diploma mill called the Minnesota Institute of Philosophy. It is known that she took the bar exam, but whether she passed is an open question. Despite her many lawsuits, she has never been admitted to the practice of law.

"People talk constantly about the problems of the world, but they don't get down to basics," O'Hair was saying. "Like, what are you going to do with all the shit? Five billion people have a bowel movement every day! Just what are you going to do with it? Let's go ahead and ask the pope—'Do you want it all accumulated and put in front of the Vatican?' "

I finally had the opportunity to ask about a curious bronze statuette on her desk depicting two animals copulating. That set O'Hair off on a discussion of the Judeo-Christian suppression of natural sexual impulses. "I know where religion came from, and don't ask me to talk about it, I'll put it out in a paperback soon, but part of it has to do with human sexuality. So, one of the things that I have been collecting over the years is those things that would show humans an understanding of the need for a recognition of sex and its normal and natural place, and here is one of them," she said, fondling the statuette. "Here is an absolutely beautiful—they're bears, I guess—example of sex in its place." She sighed affectionately. "I love them, don't you? They're forbidden."

◆

The circumstances of O'Hair's background and early life are cloudy and bitterly disputed. A 1964 *Saturday Evening Post* article on the woman who then called herself Madalyn Mays Murray states that her father's ancestors settled in the Massachusetts colony in 1650. Since then, O'Hair has given the date as 1611, although the Pilgrims didn't arrive until 1620. Her younger son, Jon Garth Murray, now says that the Mays family first appeared on American shores in the person of a man he identifies only as the Reverend Mays, a chaplain on the second ship to arrive at the Jamestown colony. In any case, eighteen generations later, on Palm Sunday in 1919, in Beechview, a suburb of Pittsburgh, Madalyn was born, the second child of John and Lena Mays. According to O'Hair's elder son, William Murray, Madalyn's mother tried to abort the child by jumping out of a second-story window. "Even Madalyn's birth had a bizarre element," Murray writes in his score-settling autobiography, *My Life Without God*. "Grandmother swore years later that Mother had been born with an unusual dark membrane covering her whole body. It resembled a black shroud, and Grandmother claimed that the doctor at hand had said it was very unusual, though he offered no explanation. He gave a portion of the membrane to her, and Grandmother kept this odd keepsake for many years."

O'Hair says that her father, whom she called Pup, was a wealthy contractor, the sole proprietor of the Pittsburgh Steel Erection Company. William Murray says that his grandfather was "a good carpenter, but the man never filed a tax return in his life." O'Hair has written, "We have always been affluent. I grew up in Cadillac cars, commodious homes, with linen damask tablecloths and heavy silver and oriental rugs and a concert-grand Steinway piano. I had fur coats and diamond rings and designer dresses." Elsewhere she states, "The chauffeur of our Rolls-Royce was black and shiny, and he rode me on his shoulders." William contends that the chauffeur was a friend who brought food to the Mays family when Madalyn's father went broke. After going bankrupt in the construction business, William writes, Pup opened a roadhouse that served as a brothel and then turned to rum running during Prohibition.

O'Hair's mixed feelings about her father may be seen in her various statements about him over the years. "My father knew only steel," she once wrote. "Master builder, engineer, contractor, he set and job fabricated the steel in every engineering feat in Pittsburgh, Pa. The banks closed their doors on his payroll money, his personal money, his business money, abruptly, overnight, and he was without resources. . . . Brutal, demanding, he kept his new job as a 'superintendent' or 'foreman' or 'pusher' by squeezing profit from the men. Then there were no more jobs, even for the 'slave driver.'" She has been quoted as calling her father, in her broad accent, a "Nazi and a *ray*shist too." On the other hand, she has also described Pup as a benevolent capitalist. "He was the only construction man in Pittsburgh then who went to the union for his 'journeymen'; paid union wages." Later, when her parents came to live with her, O'Hair and her father waged an ongoing war. The last words she said to him before she slammed out of the house to run an errand were, "Oh, I wish you would drop dead." When she returned home, she found her wish had come true.

Her feelings about her mother were never mixed. He mother was a "cowed, whipped dog." "I do think I have resolved any kind of oedipal conflict I may have had in relation to my father. I never slept with him or anything like that," O'Hair once told a student audience. "We had a very normal relationship. Now, I hated my mother's guts." According to William, O'Hair didn't speak to her mother for the final five years of her life and did not attend her mother's funeral.

In 1923 Madalyn Mays was baptized in the Presbyterian church, but that event scarcely signaled a religious conversion. The story she has told many times is that she read the Bible cover to cover one weekend while she was still in grade school, "and I was totally, completely appalled, totally turned off, filled with repugnance." She was twelve or thirteen at the time. "I came away stunned with the hatred, the brutality, the sadomasochism, the cruelty, the killing, the ugliness. Oh, I suppose that words like 'sadomasochism' were not in my vocabulary at the time, but I could see the obvious lies, the disgusting stories."

When she relates this episode, she often cites the Scriptures, such as Mark 13:12 ("Now the brother shall betray the brother to death, and the father the son; and children shall rise up against their parents, and shall cause them to be put to death") or Luke 19:27 ("But those mine enemies, which would not that I should reign over them, bring hither, and slay them before me"). She likes to quote Deuteronomy 28:27, where Moses warns that those who deny God will be smitten with hemorrhoids ("emerods"). One of her favorite passages is Leviticus 21:17–22, in which the Lord disqualifies the handicapped from the ministry: "Whosoever he be of thy seed in their generations that hath any blemish, let him not approach to offer the bread of his God . . . a blind man, or a lame, or he that hath a flat nose. . . . Or a croockbackt, or a dwarf, or that hath blemish in his eye, or be scurvy, or scabbed. . . ." According to O'Hair's exegesis, "This means that every United States veteran who has been injured in any of our wars cannot go to church. He isn't wanted there. And all of the black people in our nation, with their flat noses, aren't wanted either."

The precocious young scholar who read those passages turned to her parents for advice. "I went in and said to my dad and mother, 'You know what's in the Bible?' and for the next couple of weeks I would read little things to them. My mother just drew herself up and said, 'That's not in *my* Bible.' That ended the discussion. I never accepted the Bible after that day at all. I refused to go to Sunday school. I refused to go to church. What were they going to do, hang me by my thumbs? That ended it right there."

Despite that supposed childhood apostasy, O'Hair went on to attend Ashland College, an Ohio school affiliated with the Church of the Brethren. In October 1941, at the age of twenty-two, still a virgin, she eloped with a steelworker named John Henry Roths. Their marriage was interrupted by the Japanese attack on Pearl Harbor two months later, which inspired Roths to join the Marines and his wife to sign up with the Women's Army Corps. O'Hair claims that she served as a cryptographer on General Eisenhower's staff in North Africa and Italy. (Archivists at the Eisenhower Library, who have personal records and directories of the general's staff, could find no trace of a Madalyn Mays or Roths.) "In letters home she expressed confidence in an Allied victory because 'God is on our side,' " William Murray writes in his autobiography.

"Mother always relished telling one story in particular about her time in the army," William continues:

> Though I doubt it ever happened, it illustrates the sort of grandiose ideas about herself that her army experiences somehow fostered.
>
> While she was in Rome, serving on General Eisenhower's staff, she and some friends went out for a night on the town. After a more or less conventional round of dining and drinking, according to Mother, they arrived at the Vatican around three o'clock in the morning. Drunken and rowdy, they nevertheless gained entrance to St. Peter's Basilica by bribing a Swiss

guard. Once inside, with champagne bottles in hand, they made their way to a room where the three-tiered crown used in papal coronations was on display in a glass case. Mother never said how, but she claims they managed to remove the crown from its case. Thereupon they proceeded to act out a mock coronation of my mother as the first female pope. If true, Mother's knack for attention-getting theatrics was already fully refined.

It was in Italy that Lieutenant Madalyn Roths met William Murray, Jr., an officer in the Eighth Army Air Corps. Murray was a wealthy, married Roman Catholic from Long Island. "They became intimate," his son and namesake writes, "and I was conceived in September 1945, the same month that Japan officially surrendered."

Murray's paternity was later established in court. O'Hair told her son that his father's religion forbade him from divorcing his wife and marrying Madalyn, who was herself, of course, still married to Roths. To compound the misery, O'Hair discovered when she returned from the war that her parents had moved into a shack with no electricity or running water. "She soon learned that her father had spent on booze all the money she had sent home for savings," Murray writes. "The whole family was destitute, she was pregnant, and her husband—not the father of her child—was expected home at any time. I believe it was during this period, as she was pacing the dirt floor of that shack and mulling over the dismal outlook for her life, that her extreme anti-God views were born."

When Roths returned, he gallantly offered to stay with his wife and raise the child as his own, but O'Hair declined and proceeded to sue him for divorce. "By this time Mother's antagonism toward God had reached an advanced stage," Murray notes. During a violent electrical storm, O'Hair suddenly announced to her parents that she was going out in the storm "to challenge God to strike me and this child dead with one of those lightning bolts." The pregnant Madalyn stood in the rain waving her fist and cursing God. "You see, you see!" she cried when she returned inside. "If God exists, he would surely have taken up my challenge. I've proved irrefutably that God does not exist." Her son was born on May 25, 1946. She named him William J. Murray III, and soon after that she began calling herself Madalyn Murray, although she and Murray never married.

Like his mother, baby Bill was baptized in the Presbyterian faith. Several years later Madalyn bore a child by another man and named that child Jon Garth Murray. She baptized him in the Methodist church. "It pleased their grandparents," she explained, "and I figured the kids would think it was like any other water splashing on their heads. My attitude then was, 'You go your way, I'll go mine—you think Christ was born of a virgin; I think he's the hero of a beautiful story.' "

The Mays-Murray clan, consisting of Madalyn, her parents, her elder brother, Irv, and her son Bill, moved to Houston in 1949, where Madalyn worked as a probation officer for Harris County and studied law in night school. In 1952 Pup migrated to Baltimore, and the rest of the family soon joined him. Madalyn found work in various jobs; she says she has been a model, a waitress, a hairdresser, a stenographer, a lawyer, an aerodynamics engineer, an advertising manager, and a psychiatric social worker.

About this time she also turned to radical politics. She attended meetings of the Trotskyite Socialist Workers' Party in 1957. In 1959 she applied for Soviet citizenship. The following year, having gotten no response, she and her two children traveled to Europe on the *Queen Elizabeth* with the intention of defecting to the Soviet embassy in Paris. "The Soviet embassy didn't know what to do," William Murray told me. "It was the first time they ever had anybody trying to defect *to* them." Madalyn Murray and her sons returned to Baltimore in the fall of 1960. Almost immediately thereafter she filed her historic suit against the Baltimore schools. According to William, the suit was little more than a ploy to persuade the Soviets to accept her.

◆

Although Madalyn O'Hair is synonymous in the public mind with the Supreme Court's ban on school prayer, the truth is that her case was one of a number of suits attacking the practice of religion in public schools. In the precedent-setting *McCollum* v. *Board of Education of Champaign, Illinois*, in 1948, the Supreme Court applied the due-process clause of the Fourteenth Amendment in declaring religious instruction in the schools to be unconstitutional. That ruling still did not affect prayer and Bible reading in the public schools, which continued to be a common feature of most American children's daily life.

During the Korean War, the New York State Board of Regents voted to recommend the reading of a prayer in the public schools of that state. The prayer was "Almighty God, we acknowledge our dependence upon Thee, and we beg Thy blessing upon us, our parents, our teachers and our country." It would seem obvious now that no governmental power should have the authority to force any segment of the public into saying a prescribed prayer, but in 1962 when the Supreme Court ruled (in *Engel v. Vitale*) that such official prayers violated the First Amendment guarantee of free speech, the decision was widely attacked. "The Supreme Court has made God unconstitutional," said North Carolina senator Sam Ervin. "This is another step toward the secularization of the United States," echoed Billy Graham. "The framers of our Constitution meant we were to have freedom of religion, not freedom from religion."

The suit Madalyn Murray brought in her son's name took three years to reach the Supreme Court, but during those years the issue of prayer and Bible reading in public schools was very much on people's minds. Moreover, the *Engel* decision made the court's intent rather clear. The Murray family became the object of harassment—although according to William, it was not so intense or vituperative as his mother describes. According to her, there were death threats, the house was egged, the flower gardens destroyed, the car towed, the cat murdered. O'Hair fanned the controversy with her own provocative words and actions. "We find the Bible to be nauseating, historically inaccurate, replete with the ravings of madmen," she wrote to *Life*. "We find God to be sadistic, brutal, and a representation of hatred, vengeance. We find the Lord's Prayer to be that muttered by worms groveling for meager existence in a traumatic paranoid world.

"This is not appropriate untouchable dicta to be forced on adult or child. The business of public schools, where attendance is compulsory, is to prepare children to face the problems on earth, not to prepare for heaven—which is a delusional dream of the unsophisticated minds of the ill-educated clergy. . . ."

Not surprisingly, mail came to the Murray house in canvas bags. Much of it was hate mail, but some of it contained money—enough for the family to live comfortably, according to William.

Meanwhile, in a suburb of Philadelphia, a Unitarian named Ed Schempp had filed a suit complaining that Pennsylvania law required that his son be subjected to the reading of ten verses from the Bible followed by the recitation of the Lord's Prayer every day before the beginning of classes. Ed Schempp is practically unknown to the general public, but it was actually *Abington School District* v. *Schempp*, not *Murray* v. *Curlett*, that the court chose to consider when it banned devotional readings and prayer from public schools. The Murray case was joined to *Schempp* as a secondary litigant. Many atheists who are at odds with Madalyn O'Hair point out that the court would have made the same decision with or without her suit.

One evening in Baltimore, as she sat alone in her basement library, trying to decide whether to press ahead with her lawsuit, she reflected on the sense that she had always had of her separateness. "When we had first moved into those row houses in Baltimore, I think that I had picked out one for purchase deliberately, in the hopes that I could be 'like everyone else.' I had wanted so desperately to fit in," she writes. "I could not engage in conversation about which bleach was the whitest for the wash. I never gave a damn about the chlorophyll in toothpaste. The idiotic idea of back fence visiting left me completely cold. None of my work had ever taken up even a fraction of my thinking processes and too often I would pace that basement library floor like a lioness caged, the wrap of loneliness, of aloneness, always about me.

"I had just wanted *one person* somewhere, sometime, to understand me and I had never found any."

Certainly her parents had never fathomed her. Nor had her first husband or any of her lovers. "I just want a man," she complained in her 1965 *Playboy* interview, "a real, two-balled masculine guy—and there aren't many of them around, believe me. But I do want somebody my own age, and somebody who has brains enough to keep me interested and to earn enough money to support me in the style to which I've become accustomed. . . . I want a man with the thigh muscles to give me a good frolic in the sack, the kind who'll tear hell out of a thick steak, and yet who can go to the ballet with me and discuss Hegelian dialectic and know what the hell he's talking about. I want a strong man, but a gentle one."

For a while she thought she might have found her ideal companion in Richard O'Hair, the ex–FBI informer whom she married in Austin in 1965, a man who was "both cruelty and love, patience and anger, ignorance and knowledge," as she described him. It was his cruelty that landed him in the Travis County jail for aggravated assault against Madalyn. William Murray says that his mother intended to divorce O'Hair until she learned that he had terminal cancer; then she hung on to him for his death benefits. William believes that the disappointments in Madalyn's sex life may have colored her attitude toward religion. "It is my opinion that my mother's maniacal campaign to remove all reference to God in public schools and government . . . stems back to this issue. Madalyn Murray was mad at men, and she was mad at God, who was male."

Shortly after moving to Austin, Madalyn and Richard O'Hair formed

Poor Richard's Universal Life Church to dramatize the folly of tax exemptions for religious institutions. Richard was the "president, pastor, and prophet," and Madalyn was the bishop. Unlike her other organizations, Poor Richard's Church never did gain a tax exemption; nonetheless, Madalyn took to wearing a clerical collar for effect.

O'Hair's obsession with religion leaves some other atheists scratching their heads. "Don't you really think she is a religious person?" asks her former employee Charles Dews. "If she didn't care tremendously about all that stuff, why would she spend so much time refuting it?"

It is certainly true that religion defines O'Hair's life just as powerfully as it does the life of a priest or a television evangelist, although in O'Hair's case she finds her identity in resisting belief instead of accepting it. At times, she acknowledges herself as a religious phenomenon, even joking that she was prophesied by Jesus in Matthew 12:42 (also Luke 11:31): "The queen of the south [i.e., Austin] shall rise up in the judgment with this generation, and shall condemn it." Usually, however, O'Hair carefully separates herself from either belief or disbelief. "Atheists do *not* have 'a belief system' of any kind, even a negative belief system," O'Hair has said. "The god idea, the Christian belief package, can be demonstrated as being harmful to individuals, to groups, to countries, to whole cultures, in all eras of the history of humankind. Nothing good has ever come out of religion. I am not fighting 'a god' which does not exist, I am—rather—engaged in the effort of trying to free the human mind of some unnatural restrictions which have been placed upon it."

◆

"Mr. Wright? This is Madalyn O'Hair."

I recognized the voice on the phone. I was just preparing for another interview with her when she called.

"I just called to say that I am terminating our arrangement," said O'Hair.

"Why?"

"I don't choose to tell you," she said, and abruptly hung up.

This was puzzling. Until now, she had been cordial enough, and apparently pleased at the publicity. I had scarcely begun my research; in fact, I was still finishing another story. Had I offended her? Was there something she was trying to hide? Was it the magazine I was working for? Had she learned something about *me*? She was often accusing Christians of sending spies into her midst. Did she think I was a closet fundamentalist? It was odd to me, because my own philosophy was closer to hers than she may have realized.

O'Hair traces her intellectual lineage to the Greek materialists Democritus, who believed that nothing exists except atoms and empty space, and Epicurus, the amiable proponent of a modest life lived in the pursuit of its natural sweetness (*hedone* in Greek; thus the word "hedonism"). That philosophy was quickly seen as a threat to the established order, and in 270 B.C. Epicurus was stoned to death. Many centuries later he would become the hero and model for another great materialist, Karl Marx.

The materialist philosophy proposes that matter exists without regard for thought; there would still be a universe, in other words, if we were not here to perceive it. Thought itself is strictly a function of the brain, and dies with the death of the brain. There is no "larger" consciousness or universal life force. Nor is there a creator; matter and energy are eternal and don't require a "first cause" or a Grand Designer. "Everything traced has been found to be materialist [i.e., composed of matter]," writes O'Hair. "The physical laws of nature are always in operation. They do not step aside even for a moment to permit anything else, such as spirit, to rule. The Materialist holds that there is no spiritual existence apart from the material body."

For nearly two millennia in the West, this line of thinking went underground, driven there by intolerant Christians. But in the nineteenth century, materialism was reborn, this time as "scientific" materialism. Darwin, Marx, and Nietzsche, and soon Freud would lead the attack on religion, using reason and science as their weapons. Religion has so far proved unable to answer this attack, although it was slow to relinquish its power, especially in America, where the capacity for religious renewal has shown itself generation after generation. Nonetheless, scientific materialism in its various forms—Marxism, psychology, anthropology, humanism—took hold and gradually changed the way Americans looked at the world and their place in it.

How recent this has been is evident in my own lifetime. When I was a child in the fifties and early sixties, atheism was practically unknown in public life—and as far as I could tell, in private life as well. No one I knew admitted any doubt of God's existence, even a third of a century after the Scopes trial, where Clarence Darrow made a monkey of William Jennings Bryan and his fundamentalist faith. Of course, I lived a narrow existence in a Bible Belt city, but the reports we had from the larger world suggested that America had withstood the assault of the rationalists and emerged spiritually unshaken.

Living inside this unanimity of belief was quite terrifying, at least for me. Honest doubt was out of the question. To lose one's belief meant that one stood alone; and internally, that is how I felt, isolated and apart, because something inside me refused to melt into faith and accept the doctrines that everyone I knew appeared to believe. Consequently I was afraid to turn around and face my disbelief. It hovered behind me like something grotesque; and yet it was me, it was my own doubt, that I refused to face.

Why did it scare me so? It was not just the fear of not conforming, although that was powerful and perhaps even paramount in my thinking. There was also the question of what agnostics or atheists might be. The answer was drunkards, dope fiends, serial killers, and communists. Faith genuinely was presented to me on those terms. Without faith, the moral fabric dissolved; one lived only for the senses; gradually one became a slave of sensation. Family and loved ones lost their significance; the only lasting attachments were money, pleasure, and power—but if one pursued them blindly, they led invariably to despair and damnation. Religious conviction was not only the sole route to salvation; it was also the knot that kept one's character from unraveling. It was what saved a man from being overwhelmed by the beast inside him.

Obviously, I could look around at the mink coats in the pews and the Cadillacs in the church parking lot and see that the real values of our congregation were something other than the stated ones. Conspicuous prosperity always seemed to me to be at war with what I thought was at the core of the Christian message, which was a spirit of selflessness and a near anarchic denial of the emoluments of ordered society. The hypocrisy, the sanctimony of our unanimous civic religiousness degraded the human spirit and made cowards out of everyone who secretly doubted. At the same time, I had an investment in the status quo. There was security in living in a community where everyone seemed to have come to the same conclusions, which were that life was eternal, that the personality somehow survived, and that Jesus had paid our way into Heaven with his own bloody sacrifice. If these propositions were so easy to believe, then I supposed eventually I would come to believe them as well.

It wasn't as if I disbelieved. I just wasn't convinced. I didn't think of myself as agnostic, however; I saw myself as being in the process of accepting belief. Doubt was the dreary countryside outside my window as I traveled toward God's promise of salvation. One wouldn't want to get off here, in the wintry, unpopulated steppes, when awaiting us was the hearty, bustling, and confident City of Faith.

A few years ago, a friend of our family who had been a prominent pastor in Dallas paid me a visit. I had heard about his misfortunes. His wife had died a tortured death of cancer. He had subsequently resigned from the ministry and went to live reclusively on a little ranch south of Fort Worth. I remember him as being a humorous and insightful preacher, a rock of security to his congregation; and yet when I saw him again, he was bitter and surprisingly profane. As we talked, it became clear that he was no longer a believer. Was it because of his wife's death? No, he told me; that had only proved what he had been thinking for years, which was that life was cruel and meaningless. "The truth is, I never really believed that crap anyway," he said ruefully. "I was just going through the motions, saying what people paid me to say." I was appalled. Certainly in many respects he had been more imprisoned than I by the official piety of our culture, and one should congratulate him on breaking loose from this cage of hypocrisy. And yet my unspoken reaction was "How dare you!" I had wanted to believe in his belief.

This was the paradoxical state of my mind when I was growing up: on the one hand, I was terrorized by my own doubt; and on the other hand, I was comforted by the piety of everyone I knew. Imagine, then, the conflicting sensations of emancipation and loss that I felt when I first heard the voice of Madalyn Murray hee-hawing at religion. There was inside me a simultaneous yes and no. Emotionally, it was like watching a city burn, horrifying but thrilling. A sneaky underlying feeling of relief at the destruction of everything I had counted upon, a welcoming sense of chaos, and, above all, joy at hearing the unspeakable truth brayed out loud—what a load of powerful but ambivalent feelings I had when Madalyn Murray entered our public consciousness!

She thoroughly personified the Christian stereotype of an atheist. Rude, impertinent, blasphemous, a destroyer not only of beliefs but of esteemed values—especially sexual values—she popped off like a chain of fireworks in a sanctuary, merrily detonating everything we held dear. It was impossible not to admire her nerve, while at the same time wondering at her apparent compulsion to be loathed. Even the things we didn't know about her conformed to the stereotype. Her phony marriage, her radical politics, her attempted defection to the Soviet Union were all deeply buried secrets, but had we known them, they simply would have confirmed what we already suspected. She absorbed our hatred like a poultice.

There were many reasons I began to let go of my faith, or, to put it more exactly, my need to believe; but certainly Madalyn Murray's stormy assault on religion clarified the intellectual atmosphere and released a flood of private doubts. It became possible to discuss the troubling details of religious belief without feeling that skepticism was heresy. But once this door was opened, all the goblins we had been warned against rushed in. It seems unlikely that the skyrocketing rise in crimes of violence, crimes against property, suicide, drug use, and divorce, to cite a few alarming examples, can be tied entirely to the secularization of American society. There are many causes. But it is true that after the Supreme Court's benchmark decision on prayer and Scripture reading in public schools, the rates of increase in these statistics began their steep and remorseless climb. People were safer, institutions more revered, families more cohesive, prisons less crowded when the blanket of religious conformity was stretched across the land.

Madalyn Murray personified this secularizing force, which was both intellectually liberating and socially ruinous. It was easy to understand why she was so hated, the turmoil was so great; but as for me—and, I suspect, millions like me—there was a debt of gratitude for being set free from orthodoxy.

When I was finally able to face my doubt, and then forced myself to imagine life as Madalyn sees it, as a brief and difficult journey to oblivion, I understood what an escapist fantasy religion had been for me. I didn't picture pearly gates and angels—I didn't have a real image of an afterlife at all—but the prospect of there being something more than the life I was living had allowed me to live partly outside of my everyday existence. Even when I no longer considered myself religious, I had protected this fantasy of an afterlife by claiming to be agnostic. There was probably no reason to hope—but I might be wrong. I was willing to be surprised. This had seemed to me an entirely innocent and defensible position, and in fact the only possible conclusion any thinking person could come to without further evidence. It never had occurred to me how laden my agnosticism was with longing. To be agnostic, to take no position on spiritual matters, was to accept the possibility of divinity and the meaningfulness of life. Not to have a conviction meant that the jury was still out. I admit this was ideal for me in many respects. I could be honest with myself intellectually while still entertaining the alternative of life everlasting. Doubt, that clever word, allowed me to embrace all options.

It wasn't until I realized that doubt was a cover for my disowned beliefs that I made myself imagine life without it. "There is nothing more," I said to myself once in the middle of the night when I was forty years old and struggling once again with the questions life poses at that hour. I am sure I have often said that to myself in the past, but for some reason this statement now rang with truth. I had an image suddenly of the spinning planet; behind it was a great screen, like a portable home-movie screen that rolls out of a tube. It was there to capture my projections. Then the screen snapped and rolled itself up, and I was looking into the stars. It was as if I had never seen them so clearly. I realized that the screen had always blocked my view. I think it was also there to protect me from the coldness of space.

My reaction to spiritual hopelessness was not despair but gratitude. If this is all there is, I thought, then how fortunate I am to be loved by my family, to be healthy, not to be poor—to be able to enjoy so many pleasures that this astonishing world has to offer. Atheism forced me to focus on the life I was actually living. Never before had I savored the sweetness of existence so intensely, and that surprised me, because I had always associated that sense of joyousness and serenity with profound religious faith. I felt comforted by the thought that I was living the truth and not flirting with possibilities. I lived for about a year in this state of crystallized certainty. Then the doubts crept back.

Perhaps I am unable to cling to the absolutes that belief, and the rejection of belief, require. Now my doubting took the form of being open to mystery. My particular weaknesses were wonder at the majesty of nature and an occasional moment when the beauty and intelligence of another human being made me reconsider the notion of divinity. I'm expressing myself too dryly. What I mean to say is that sometimes I felt myself overflowing with love. It didn't seem to me that this was just an evolutionary response to my environment, although who can say that evolution itself is not a loving response to creation?

I once read about a unified field theory that imagined the four physical forces of nature—the strong force, the weak force, electromagnetism, and gravity—as manifestations of love. The attraction of the electron to the atomic nucleus, or the earth to the sun, were, in some sense, emotional. Love was the bond, the matrix of existence. This theory appealed to me in the same symbolic way that certain religious beliefs did. It offered an explanation for this unaccountable rush of love that tied me to friends and nature and my community and even to ideas and values that were particularly dear to me. I recognize that this is just another way of envisioning God. I don't *believe* in this theory; I just like it. And it makes me wonder why the God idea is so resonant that it keeps echoing inside me.

◆

"My mother is a cult leader, in case you haven't noticed," said William J. Murray III, as he raced toward McKinney, Texas, to deliver his Christian testimony at a crusade in a junior high school. "Madalyn Murray O'Hair makes Reverend Moon look mainstream! She could not survive in a competitive society. She lost *dozens* of jobs! She was forced out of homes for not paying, had furniture repossessed. Her personal life is almost a duplicate of the personal life of Karl Marx! What she and Marx and Charlie Manson have in common is magical thinking—the ability to think that somehow through the destruction of other individuals or classes their own personal problems will get better."

Murray is a sandy-haired man with O'Hair's light green eyes and a similar tendency to speak in diatribes. Since Mother's Day, 1980, when he announced that he had found God, William Murray has been preaching salvation and telling the world about life with America's most famous atheist. In the trunk of Murray's Mercury were several boxes of books that he would sell after his testimony. He is the author of four books, including *The Church Is Not for Perfect People* and *Nicaragua: Portrait of a Tragedy*. When I met him, he was dividing his time between evangelism and soliciting private aid for the contras.

Murray has often voiced the hope that his mother would repent. In his fantasies he sees her walking up the aisle of a church as he is giving the invitation to salvation. O'Hair, on the other hand, refuses to discuss her elder son's conversion. "Bill simply got fed up with being poor, and he has sold out to the highest bidder: religion," she observed when she first heard the news. Years later she would only comment, "My son is disturbed."

Sitting on the stage, Murray listened as Paul Jackson, a Little Rock evangelist, introduced him to the half-filled school auditorium. It must have seemed an odd moment to a man whose life was changed in another junior high school in September 1960, when his mother went to register him for the ninth grade and overheard students praying aloud. The lawsuit that followed would make Madalyn Murray a household word. But Bill Murray had to continue his life in the Baltimore public schools. "He was pummeled, hit, shoved, pushed, tripped," his mother once wrote. She told the *Saturday Evening Post* that her son had been beaten "more than a hundred times." Once a group of thugs cornered him in a barbershop and serenaded him with "Jesus Loves Me." When Bill tried to escape, the boys pushed him in front of a city bus.

And yet the adult William Murray renounces the atheism he has suffered to defend. He is rueful about the legacy of the suit his mother brought in his name. "If all it took out of the schools was organized prayer, then who would care?" he says. "But they took everything out of the schools that had anything to do with religion, including the instruction of morals. Now, a quarter-century after the court decision, we have a nation that is basically devoid of any moral principles." In 1980 he wrote a letter to the Baltimore *Sun* and the Austin *American-Statesman* confessing that "the part I played in removing prayer from public schools was criminal" and apologizing for his role in "the building of the personal empire of Madalyn O'Hair."

He maintains that his conversion to Christianity had nothing to do with his mother's atheism; rather, it was a reaction to the "total swirling chaos that surrounds *everything* to do with my mother." He didn't even realize O'Hair was his mother until he was in grade school. She had taken him to a supermarket, and he asked, "Madalyn, can I get some Coke?" And she responded, "Why do you keep calling me 'Madalyn'? I'm your mother." Until then, he had thought his grandmother was his mother; he had never really known what his relationship with O'Hair was.

By the time William was eighteen, he says, "my mind was totally scrambled." He had already fathered a child, Robin, whom he later abandoned to his mother's care. He paid off O'Hair for her trouble with an old mailing list he had left over from a failed effort as a magazine publisher. After serving in the Army, he went to work for Braniff Airlines as an operations agent, later working his way up to manager. In 1975 he decided to rejoin his mother and his daughter in Austin, to "help with the family atheist business. All of a sudden I was back in all the irrationality—the screaming, the hollering, the profanity, the drinking. I started to drink heavily myself." He launched a brief, aborted political career by running in the Republican primary for the congressional seat held by J. J. "Jake" Pickle. Murray described himself as a conservative businessman who opposed school busing. A year later, in October 1977, he left Austin, "in total emotional distress." He drove to Tucson, Arizona, and opened a bookstore.

Soon he drifted to San Francisco and went back into airline management. In July 1979 he was charged with the attempted capital murder of a police officer who had answered a complaint about a domestic disturbance in Murray's home. In the midst of his personal turmoil, Murray began seeking God. In large part, this was due to the influence of Alcoholics Anonymous, which had helped him stop drinking. "But I was praying to a god I didn't know. I said, 'Please, God, get this garbage out of my mind about my mother. Let me walk away from my past and do whatever it is I need to do. It took me two years after I had said, 'Yes, I want to believe that Jesus is the Christ' to convince myself that that's what I actually believed."

During this period of spiritual questioning, Murray had a powerful dream. A great winged angel stood before him with a sword in his hand. Inscribed on the sword's hilt were the words IN HOC SIGNO VINCE, meaning "In This Sign Conquer." The tip of the sword touched an open Bible. "Well, I got up in the middle of the night," Murray told the audience in McKinney, "and drove to downtown San Francisco to one of those all-night discount department stores. There, under a stack of porno magazines, I found a Bible. It was there, in that Bible, that I learned the *truth*: that Jesus Christ was not some local politician of some two thousand years ago; no indeed, he was already a king, a king who had come down from his throne in heaven to this earth, to minister here, to die on the cross of Calvary so that the sins of mankind—the sins of Bill Murray—could be washed away in his blood. And when I realized that, I was able to get down on my knees and repent of my sins and ask him into my heart.

"Some here would say, 'That's all fine and good, Bill Murray, but how can you say all those terrible things about your mother?' " Well, I've tried to tell this story without saying a single derogatory word about anyone. I soon found out it was impossible to tell the story without the truth. That doesn't mean I don't love my mother. *I don't love the one who reaches up from his fiery pit to direct her!*—but I can and do love my mother. Because I want you to listen very closely to what I am going to say: she is no different than a single person in this place tonight before they accepted Jesus Christ as their personal lord and savior. She's just another sixty-nine-year-old white-haired woman that needs Jesus."

✦

O'Hair and her younger son, Jon Garth, were in a television studio taping their weekly cable TV show when I came in and took a seat behind the crew. O'Hair glowered when she noticed me. "You're really dogging us, aren't you?" she said when the camera blinked off. She combed her hair in furious strokes and trapped it in a yellow hairband. Jon Garth sheepishly glanced away. He had invited me to the taping.

"Hello, I'm Madalyn O'Hair," she suddenly said with a broad smile when the red eye of the camera opened again. It was easy to see the charm she has in store when she chooses to call upon it, and easy to see as well her courageous, witty, but also bitterly sarcastic intellect. Her intelligence is real, despite her gruff nature and the fabrications of her background. Tonight she and Jon Garth were discussing the recent purported appearance of the Virgin Mary in Lubbock at a small church that O'Hair labeled a "Texas Lourdes among the mesquite." "Two different cripples jumped out of their chairs, and people cried, 'They're healed! They're healed!' " Jon Garth reported. "Except that when the media got to them, these individuals said that they were in wheelchairs for other purposes—they could walk perfectly fine."

This has been one of the valuable functions of the American Atheist Center—exposing the credulousness of mistaken believers and the occasional religious fraud. With an increasingly conservative Supreme Court, O'Hair acknowledges that the groundbreaking lawsuits are mostly a part of the past. In any case, her victories have been scattered and rather marginal. A 1969 suit she brought against "religious exploitation of outer space" was eventually thrown out of court, but in the meantime it succeeded in preventing *Apollo 11* astronaut Buzz Aldrin from taking a televised Communion on the moon. In *O'Hair* v. *Hill*, which became one of her most important victories, she sued the State of Texas over a constitutional provision that anyone holding an office of public trust be required to believe in a Supreme Being. That requirement is no longer enforced. Her suit to block Pope John Paul II from saying Mass on the Mall in Washington, D.C., in 1979 backfired when it helped to establish the precedent of equal access of religious groups to public facilities. Her campaigns to eliminate tax exemptions for churches and to remove "In God We Trust" from the coinage have also failed.

In the past, Madalyn has claimed as many as 100,000 members in her organization. If that were true, the revenue from the $40 annual dues would exceed by more than five times the $750,000 budget of the American Atheist Center. Sometimes Madalyn uses the more ambiguous figure of 60,000 or 70,000 "families." When William Murray resigned from the center, he said that the organization's mailing list comprised only 2,517 people, less than half of whom were actual members. "If I headed the atheist movement for twenty years and had only twelve hundred and forty members, I'd look for something else in life," he remarked. The latest official numbers are 55,000 members, representing 45,000 families. Brian Lynch, the former treasurer of American Atheists, whom Madalyn fired for alleged sexual misconduct (he emphatically denies the charge), says that the actual membership is about 2,400, "the highest total she's ever had. That's pretty pathetic considering that there are somewhere between eighteen and twenty-three million atheists in the United States and that when you mention atheism to most people, the only name they can think of is Madalyn Murray O'Hair—a loudmouth who has a bad family life, communist ideas, and a negative personality. She's brought atheism into a position of intellectual disrepute, accomplishing in twenty-five years what churches haven't been able to accomplish in centuries. I think she ought to get a check from the pope."

The checks O'Hair counts on come from the estates of deceased atheists. Lynch maintains that O'Hair's organizations (besides American Atheists, there are the Society of Separationists and the Charles E. Stephens American Atheist Library and Archives) took in $1.9 million in 1987 alone, most of it from estates. "Madalyn told me she learned from Jerry Falwell that if you create a crisis every month, people are more likely to respond with money," says Lynch. Although O'Hair does occasionally report bequests to her members, it's also true that her complaints about money are legendary. Her newsletters are filled with urgent requests for funds. "In a continuing way, I feel like an old dog outside the stoop of your house, waiting for you to throw me a well-chewed bone, devoid of meat," O'Hair complained to her members. Frequently she has told her employees that she cannot meet their payroll that month. At the annual American Atheist convention she hectors her loyal followers about the need to include her organization in their wills. "Madalyn is not an atheist activist," wrote G. Richard Bozarth, Madalyn's former printer; "she is an atheist mendicant."

Now the camera was shut off again while a trailer ran, promoting the upcoming atheist convention in San Diego. O'Hair's face went slack. It was then that I saw the frightened look in her eyes once more. It's an expression her friends know well. "Yes, I know what you mean," Frank Zindler told me. "I think it's because she's been betrayed so many times. Madalyn does indeed have to worry about physical assaults and betrayal. Fear is not an irrational response given what's happened to her over the years. Also, Madalyn is very sensitive to the reality of mortality." Charles Dews remembers the first time he saw "that scared look" on O'Hair's face. "We were both in the employee kitchen and she began talking about feeling ill," says Dews. "She was worried that she was not going to live much longer. There was a vulnerability about her that I wasn't expecting. It seemed to me that she must have lived a hard life, a hard life and an empty life—not because her life is not full of God but because she has no real friends. I intuited something that made me feel really sad. It wasn't that she imagined that she was going to hell or anything like that. It was that she had created a nothingness out of her life."

O'Hair turned to watch the convention promo on the monitor. At that moment it was advertising the marvels of San Diego, which include the famous zoo. A female orangutan was idly chewing a banana on the screen. O'Hair suddenly guffawed. "Well, look at that," she said. "The Virgin just made another appearance."

When the taping was over, the crew ordered pizza and I chatted with Jon Garth. O'Hair went into the control room for a few moments, then came storming over to where we were talking. "Why don't you tell him about that gawddamned *Texas Monthly*," she said to her son. "Tell him what?" asked Jon. "You know—that ad!" she said. "The ad they refused to run!"

At last, I thought to myself, the source of Madalyn's anger at me. But Jon Garth looked blank. "Oh, you're talking about that ad that got lost," he said finally. "But Mother, that wasn't *Texas Monthly*—that was the *Texas Observer*."

There was a momentary, very pregnant pause.

"Well, whatever," said Madalyn. "It really pissed me off."

◆

I was sitting in Jon Garth Murray's nicely appointed office. He succeeded his mother in 1986 as the president of American Atheists. "Most cause people think that part of being a dissenter is that you need to be poor or look poor," Murray said. "Madalyn and I and Robin just don't fit into that role." Murray, who was thirty-four when I talked to him, has dark brown eyes, a mustache, and the mulish jaw and sprinkle of freckles that are his mother's mark. He never knew his father, whom he describes as being "of Neapolitan extraction . . . one of the nation's outstanding aerodynamics engineers." Murray's radio was set on an easy-listening station. On a credenza behind him was a photograph of O'Hair cuddling her late, beloved dachshund, Keegan. "We're accustomed to good food, to eating in dining rooms with tablecloths, good dishes, a good bottle of wine. Even when we go out for lunch, we go someplace nice. You'd never see us at McDonald's or Burger King—that's just not our lifestyle. All of us have nice clothes. My suits costs a minimum of five, six hundred dollars. My shirts are custom made; my ties are all silk. We have a nice house in Northwest Hills, nice automobiles—we get a tremendous amount of flak over the fact that I drive a Mercedes, Madalyn drives a Mercedes, and Robin drives a Porsche. We've been around the world three times. . . ."

One of the complaints that atheists have about the Murray-O'Hairs, as the triumvirate is called, is that they run the center as a family business. Jon Garth is not apologetic about that. "When it comes to 'cause' organizations," he once wrote, "democracy kills." The Murray-O'Hairs live together, travel together, and tend to spend all of their remaining waking hours, seven days a week, at the center. "At lunchtime the three go out together, generally in three different cars," Charles Dews observed, "and of course they come back in three different cars. I used to wonder about that. Then I realized it's probably the only time they ever have to be alone."

O'Hair has claimed, "I work full-time on a volunteer basis for the American Atheist Center—that is, without a salary." Yet the Murray-O'Hairs obviously live an opulent life. Jon Garth says that his lifestyle is no different from that of Jerry Falwell or Jimmy Swaggart. "I kind of understand somebody like Swaggart," he says. "I understand why he has the mansion, the limos, the Rolexes, and so on. He's in with a particular set of folks, and he's got to compete. The people in his church are happy for him to do that. It's just the outsiders who don't understand."

"People say that one of your mother's goals is to see you elected president of the United States before she dies," I said.

"Yeah, it is," Jon Garth acknowledged. "She would like to see me run for office. I haven't ruled it out."

I asked him what his politics were.

"I don't think you could actually call me a communist at this time, but I'm very close to that."

I was surprised, because all of her life O'Hair has fought her image as a subversive. In fact she has said: "My most exciting victory never got near the courtroom. I am the single person who disassociated atheism from communism. I taught the American people that there is such a thing as an American atheist, just as there is an American Democrat, an American Republican, an American fascist, and an American socialist." She purged her own organization of Marxists. "The moment we mix politics with us, we're dead," she warned. "We do not pretend to be one thing when we're another." Her attempted defection to the Soviet Union was a deeply buried secret.

In 1970, after the student movement made leftist politics more acceptable, O'Hair began calling herself an anarchist. In 1976 she contemplated a race for governor of Texas, but turned her attention to the Austin City Council instead. She received 6 percent of the vote. Undaunted, O'Hair briefly considered running for president. Instead, in a move that upset many of her members, she became the chief speech writer in the bizarre 1984 presidential bid of pornographer Larry Flynt, publisher of *Hustler* magazine. It certainly was an odd alliance. Only a few months earlier Flynt had declared himself "saved" and had returned to his native Kentucky to be baptized in Stenson Creek. The main plank in his political platform was the elimination of venereal disease.

Flynt's campaign was cut short by his imprisonment for contempt of court when he refused to disclose the source of the secret tapes he had released in connection with the drug arrest of car maker John DeLorean. While Flynt was in prison, O'Hair persuaded him to sign over a power of attorney, giving her and Jon Garth "every cotton-picking thing that he owned, all real, personal, and mixed property," including *Hustler* magazine. "To those of you aghast at our turning to a big pornographer for help," O'Hair scornfully advised her members, *"you had your chance to keep us afloat."* O'Hair privately estimated Flynt's fortune at $300 million. This coup was blocked by Flynt's brother Jimmy, who filed suit in Los Angeles for a conservatorship of Flynt's estate. By the time Flynt got out of prison, he had apparently changed his mind and decided to keep his fortune for himself.

◆

"My gawd, you're persistent!" O'Hair yelled at me as she came into the office to deliver a message to her son. She walked out of the room, then abruptly returned. "You've got no business writing this story!" she shouted. "You don't have a radical mind. There's no way you could ever even attempt to understand what we're trying to do here. You're a classic liberal!"

Two weeks later, when I called her on the phone, she laid into me again. "You're a gawddamn liar!" she cried. "It is absolutely incredible that you're calling people up and telling them that I am a thief, and that you are telling them that we are in serious trouble with a number of government agencies, and that we're under criminal investigation. . . ."

She was upset because I had been digging into various charges, most of which had been leveled at her by Brian Lynch. Lynch maintains that the IRS was following up his assertions with an investigation into the finances of O'Hair's tax-exempt corporations. She was also facing a civil racketeering suit in a weird episode surrounding the estate of James Hervey Johnson, a deceased atheist and white supremacist who had published a magazine called *Truth Seeker*. Even before Johnson's death, O'Hair had made a claim on his $15-million estate and went so far as to have stock certificates made up in her own print shop in the name of the Truth Seeker Corporation; she then held a board meeting of her friends and allies and voted Johnson out of power. "It's like you and me deciding that we're going to take over Chrysler and kick out Iacocca," says San Diego attorney Roy Withers, who represents the Johnson interests in this case.

As a matter of fact, I had never been much interested in doing an exposé of O'Hair's finances, as she feared. It was the woman herself I sought to understand. I had wanted to study a life lived in defiance of convention, a life that was recklessly authentic and accepting of the consequences. But when I looked into Madalyn Murray O'Hair, that was not the life I found. O'Hair stood aside from the world of belief and longing-for-belief and said it was only imaginary. She had been willing to state the awful truth as much as she understood it, no matter what the consequences. I admired her courage. But I had discovered that much of her own life was imaginary as well. As I had peeled away each layer of O'Hair, Murray, Roths, Mays, looking for the Madalyn inside, I began to have a sense of the sadness of that life. It seemed a commonplace observation about her, one that her detractors and even her friends frequently made, but I came to see O'Hair as a religious phenomenon, in the same way that antimatter is an expression of matter. She was a black hole of belief.

Long ago O'Hair understood the power of disbelief. She used it to change our country and to rattle our ideas about who we are. Now I had glimpsed how fragile her own identity was. She had made us examine our own beliefs, perhaps at the cost of her own. But "what the hell," as O'Hair observes. "We have to live now. No one gets a second chance. There is no heaven and no hell. There is no 'after' life. You either make the best or the worst of what you have now or there is nothing. Laugh at it. Hug it to you. Drain it. Build it. Have it."

Anton LaVey:
Sympathy for the Devil

There are three possibilities where Anton LaVey is concerned. The most likely is that he is a complete fake. It is also possible that he is a tortured psychotic with grand delusions. The most frightening possibility, however, is that he really is the Devil incarnate—perhaps without even knowing it.

He certainly looks the part. I first saw him getting out of a black Jaguar and coming through the glass doors of a restaurant with a blonde on his arm. His devilish appearance is cultivated, of course: the shaved head; the black slacks, black shirt and ascot, black leather jacket, and black fisherman's cap; the Leninesque goatee, also still shimmeringly black, although LaVey is now over sixty years old; and a tiny gold ear loop in his left lobe. That much, however, would describe most of the leftover beatniks still wandering around San Francisco. No, there's definitely something more, something sinister about this man.

His ears, you notice, are slightly pointed, and when he doffs his cap, you see his gleaming head is as well. He has a peculiar walk, a splay-footed, simian shuffle he says he picked up during his days in the circus and the carnival. Pale skin, which you would expect in a man who never sees the sun, but unnaturally youthful and lightly freckled—there's a boyishness about him. A gap-toothed smile that is missing an upper left incisor. Amber eyes, which scarcely look human at all, more like the eyes of a big cat, with a cat's sleepy intensity and implacable indifference. It is a wicked face, which is to say that it is charming, defiant, jaded, beguiling, humorous, bitter, knowing, and even a bit insouciant. How else would the Devil appear?

LaVey started the First Church of Satan in San Francisco in 1966. His book *The Satanic Bible* was published three years later and has sold more than 600,000 copies through twenty-eight printings. It is this work, a romantic celebration of indulgence, vengeance, and existential doubt, that has earned him the reputation among many religious believers as the most evil man in the world, or at the very least a symbol of Satan's resurgence. It has also made him a dark hero to the disaffected, the alienated, the marginal personalities for whom his philosophy rings chords of recognition and identity.

"Anton LaVey is the pivotal figure in the growth and dissemination of satanic theology in America. He is the Saint Paul of satanism," says Dr. Carl A. Raschke, author of *Painted Black*, which surveys the spread of satanic activity among the young and the phenomenal rise in reported cases of ritual abuse. As LaVey points out, however, "I've never presented myself as having spoken directly to Satan or God, or being in touch with any sort of divinity or having any sort of spiritual mandate. I just feel that what I'm doing is part of my nature."

Reviled as a despoiler of youth, dismissed as a con man and a carny trickster, pursued by thrill seekers and Bible thumpers and occult weirdos, LaVey has become increasingly reclusive over the years. Indeed, he is often rumored to have died long ago. His church, which once had "grottoes" in many major cities in the country, is now largely disbanded. During the sixties, LaVey had fashioned himself into an archetype of our depraved unconscious; he hobnobbed with movie stars and boasted of affairs with Marilyn Monroe and Jayne Mansfield; he was our libido let out of its cage; he was the "Black Pope," raging and blaspheming and flaunting our taboos. Back then, satanism was new to America, and shocking, and LaVey was its most conspicuous practitioner. The post office would deliver mail to him addressed only to "Satan." Now, in the nineties, satanic cults are springing up, it seems, in every little township and crossroads in America. Rock groups openly worship the Devil. Police departments all over the country are coping with rumors of human sacrifice, and hospitals with survivors of ritual abuse. The signs of satanic activity can be found not only in the graffiti on subway trains but in the growing number of teenage suicides and in some actual cases of ritual murder. Meanwhile, the spiritual father of this movement has retired to his gloomy house in the Richmond district of San Francisco, where he lives a self-consciously ascetic life, surrounded by his books, weapons, and keyboards, by his pets and his magical artifacts, and by Blanche Barton, his Boswell and omnipresent companion.

I had read the increasingly sketchy reports about LaVey's present existence and wondered whether he was sick, or in hiding, or even if, in some secret fashion, he had reformed. LaVey has made a career out of exploring the shadows of the human psyche. "I am all that is vile, reprehensible, and evil in the world," he brags. "I am people's worst nightmares." Despite the absurdity of this claim, I did feel some anxiety about our meeting. I wasn't worried about what I was going to find out about LaVey—it was what I might discover about myself. After all, the danger that LaVey represents to society lies not in who he is but in who we are.

◆

"What dressing would you like on your salad?" the waiter inquired.

"Bleu cheese," I said.

LaVey and Barton exchanged a look, then returned to their menus. Unknowingly, I had just failed the LaVey Salad Dressing Test. According to *The Satanic Witch*, his guide for lovelorn sorceresses, "dominant, masculine archetypes [like LaVey] prefer sweet dressings, such as French, Russian, Thousand Island," because the smell resembles the odor of a woman's sexual organs. Bleu cheese, on the other hand, is "reminiscent of a locker full of well-worn jock straps." It is suitable, really, only for wimps, homophiles, and submissive females. LaVey ordered the twenty-two-ounce porterhouse steak, rare.

We were talking about violence and the corruption of art, which LaVey blames on television. "But a lot of what has been unleashed is because of the Church of Satan," said Barton, a plump and intensely pale young woman with a little spit curl poking out from under her blue pillbox hat, a sort of blond Betty Boop with a Phi Beta Kappa pin on her dress.

LaVey agreed. "I promoted the idea where everybody is a god. That's the Pandora's box I'm partly responsible for opening. I helped create this big-shot-ism in everybody."

"And are you glad you opened Pandora's box?" I asked, innocently enjoying my salad.

"Yeah, because things have to get worse before they get better. But I think we've already reached the lowest level of artistic expression as a result of this newfound sovereignty in every man." Although he spoke quietly, a brooding cloud had come over his features. "Here we're dealing with the 'dignity' of the human animal. I find more dignity in the movement of a fish, the shape of a horse. . . ."

He was off on one of his misanthropic rants. I would hear that theme played again and again over the two weeks we would spend dining together and hanging around the purple parlor of his famous black house. During those sessions, which lasted until I staggered away in exhaustion, usually around four in the morning, I often wondered what it was that had caused him to become so alienated from the human race. I thought if I could get to the bottom of LaVey's rage, then I would find some great truth about the human need to pursue evil. Later, I would realize that was itself a satanic idea, perhaps the ultimate satanic idea—that one could find truth and perhaps even salvation through the exploration of repressed human needs.

"I actually have more respect for vegetables than I do for people. I hate to even leave a pea on my plate," LaVey said as he pronged one with his fork. "This little pea died for me. I know I'm beginning to sound like Albert Schweitzer, but for this pea to be able to grow and fulfill its purpose on the planet, that's more than most humans accomplish."

"Do you believe that peas have souls?"

"Well, I wouldn't use the word 'soul,' but I do believe there are living entities beyond what we normally understand. Anything can have life bestowed upon it; a car, a good faithful car; a typewriter. A house, certainly, becomes a living entity. Who can say these objects are not alive?" With that, the pea moved on to its final reward.

"Doctor LaVey has had to keep a very low profile," Barton said. "He got tired of the capes-and-horns scene."

In that case, why had he chosen to talk to me?

"I have come out from under my rock because the climate is more conducive to what I've been saying," LaVey remarked. "The zeitgeist now happens to be right. These are salad days for satanism.

"And besides, what's the worst you can say—that I'm a monster, a phony, a charlatan? That I'm mad? That I'm a murderous mastermind? That I'm some Jew gypsy roustabout who looks at the world through a carny's eyes? I've been accused of being everything from an agent for the KGB to the chief ideologue of Nazism. In the roll of twentieth-century villains, it's Hitler, Charlie Manson, and Anton LaVey."

✦

"I've always been fascinated by the underbelly of humanity," LaVey told me in one of those early-morning discourses in his purple parlor. He was sitting in his favorite armchair, beside a bookcase predictably filled with obscure occult literature, but there were as well a number of coffee-table books on Hollywood, biographies of Marilyn Monroe, books on circus and carnival lore. I noticed Yeats's *Memoirs*, as well as several rare books by one of my favorite authors, Ben Hecht. Also *The Complete Jack the Ripper*, *Eros and Evil*, and *My Father* by Maria Rasputin, which was inscribed "Happy Winter Solstice to my father, Love, Karla." On the mantel above the fake fireplace (it is actually a secret entrance to a ritual chamber) are pictures of his two very pretty daughters, Karla and Zeena. There are no windows in this room. The only light comes from what I supposed to be a twenty-five-watt bulb in the lamp behind LaVey's chair. He claims to be photophobic—one of his many vampiric qualities, which include an allergy to garlic. When he reads, even in this light, he wears a pair of bifocal sunglasses. Beside him, on one side of his chair, is his crystal ball and a bullwhip; on the other, a stuffed armadillo and a machine gun. "I guess," LaVey continued, "it's because I've lived a sort of noir existence since I was a kid."

He was born, he says, Anton Szandor LaVey on April 11, 1930, in Chicago, to Joe and Augusta LaVey, although even these initial details have been the subject of some dispute. (There is no such name as LaVey listed in the Cook County birth records; however, there was a Howard Stanton Levey born on that day to parents Mike and Gertrude. Even the date of that birth is in question; originally it was listed as March 11, but Gertrude amended the certificate to make it one month later.) He had what he calls a "subjective childhood." His parents were "very normal," with no interest in the dark side. "The story of my father's life was to blend into the woodwork. My mother was the same way. They were very paranoid about the neighbors and what people thought of them. In a way it was good. I was allowed to take my own lead. In that sense, I couldn't have chosen better parents."

Being a child was a miserable experience for him. "It was not a real structured lifestyle. Home was just a place to eat or sleep. And anyway, I was not an average kid, I was more like a midget. I wanted to be an adult. It was a matter of biding my time."

His religious upbringing was "very iconoclastic and extremely permissive. My own family were nonparticipants. I was never pushed into a religious formula. The only thing I ever heard about religion was 'Another name for God is nature.' We did have relatives who were Christian and Jewish. I had an aunt who was Christian Scientist and an uncle who was an atheist. You could say I grew up a second-generation nonbeliever or cynic." Although Tony, as the boy was called, was pleased that he didn't have to go to a priest or a minister or a rabbi ("so I never had any lies told to me"), he was guarded about his agnosticism. "To say you didn't believe in God back then was like saying you were a communist. I would say, 'Of course I believe in God.' I didn't want to get clobbered."

The family moved frequently in LaVey's early years. "As soon as I got used to one school, I'd get pulled out and put in another," he recalls. They eventually wound up in San Francisco, where his father had obtained a liquor dealership.

One of Tony's most vivid memories is attending the 1939–40 San Francisco World's Fair, where he snuck into Sally Rand's Nude Ranch and watched topless cowgirls twirl lariats. Over in the Illinois Building, he discovered a miniature replica of Chicago, his old hometown. It was so exact that Tony was able to find the school he went to, the street he grew up on, the house he lived in. Inspired by this exhibit, Tony went home and began construction of his own miniature city on four-by-eight sheets of plywood on the floor of his room. He made balsa wood mansions on the hilltops and slums in the back of the town. There was a harbor filled with rowboats and yachts and freighters. "It was my first true magical exercise," he says. "I could throw my consciousness down to any one of the buildings and imagine the life inside."

According to LaVey, most satanists are stigmatized as youths. When I asked him about the stigmas of his own childhood, he spoke vaguely about his unpopularity with other kids and his inability to dance. "My life wasn't awful. My only stigma was up here," he said, pointing to his angular, menacing face. "I was odd looking. By today's standards I would have looked fine, but in nineteen thirty-nine I was not cute. I was certainly not a Van Johnson or a John Wayne." He did talk about his horror of going to gym with the other boys, which was so great that he managed to get a doctor's excuse to avoid it. He spent his gym periods in the clinic eyeing the sexy school nurse.

These experiences did not seem so traumatic that they would catapult a person into satanism. I was still groping for some catastrophic incident in LaVey's childhood as I read the manuscript of Barton's authorized biography of him, *The Secret Life of a Satanist*. There, I ran upon this abbreviated and oddly impatient passage: "Had tail removed. Extra vertebra removed near the end of Tony's spine which formed a prehensile tail, a caudal appendage, which seems to occur about one in every 100,000 births."

"You had a *tail*?"

"Yeah. I had it removed when I was thirteen or fourteen, under very painful circumstances."

"Don't you think that might have been stigmatizing?"

"I never thought about it," said LaVey, "although it really was profoundly disruptive to everything I did. I couldn't sit straight in a chair because it would get inflamed. Several times it had to be lanced and drained. The last time it happened we were camping on rocky terrain. I rolled around and must have banged it. Next day it started itching. Two days later it really flared up." This was during wartime, and there was a shortage of hospital rooms and anesthesia. LaVey says he was operated on while he lay on a gurney in the hospital hallway, with a local anesthetic that was not very effective. He remembers biting through the rubber cover of his pillow.

I didn't know what to make of this story. His previous biography, *The Devil's Avenger*, by Burton Wolfe, makes no mention of a tail except to state specifically and ironically that LaVey was born without one. Either LaVey had not thought enough of the incident to tell Wolfe about it, or else it never happened—LaVey simply had invented it in order to dress up the myth he cloaks himself in. This latter possibility I found more interesting. The offhandedness of this story, the wealth of persuasive details, I had to admire. He has made an allegory of his life—not his real life but the fantasy life of the Anton LaVey persona. These ornamental embellishments were painted onto the façade. One can look at them as lies or as art.

LaVey's father went to work in the shipyards during the war. This was a thrilling period in Tony's life. He would wear military outfits to school, and occasionally he got to go on submarine patrols in his uncle's boat, which had been recruited by the Coast Guard Reserve. In the summer of 1945 that same uncle got a contract from the Army to reconstruct air strips in Germany. He invited Tony to come along. "The smoke was still clearing," LaVey recalls. While he was there he had the chance to see the *Schauerfilmen*, or horror movies, that were a notable feature of German decadence. He particularly recalls Fritz Lang's futuristic *Metropolis*, which depicts a scientific wizard who constructs a humanoid, through which he is able to control the entire population. The themes in this movie would influence LaVey profoundly, as would its dark mood. LaVey says he came home with malaria, which left him smelling like scorched silk.

"The Second World War and its permissiveness were not lost on me," he says. "Prurience was the order of the day." He had already experienced what he would later term an ECI (for "Erotic Crystallization Inertia") when he was five years old. A girl at a birthday party invited him into her room. When her mother suddenly came to find them, the little girl was so upset she peed in her pants. "The ECI is the split second of sexual awakening," LaVey explains. "A switch goes off inside." After that, the sight of women urinating became a fetish for LaVey. He associated it with carnivals, because that was a place where girls became giddy and excited on rides; it felt like a lustful environment. When he was eleven, he was earning money picking up bottles around an outdoor dance pavilion, and he discovered a hole under the ladies' restroom. "Tony made sure he was front and center whenever he spied an especially interesting woman going to relieve herself," Barton notes.

When he was sixteen, he experienced another erotic crystallization. He was at another party; some of the kids were wrestling, and a girl's dress was hiked up so that Tony could see her plump thighs and pale skin. She was a blonde. "She was just another schoolgirl," LaVey says. "I wasn't even interested in her." But forever after, blondes were it for him—an unending source of love and trouble.

We had moved into the kitchen, where LaVey keeps his eight keyboards, his two house cats, and his pet boa constrictor, Boaz. Music has always been at the center of LaVey's life and of his magic as well. "I play kitsch music—bombastic, schmaltzy, corny—the kind of music you hear in the background of cartoons," he said unapologetically, as he took a seat inside his nest of synthesizers and samplers. Music is the heart of his theory of magic. "Satanic music is not heavy metal rock and roll," he contends. The music of supposed satanic groups such as AC/DC, Black Sabbath, and Slayer is not really occult, because millions of people hear their songs every day on records and radio and in concert. Occult is what no one ever listens to anymore, songs that once were popular but now are long forgotten, such as "Telstar" and "Yes, We Have No Bananas." LaVey keeps a list of such lost songs. He believes that by playing them he releases their suppressed power.

"Music is a magical tool, a universal language," he says. How does that magic work? "If you wanted it to rain, for instance, you could play every song with 'rain' in the title. If no one else is playing those songs, there is still a certain charge in them. It might just rain." That sounded pretty tame to me, although LaVey has claimed in the past that he went cuckoo on the keyboards one night and caused the 1986 earthquake in Mexico City.

His musical career began, he says, at the age of five when he went into a music store with his mother and spontaneously picked out a tune on the harp. Soon he was studying violin, then drums and oboe. By the time he was fifteen, he was sufficiently accomplished to play second oboe with the San Francisco Ballet Orchestra. (According to San Francisco's Performing Arts Library, there was no such orchestra in 1945. The ballet employed the local symphony for its performances, and none of the three oboists was named LaVey or Levey.)

LaVey's kitchen is painted black, with fiendish murals on the walls, and draped with cobwebs like a high school gym decorated for a Halloween dance. There was a small electrical hum when he turned on his synthesizers, which aroused Boaz in his lighted box on the kitchen table. LaVey became visibly energized, as if the current were running through him as well. His life story resumed, this time set to music.

He began with "Entrance of the Gladiators," the traditional opening song of the circus, which he played with a wheezing calliope sound. LaVey's legend, as he has told it many times, is that in the spring of 1947 he ran away and joined the Clyde Beatty Circus. "I got in trouble with the law and had to take off," he says elliptically. He signed on as a roustabout and cage boy. "After a short time, 17-year-old LaVey was handling eight Nubian lions and four Bengal tigers in the cage at once," says Barton's book. LaVey learned some elemental lessons in magic upon being knocked to the ground and finding himself on his back with the hot breath of a lion in his face. "You have just one defense left: willpower. Any good cat trainer has to learn how to use it, how to charge himself full of adrenaline, to send out gamma rays to penetrate the brain of the cat," says LaVey. "That's when you really learn power and magic, even how to play God."

One day the calliope player, Fred Mullins, got drunk, and LaVey was pressed into service. He played the *William Tell* Overture—to such enthusiastic reviews that Mullins spent the rest of the season on the sidelines. "Anton would subsequently perform mood-setting, emotionally-charged music to accompany some of the world's most famous circus acts: the Hannefords' riding team, the Concellos, Harold Alanza, the flying Wallendas, the Cristianis, and others," says the Barton biography. (According to the Circus World Museum in Baraboo, Wisconsin, the 1947 route books of the Beatty Circus list no one named LaVey or Levey in either the cages or the band, which does not mean that he might not have been employed in some other capacity for a brief period of time. Several of the acts that Barton lists in her book, however, such as the Concellos, Harold Alanza, and the Cristianis, were actually Ringling Brothers performers.)

Now the music changed. It was the snaky sound of "The Billboard March"—the melody of the midway, the freak show, the hootchy-kootchy girls. This next stop of the LaVey legend is the carnival, where in the late forties and early fifties, he says, he played the Hammond organ and learned the "mitt trade"—that is, fortune telling. "I got to rub elbows with human oddities—freaks, dancers, showgirls who wanted to be stars—it was a chance to meet people who were really marginal." LaVey says he received a critical insight into the nature of religion during this period, because he was often recruited by itinerant evangelists to play gospel tunes. "My exposure to grass-roots Christianity was on a real dirt-lot, tent-show level," he recalls. "I used to have to duck the crutches and braces at the healing show. They'd really slam them down on the stage." While he was playing "Bringing in the Sheaves," he would look out at the audience, which was clamoring to be saved. "I'd see the same god-damned faces that had been ogling the half-naked girls at the carnival the night before." It was, as he has said many times before, a revelation: "I knew then that the Christian church thrives on hypocrisy, and that man's carnal nature will out no matter how much it is purged or scourged by any white-light religion." (According to Ward Hall at the New Museum of the Carnival in Gibsonton, Florida, LaVey was employed by sideshow operators at one time, probably by the Pike Amusement Park in Long Beach, California. "I'm quite sure he was a fire eater," Hall told me, although that's one profession LaVey has never claimed.)

When winter came in 1948, the carnival closed for the season, and LaVey started playing burlesque houses in southern California—in particular, a theater called the Mayan in Los Angeles. "That's where I met Marilyn Monroe, at the Mayan," says LaVey. "The guy who ran it was Paul Valentine." Monroe was down on her luck as a starlet and had taken up stripping to get by.

As he related this story, LaVey played "Slow Boat to China," which was one of Monroe's numbers, followed by "Harlem Nocturne," a classic stripper's tune. He performed it in the organ mode, with a bawdy snare drum in the background outlining the bumps and grinds, and a lonely trumpet crying out for love and attention. "She was what the girls would call a 'chain dragger,' which meant she was slow to take her clothes off,"

LaVey explained. He had not been interested in her until he noticed her white, marshmallowy thighs, with a trail of blue bruises, which he thought added an air of vulnerability. His old fetish for pale blondes made a sudden entrance, and within a few days he and Marilyn were lovers. The affair lasted about two weeks.

"I think she was attracted to your darker elements," Barton observed.

"She did have a strange fascination with the dark side," LaVey agreed. "I've tried to retrace all the places we stayed, like the fleabag motel on Washington Boulevard where we lived together, the whole West Adams section of L.A., where we drove around in Marilyn's Pontiac. . . ."

As a souvenir of those days, LaVey produced a copy of Monroe's famous nude "Golden Dreams" calendar, which he claims she sent him. There she is, lusciously recumbent against a red satin drop, her legs curled under and her left arm raised invitingly, her body so white but her open lips so red; even her nipples look red against that pale, pale skin. "Dear Tony," the inscription reads, "How many times have you seen this! Love, Marilyn."

"Her big break came right after we broke up," LaVey continued. "She did a walk-on in a Groucho Marx movie. Then John Huston gave her a great part in *Asphalt Jungle*." (As it happens, the romantic lead in that Marx Brothers movie, *Love Happy*, was Paul Valentine, the same man who directed the Mayan Theater. "I don't know if Marilyn ever performed at the Mayan," Valentine told me, "but I do know that she was never one of my dancers." In any case, Valentine says he operated the Mayan as "a legitimate theater. It was never a burlesque, never a bump-and-grind." He says LaVey never worked for him, either.)

While Monroe moved quickly on to stardom, LaVey drifted back to San Francisco. It was there, in 1950, that he met a tiny teenaged blonde named Carole Lansing. They married a year later, even though Carole was only fifteen. The Korean War was going on at the time, and in order to evade the draft, LaVey signed up to study criminology at San Francisco's City College. His first daughter, Karla, was born in 1952. To support his young family, LaVey got a job as a police department photographer, which exposed him to the savagery of human nature. He saw children splattered by hit-and-run drivers, women cut to pieces by jealous husbands, the bloated bodies of suicides fished out of San Francisco Bay. He came to the conclusion that if this brutal carnage was God's will, then he wanted nothing more to do with God. "There is no God," he decided. "There is no supreme, all-powerful deity in the heavens that cares about the lives of human beings. There is nobody up there who gives a shit. Man must be taught to answer to himself and other men for his actions." (According to the San Francisco Police Department, no one named Howard or Anton LaVey or Levey ever worked for them; nor does City College have a record of his enrollment. Frank Moser, a retired police officer who was in the photo department during that time, says that LaVey was never in that department under any name. LaVey himself suggests that the records were purged by the department to avoid embarrassment. The first time the name LaVey—or actually, La Vey—makes an appearance in the official records is the wedding application filed in Reno on September 4, 1951, between Carole Lansing and Howard Anton La Vey. They were divorced in 1962. Karla LaVey says that her mother died in 1975.)

In 1951, about the same time he married Carole, LaVey claims to have visited the Church of Thelema, a satanic cult in Berkeley that was run by a Cal Tech rocket scientist named Jack Parsons. Apparently the church did not make much of an impression on LaVey, because he never returned, and the following year Parsons blew himself up in a secret experiment he was conducting in the basement of his Pasadena mansion.

More important to LaVey's future was the publication in 1952 of John Symonds's biography of Aleister Crowley, *The Great Beast*. Here LaVey found a model for the antihero he would fashion himself into. Crowley, the son of an English brewer, was born in 1875. Strong-willed, adventurous (despite his personality, he was a well-regarded mountaineer), famously lecherous with either sex, Crowley cultivated an international reputation as the most hated man in the world. He had been a member of the Hermetic Order of the Golden Dawn, a magical fraternity of literati that included Bram Stoker and William Butler Yeats. The Golden Dawn was an amalgam of cultish mysteries drawn variously from the Rosicrucians, the Theosophists, and the Cabalists. Crowley got booted out of this group after alienating most of the membership, especially the immortal Yeats, whom Crowley accused of being jealous of his literary superiority. In 1912 he joined a German society called the Ordo Templi Orientis, which specialized in sexual magic. Soon Crowley became the leader of the OTO. He moved the headquarters to a Sicilian farmhouse that he called the Abbey of Thelema (a word that means "will" in Greek) and there performed barbaric rituals that brought widespread notoriety and condemnation. Although Crowley was himself enthusiastic about fascism, Benito Mussolini, the Italian dictator, finally expelled Crowley and his band.

The OTO survived in various chapters, including Jack Parsons's Church of Thelema. Crowley himself died a broken drug addict in 1947. But he left behind a legacy: his body of literature about "magick," as he spelled it, and a demonic role that was waiting to be filled. Although LaVey pays Crowley less homage now than he did in the past, there are obvious debts to the Great Beast's writing as well as to his shaved head and even to such details as the use of the pitchfork motif in his signature.

A switch here, a switch there, and the sound deepened into a throaty theater organ. It was "Deep in the Heart of Texas," which LaVey slyly played in my honor. He said he was the official organist of the city of San Francisco until 1966, playing "the largest pipe organ west of Chicago" in the Civic Auditorium, where so many conventions are held. "I played official banquets, political functions, basketball games." (There actually was no such position as city organist in San Francisco. Carole LaVey's divorce pleadings state that her husband's sole income was $29.21 per week, derived from playing the Wurlitzer organ at the Lost Weekend nightclub as well as "various infrequent affairs at the Civic Auditorium.")

◆

> *Blessed are the strong, for they shall possess the earth—*
> *Cursed are the weak, for they shall inherit the yoke!*
>
> *Blessed are the powerful, for they shall be reverenced*
> *among men—Cursed are the feeble, for they shall be blot-*
> *ted out!*
>
> *Blessed are the bold, for they shall be masters of the*
> *world—Cursed are the righteously humble, for they shall*
> *be trodden under cloven hoofs!*
> *"The Infernal Diatribe" from* The Satanic Bible

"I've met kids who have completely memorized *The Satanic Bible*," said Sergeant Dan LeMay of the Round Rock (Texas) Police Department. He was speaking to a Mental Health Association conference entitled "Children, Cults & Consequences." LeMay, like police officers all over the country, has been overwhelmed with the increase in reports of satanic or ritual abuse. His own investigations have persuaded him that 50 to 60 percent of adolescents dabble in the occult. Most of those who then proceed to join cults or become self-styled satanists have been sexually or emotionally abused as young children. As LeMay outlined the profile he uses to diagnose kids at risk ("intellectually curious; creative and artistic; low self-esteem but narcissistic; alienated from family, peers, and mainstream religion; bored and understimulated; obsessed with fantasy role playing; intense unresolved family conflicts . . ."), I was struck by how well these characteristics described the young Anton LaVey.

For several years now I have been informally investigating this enormous rise in satanism and the reports of ritual abuse. Are we really in the middle of a satanic crime wave? Certainly, popular interest in satanism is apparent; it's the subject of countless talk shows and newspaper stories; anyone who is familiar with rock music can testify to the flagrant devil worship of some heavy metal groups; and of course, there are proven cases of satanic slayings, as in the voodoo murders in Matamoros, Mexico, which were discovered in 1989, and the Richard Ramirez "Night Stalker" mutilations and murders, which terrorized southern California during the summer of 1985. There seems to be a parallel and related increase in reported ritualistic child abuse, often with satanic overtones, in day care centers. The McMartin preschool case, the most notorious of these, ended in the acquittals of Raymond Buckey and his mother, Peggy McMartin Buckey, on fifty-two counts of child molestation after the longest and most expensive trial in American history.

Frequently, these reported satanic crimes have some tentative link with Anton LaVey, such as the case of Bunny Nicole Dixon, a Florida teenager convicted of murdering and mutilating a Vietnamese immigrant named Ngoc Van Dang. "According to the court hearings," writes Carl Raschke in *Painted Black*, "Dixon had been inspired to commit the crime through her constant reading and study of *The Satanic Bible*. She wanted to have sex with the Devil and 'to bear the Antichrist.' The accused had carved a large, upside-down cross on Dang's chest to mark him as a sacrifice, then hauled him into the woods and shot him seven times." Raschke also cites the case of eighteen-year-old Scott Waterhouse of Stanford, Maine, who was convicted of strangling a young girl "after carefully studying Anton LaVey's *Satanic Bible*." Another teenager, named Patricia Hall, was arrested for flogging a girl in New Orleans with a cat-o'-nine-tails; she later was extradited to Florida and convicted of murder. Hall claimed she had been baptized into satanism by LaVey. LaVey denies this; on the other hand, he frequently encourages the idea that Charles Manson was a sometime follower of his. "Manson makes a lot of sense," he told me, "and obviously he didn't commit those crimes. He may well be dangerous, but he was charged with *influencing* people. That's scary. If a person can be charged and prosecuted and imprisoned for *influencing* someone, where does that line cross over? How many people have I influenced?" LaVey also told me about a brief encounter with Richard Ramirez: "I met him when he was on one of his sprees. He was rather pale, dressed in black, wearing a Baphomet medallion [an emblem of the Church of Satan]. He said, 'Mr. LaVey, can I speak to you?' I told him, 'I don't do business on the street,' and suggested he write to my post office box. I thought he was a sensitive, polite young guy. I shouldn't have been so rude to him. He said, 'Have a pleasant solstice.' He reminded me a little of myself."

Psychiatrists and psychologists who study satanism generally divide it into three related types. The first is religious satanism, represented by the Church of Satan, the Temple of Set, and various other aboveground, organized sects. Even the United States Army recognizes the Church of Satan as an established religion in its *Handbook for Chaplains*, which lists the membership of the organization at ten thousand to twenty thousand (figures supplied by LaVey). The second is self-styled satanism, mainly a phenomenon among adolescents. How widespread it might be is impossible to determine, but even such a middle-American publication as *Seventeen* magazine conducted a survey in 1989 that found 12 percent of teenagers have "some or a lot of faith" in satanism. The last type is multigenerational satanism, in which the religion is passed from parent to child, along with accompanying traumatic abuse. It is this third category that produces most of the "adult survivors" of satanic abuse, whose stories of incest, torture, ritual murder, and the sacrifice of their own children have shaken therapists and police officers, titillated talk-show audiences, and made many Americans wonder if there is a nationwide satanic conspiracy.

Along with the increased reports of ritualized abuse, there has been a corollary rise in the number of patients diagnosed as having multiple personality disorder (MPD). This syndrome had great currency in the mid–nineteenth century, but it had almost completely disappeared by the 1920s. In 1957, after a best-selling book, *The Three Faces of Eve*, revived interest in this confounding disorder, psychiatrists began seeing more multiples in their practice. In 1974 another popular book, *Sybil*, about a woman with sixteen different personalities, brought multiplicity more into vogue. I'm not suggesting necessarily that these books caused people to model their behavior on the characters described in them; a more interesting proposition is that every age is partly defined by its own forms of insanity. Probably there was a mutual correspondence: these books were merely describing a trend that was already under way and managed to enlarge it.

Then in 1980 another book, *Michelle Remembers*, by Michelle Smith and her psychiatrist (later her husband) Lawrence Pazder, explored Smith's childhood memories of ritual abuse by a satanic cult. Although she was not diagnosed as a multiple herself, Smith's story—that she was sexually abused, thrust into an open grave and buried under the carcasses of dead cats, imprisoned in a cage filled with snakes, and frequently rubbed with the severed limbs of human babies—would become an archetype of many similar tales that would follow. Whether Smith's recollections are true memories of actual events or a kind of personal mythology based on a fanciful distortion of a childhood that was filled with neglect and other forms of trauma, her book opened the gates for an outpouring of similar stories. According to Ken Lanning, a child abuse specialist with the FBI, the phenomenon of cult survivors began after the publication of Smith's book; indeed, he could not find any survivor stories before that date.

I myself have spoken to several adult survivors, who have provided gruesome accounts of being tortured, thrown into coffins with decomposing bodies, scalded and forced to walk on hot coals, nailed upside down on crosses, forced to eat human body parts, and witnessing or actually participating in the murder of babies. One woman told me that she had seen thirty-three baby murders in a two-year period; another said she had watched sixty babies die and "I couldn't guess how many adults and kids." These stories are not at all unusual; indeed, most survivors' stories are profoundly alike. In a study of thirty-seven patients reporting satanic abuse in childhood, every one of them said that they had been serially raped and tortured, witnessed animal mutilations, and received death threats; thirty said they had eaten human body parts; thirty-one said they had witnessed or participated in adult or infant sacrifices; and twenty (of the thirty-three females in the report) said they had been forced to sacrifice their own child. "It can't be just a coincidence that kids are telling these same stories across the county," says Sandi Gallant, a cult investigator with the intelligence division of the San Francisco Police Department. "The problem is we are not finding any bodies. We are not finding any bodies, period."

At the Dissociative Disorders Program at Chicago's Rush-Presbyterian Hospital, which puts on a conference every year to chart the developments in this field, about 50 percent of the MPD patients admitted are reported to be victims of ritualized sexual abuse in childhood. Oddly enough, the doctors at Rush-Presbyterian were far more secretive and reluctant to speak to me than the patients and even the satanists I interviewed. Many social workers who deal with MPD patients and adult survivors believe that there is a worldwide, mafialike conspiracy of devil worshipers who are spreading their occult faith through a satanic underground. One year at the annual Dissociative Disorders conference, according to a participant I talked to, the level of paranoia was so high that the psychologists attending it seriously considered evacuating the hotel. They were convinced that satanists were going to blow them up.

The chief wizard of this conspiracy is often said to be Anton LaVey. He is, of course, the most conspicuous satanist in the country as well as the head of an actual multigenerational satanic family. Perhaps because his own children have not come forth with the same tales of abuse, and because he is himself such an obvious showman, LaVey is a problematical figure for the conspiracists. Carl Raschke, who supports the idea that satanism is a feature of a larger conspiracy involving drug trafficking and child pornography (he calls satanism the "ideological bonding mechanism" that knits these disparate pursuits together), says that LaVey is "far more powerful within the occult underground than his cultivated reputation as a buffoon and a cynical P.T. Barnum huckster would suggest." "If LaVey says jump, you jump," one of Raschke's anonymous informants tells him. "There is nobody in the world more powerful than LaVey."

Raschke quotes LaVey's boast "We are the new establishment." "The spreading incidence of satanic murder cases may vindicate his words," writes Raschke. "Did LaVey create the 'new establishment'? With his own furry and clawed hands did he perform confirmation ceremonies for tomorrow's streetside child molesters, cannibals, and heavy-metal perverts? A young man . . . who had been raised since a tender age as an acolyte in the local parish of the Church of Satan before turning to Christianity, said with a straight face, 'LaVey knows all, sees all. You can't do anything in the religion without LaVey's authority.' "

◆

Blanche Barton had a cold. She stuck a package of tissues in her purse and glanced outside. "It's nice out," she said, looking at the fog and the light, chilly rain.

It was sundown, and LaVey was just rising. He sleeps, he says, in four-hour stretches. While we waited for him to emerge, I roamed around the small parlor, to which—with the exception of the kitchen and the bathroom—I had been restricted. It was a great frustration for me, because I knew from old newspaper accounts and from speaking to former associates of LaVey's that there really were secret passages and amazing artifacts buried in this thirteen-room house. A trapdoor to the basement, for instance, leads to his famous "Den of Iniquity," where he keeps his Hammond organ, a Rock-ola jukebox, and his mannequins—Steve the sailor, Bonita the whore, Fritz the cabbie, and Gwen the drunk, who is passed out on a bar stool with a puddle of urine on the floor beneath her. It is LaVey's latest attempt at a "total environment," one in which time stands still. Downstairs, it is 1944.

"Anton literally has created an underground world in his basement," says his old friend Kenneth Anger, the filmmaker and author of the scandalous exposé *Hollywood Babylon*. "We share a fondness for mannequins," Anger says sweetly. When he and LaVey met, "it was just like a friend I should have known forever. We've never had a quarrel."

They met in the sixties, when Anger was working on *Invocation of My Demon Brother*, a film version of the black mass. Anger fell in with an informal group of friends who met every Friday evening in LaVey's house to discuss the occult. They called themselves the Magic Circle. It was this group that eventually became the nucleus of the Church of Satan. They included novelist Stephen Schweck; a Danish baroness named Carin de Plessen; Donald Werby, one of the wealthiest property owners in the city, and Werby's wife, Willie. Along with this group was a selection of science-fiction writers, a tattoo artist, a dildo manufacturer, and a handful of San Francisco policemen. These meetings became famous in the city, and eventually LaVey opened them to the public, charging $2.50 a head to hear him lecture on "Fortune Telling and Character Analysis" or "Love Potions and Monkey Glands." Vampires, werewolves, freaks, homunculi, bondage and torture, moon madness—it was a survey course in the weird and forbidden. One memorable evening LaVey spoke on the subject of cannibalism, and his wife—his second wife, a slender blonde named Diane—served a small portion of a human thigh, which a doctor friend had salvaged from an autopsy.

Eventually Anger would cast LaVey in his film, in the role of His Satanic Majesty. The film also featured Anger's roommate and protégé, Bobby Beausoleil, as Lucifer. By the time the film was released, Beausoleil had run off to join Charles Manson. LaVey says Manson himself was an occasional visitor to his lectures on magic.

I had run into Anger in Los Angeles, in the company of LaVey's younger daughter, Zeena, an exotic blonde in her early twenties. "Zeena is trying to gain recognition," LaVey had told me with apparent mixed feelings. "She feels she has a legacy to gain. But what they've set up is a much more authoritarian structure. I think she's got a father fixation." Zeena was with her boyfriend, Nicholas Schreck, who is a member of a Naziophile rock band called Radio Werewolf. (Schreck also has produced a film of his prison interview with Manson, called *Charles Manson, Superstar*, in which Manson makes the notable statement: "Who am I? I'm anyone I can get away with being.")

Zeena and Schreck are carrying satanism to a new generation. Half a dozen young members of Zeena's "wolf pack" sat glumly on couches in the lobby of the Hollywood hotel she had selected for the meeting. They formed a solemn audience for my interview with Anger. I felt a bit like Oprah Winfrey.

Anger was looking at Zeena and trying to remember exactly what their connection was. He had been present at her highly publicized baptism into the Church of Satan in 1967. "I'm your godfather, right?" Anger asked.

"Right," said Zeena.

Now here I was back in LaVey's parlor, feeling much as his pets must have felt as I paced back and forth in the small room. LaVey first began cutting a conspicuous public figure in San Francisco in 1964 as a "psychic investigator," who drove a coroner's van and could be seen strolling with a black leopard named Zoltan. Zoltan used to sleep in the crib with Karla. When the leopard was run over by a car, he was quickly replaced by a ten-week-old Nubian lion named Togare. Whatever LaVey's actual connections were with the circus, people who visited him were impressed with his ability to handle the lion in his own house. Togare could be rambunctious—he left a scar on Karla's back—but Anton had him trained so that he would not eat until his master had taken a bite of his own dinner. "I used to call him to his meal by playing 'Onward, Christian Soldiers,' " LaVey recalls. Unfortunately, Togare had a habit of roaring at night, which kept the neighbors awake. Eventually a city ordinance was passed forbidding lions in private homes, and Togare was taken to the city zoo.

His successor was a beaten-down German shepherd named Bathory, who was confined to the pitch-black narrow entranceway between the front door and the door to the parlor. My heart went out to this pathetic creature. I could hear her breathing; she had her nose stuck under the door as if she were craving even the minimal light in the parlor. Her odor, and what seemed like generations of leftover animal smells, suffused the room. Somehow the overarching essence in this clammy parlor was that of snake, although as far as I knew Boaz was seldom let out of his box.

Beside the couch was an antique examination table with stirrups on the side, which seemed to me the most sinister object in the room. I had heard about various implements of torture LaVey is supposed to own. Some of these items had surfaced in the press during LaVey's ongoing, rancorous palimony proceedings with Diane (they never formally married). The knickknacks they were contending for include an Egyptian skull, a Byzantine phallus, a shrunken head from Ecuador, an Aztec sacrificial knife, a stuffed wolf, a coffin, a bed of nails, a horned mask from the Inquisition, two crossbows, and a General Electric toaster oven. LaVey also claims to own Rasputin's sled chair and the "chair of confession" from the eighteenth-century British "Hell Fire Club," which Benjamin Franklin frequented during his ambassadorial days. Although LaVey has often alluded to having property all over the world, owning as many as three houses in the Bay Area alone, a nunnery in Tuscany, a 185-foot yacht, and three oceangoing salvage ships, the only real property mentioned in the suit is his longtime home in San Francisco. There LaVey has been living under a court order not to enter the upper story of his own house, where Diane had taken up temporary residence. She has long since gone. Eventually the judge would order LaVey to sell his house and all his beloved belongings to settle their suit, but that ax had not yet fallen.

Next to the examining table was a chair stacked full with LaVey's dozen black hats. Above that, in a light so dim I could scarcely make it out, was a framed sign:

> MY WORST ENEMIES ARE THOSE WHO PRESUME ME HARMLESS. THEY CANNOT IMAGINE HOW MUCH I RESENT AND DISDAIN THEM, OR JUST HOW GREAT A THREAT THEY WOULD FACE IF I COULD GET AT THEM. . . . SOME DAY, WITH THE HELP OF TIME, SPACE, AND CIRCUMSTANCE, I WILL BE ABLE TO HUMILIATE THEM PROPERLY—IN A MANNER THEY WOULD ENJOY, BUT IN A STYLE CALCULATED TO MAKE THEM WISH THEY HAD NEVER BEEN BORN.

Just then, LaVey entered and greeted me with his gap-toothed smile. The missing teeth, he had already admitted, he had extracted himself. "I don't get them fixed, I just pull them out when it's time." I supposed it would be difficult to get a dental appointment in any case, given his schedule.

LaVey stuck a Smith & Wesson .38 into his holster in the small of his back and a nifty five-shot derringer into the pocket of his leather jacket. "I never go out without armament," he said. He claims to be a champion marksman and a trick shot.

"Do you have a permit for those?" I asked.

He laughed and flipped open his wallet. Inside was a San Francisco Police Department badge. "Look at the number," he said. It was number 666.

This evening we were headed over the Golden Gate Bridge to Marin County for dinner. Barton was driving, despite her miserable cold. First we were going to swing by Karla's for a drink.

On the way LaVey talked about androids, his favorite hobbyhorse. He has spent years working on his own android prototypes—his mannequins—preparing for the day when the science of robotics will enable industry to begin the production of artificial human companions. "The forbidden industry," he calls it. "Polite, sophisticated, technologically feasible slavery." He sees it as the next great consumer revolution, a "do-it-yourself God kit that will be as big as Henry Ford's Model T and David Sarnoff's box. The timing is right, the zeitgeist is right."

Most of his dolls are store mannequins with the faces sawed off, replaced by latex impressions taken from his friends. "I sculpted one entirely out of polyurethane foam," LaVey said as we edged across the bridge through the fog. "I inhaled all those fumes trying to create a realistic woman with actual sexual parts. I put so much of my personal fetishistic desire into it that I became like Pygmalion. I kept expecting her to show up on my doorstep."

How do androids fit into satanism? "Part of the programming of artificial human companions would be to provide fetishistic human ideals in a total environment," he said. Of course, that is his longtime dream, going back to his childhood when he made artificial cities on the floor of his bedroom. In the past, he has spoken about how androids would be more stimulating, and in some respects more alive, than their human masters: "Like an old Duesenberg sitting at the curb is more alive than the people crowding around it, drawing energy from its beautiful chrome pipes, the object will become more valuable than the people watching it. When things become precious and people expendable, that is the horror of the true satanic society. That is when the nightmare begins."

His interest in actually making androids started with his introduction to Dr. Cecil E. Nixon, perhaps the only dentist he has ever associated with. Nixon was famous for his soirées, which were attended, LaVey says, by such dignitaries as Houdini, Paderewski, and Rachmaninov. LaVey's entree into this circle of luminaries was through San Francisco socialite Brooks Hunt. (Both Nixon and Hunt are now dead.) Nixon's life's work, aside from teeth, was a carved wooden music box that was a full-scale woman he named Isis. There is a photograph of her in a book of famous music boxes in the world, which is in LaVey's library. The dusky voluptuary is recumbent on a daybed, with a zither in her left hand, upon which she can play up to sixty-three tunes. She is one of the most beautiful objects I have ever seen. Her perfect form is draped with a sheer veil. "I am all that was, and is, and is to be, and no mortal hath lifted my veil," says the legend at the foot of her bed. According to the literature, when the room temperature grows warm enough, Isis removes the veil herself. She was sold to a collector in 1986 for $33,000.

"She was an unobtainable, haughty creature," LaVey said with a touch of derision. "I told Nixon I thought it was a waste of time for him to make a woman who was so intricately carved and technologically advanced without being able to have sex with it."

"Do you have sex with your dolls?" I asked.

Pause.

"I tried to," he said after a moment. "It was going to be my great test run. Just as I was entering her, the damn room started shaking. An earthquake hit. I figured it was God's way of trying to tell me something. So I ceased"— he laughed—"my activities of the moment."

I thought how LaVey himself has been made into a doll of sorts. He is in the wax museum in San Francisco (in the Chamber of Horrors), as well as Madame Tussaud's in London. He says that after he dies he would like to be stuffed and brought out for display on ceremonial occasions, like the corpse of Jeremy Bentham, the nineteenth-century British philosopher who is stored in a closet at the University of London.

LaVey suddenly turned solemn. "When I say 'God,' you know, it's just a figure of speech."

His theology is a puzzle, perhaps deliberately so. "It is a popular misconception that the Satanist does not believe in God," he writes in *The Satanic Bible*. "The concept of 'God,' as interpreted by man, has been so varied throughout the ages, that the Satanist simply accepts the definition which suits him best." Man creates his own universe; he may even people it with gods of one sort of another, but they are all projections of parts of his ego that he is afraid to accept. If, on the other hand, he is courageous enough and defiant enough to acknowledge in himself those fiendish qualities metaphysically associated with the Devil—self-indulgence, carnality, vengeance, pride, greed—then he is empowered to act in the world. "When all religious faith in lies has waned, it is because man has become closer to himself and farther from 'God'; closer to the 'Devil,' " LaVey writes. "If this is what the devil represents, and a man lives his life in the devil's fane, with the sinews of Satan moving his flesh, then he either escapes from the cacklings and carpings of the righteous, or stands proudly in his secret places of the earth and manipulates the folly-ridden masses through his own Satanic might, until that day when he may come forth in splendor proclaiming 'I AM A SATANIST! BOW DOWN, FOR I AM THE HIGHEST EMBODIMENT OF HUMAN LIFE!' "

For the most part LaVey has tried to define satanism in nonreligious terms. "Satanism is not just an occultnik-type thing," he told me. "It is a way of life, an aesthetic ideal, a code of behavior." Perhaps what he stands for is best understood this way. More than anything else, LaVey's life is spent evoking a mood, a moment in time, a frame through which we can look at the world through his art. He sees this as a satanic exercise, a way of replacing the externalized concept of God with an acknowledgment that man is responsible for everything. By seizing control of his own destiny, man can make the universe accord to his needs and enhance his life—perhaps even his lifespan. "I think you could keep people going one hundred and fifty years if you controlled the environment," LaVey says. "Just playing the music, wearing the clothes, even listening to the news of the old days, would be rejuvenating. You could shut the present out and let them live in a gestalt vacuum, in suspended animation or a suspended state of decay, on cultural reservations."

LaVey himself is still mourning the lost moment of the forties. That's the world he satanically calls forth. "I like dark, wet environments with streetlights reflecting in the wet pavement, little towns with farmhouses in the distance, all-night gas stations in the middle of nowhere, bars with glass-brick fronts that are dark inside even at two in the afternoon, back alleys in the lost parts of town, streets that wander off into the fields, general stores that double as Greyhound depots, the sound of a siren in the night, automobiles with long hoods and short rear ends, women with moll-like qualities who are real sidekicks, the clicking of high heels on the pavement. . . ."

In LaVey's world, women still wear bright red lipstick and the music swings softly and sex is there but not there in the teasing, exaggerated fashion of the DC comic books that he used to read and save and still has inside plastic envelopes, and men had undreamed-of powers just like the film noir antiheroes he grew up on: the Green Hornet, the Shadow, the Avenger. "Batman," he says, "is the perfect manifestation of the satanic ethic. These are heroes who work in the shadows, doing what officials cannot do or will not do." Good and evil for him are not very interesting concepts. What is good feels good, what is evil feels bad; but the true satanic hero doesn't traffic in such terms—he lives beyond them, in the realm of the forbidden. Often he must endure the condemnation of small minds who are fixed on narrow definitions of morality, who resent his genius and long to see him destroyed. "The villain becomes the hero, eventually," LaVey once observed. "I've seen this so much with people I've been fortunate enough to meet or be inspired by . . . the alienation makes them much more heroic. I remember going to see Paul Robeson in concert, years and years ago, when this guy couldn't sing in the Opera House and people had to wait around the block of this little old church building to listen to him sing. . . . Chaplin was another one. He was absolutely alienated from this country, although there were still people who went to see his films. . . . He was castigated, unfairly, alienated, and was, in my eyes, a much greater man because of it."

LaVey's music, his mannequins, his writings, the total environments he attempts to create, his taste in just about everything are reflections of this satanic pursuit of making his own world. Later, as I began to take apart the literary creation he has made of his life, I would realize that "Anton LaVey" was itself his supreme creation, his ultimate satanic object, composed of all the taboo elements his mysterious creator had chosen from the universe of dark possibilities. LaVey was ten years old in 1940; the world he created and the self he placed inside it are really the property of that shunned and solitary child's imagination.

Boiled down to its essence, says LaVey, the philosophy of satanism is indulgence. "The best way to deal with temptation is to yield to it," he once said; "the highest form of spirituality is the carnal and this is the seat of all spirituality." The satanist should enjoy all seven of the deadly sins, as long as he does not hurt others who don't deserve to be punished. "Satanism *does not* advocate rape, child molesting, sexual defilement of animals," he writes in *The Satanic Bible*. Given to making lists of all sorts, LaVey codified what he calls "The Nine Satanic Statements":

1. Satan represents indulgence instead of abstinence!
2. Satan represents vital existence instead of spiritual pipe dreams!
3. Satan represents undefiled wisdom instead of hypocritical self-deceit!
4. Satan represents kindness to those who deserve it instead of love wasted on ingrates!
5. Satan represents vengeance instead of turning the other cheek!
6. Satan represents responsibility to the responsible instead of concern for psychic vampires!
7. Satan represents man as just another animal—sometimes better, more often worse, than those that walk on all-fours—who, because of his "divine spiritual and intellectual development," has become the most vicious animal of all!
8. Satan represents all of the so-called sins, as they all lead to physical, mental, or emotional gratification!
9. Satan has been the best friend the Church has ever had, as He has kept it in business all these years!

Despite these many declarations, there was still a question in my mind about what he actually believed. In *The Satanic Bible* he speaks of an "immortal spirit," but he also says that there is no heaven or hell: "Here and now is our only opportunity." "Life is the one great indulgence," he wrote, "death the one great abstinence." And yet he told me he has seen evidence of personality survival after death, declaring that "it is not dependent on a belief system but upon the strength of personality. If something has the will to live so strongly, it becomes part of an adrenal burst"—an apparition, in other words, or a ghost. "I believe we are placed here for a purpose," he said one night in his parlor. "I think my efforts are a tiny step on the evolutionary march we like to think we're capable of performing." He believes in "a balance of nature. A natural order. That's God. And that's Satan. Satan is God. He is the representation of the state of flux; he is the action-reaction; he is the cause and effect; he is all the elements interwoven in what we call evolution." That statement seemed to me little more than an elaboration of his parents' single religious dictum: Another word for God is nature. Another word for God is Satan. Another word for Satan is evolution.

I recalled a queer passage in a book by Susan Atkins, who was a topless dancer in LaVey's short-lived North Beach nightclub act, the Witches' Workshop, before she joined the Manson family and became a killer. At that time, Atkins was dancing under the name Sharon King. While LaVey was trying to recruit her for the vampire role in his act, he invited her to attend one of his satanic services. She told him she preferred not to, since she didn't believe in the Devil. "But Sharon," LaVey said, "we don't believe in God, either, but that doesn't mean he doesn't exist."

"I am a skeptic, although I want to believe in something," he admitted when I pressed him on the subject. "And whenever we want to believe in something so strongly, we do speculate on its existence. But I need something more than pap or clichés. Maybe I'm practicing solipsism." Solipsism is one of "The Nine Satanic Sins."

Was there anything he believed in?

"Farting, but that may be speculative, too. Whatever I have faith in is based on prior experience, which would lead me to believe that this can or will happen again." Then he told a parable about a bull terrier he once owned named Typhon, who he said would pray to the electric can opener because he believed that dog food would come from it. Once LaVey was having a party and served little Russian sandwiches called piroshki. After the party Typhon discovered the uneaten piroshki in the garbage can and eagerly devoured them. "Every night from that moment on I'd hear a clank when his metal chain hit the can. He was checking to see if there was another piroshki. So every Saint Patrick's Day on his birthday we'd put another piroshki in the garbage can to reinforce his faith.

"And it's the same story with the religion of mankind."

He wasn't always so unbelieving, according to LaVey's former acolyte and now his chief rival, Michael Aquino. Aquino says that when they first met in 1969, LaVey believed in a literal Devil. "I think Anton's loss of faith came later," says Aquino. "It was a side effect of his insecurity at being the head of an institution that had grown beyond him." In Aquino's eight-hundred-page history, *The Church of Satan*, he asserts that LaVey signed an actual pact with the Devil. "He did not speak of this pact nor display it, but it existed among his most private papers—at least until August of 1974." At that time, according to Aquino, LaVey issued his "Ninth Solstice Message," in which Satan declares LaVey "my anointed man, in whose mortal flesh I, Satan, have chosen to inspire my material Self." Satan goes on to say:

> Recall first the pact which, years ago, you [LaVey] drew up before me, and to which you set your own name. Think not that I have been unmindful of that act long past, pale and lonely though it might seem beside the wreaths you have won for your own kind. . . .
>
> Take now the pact. In that chamber which you know to be most beloved of me, build now with your own hands a Flame that is sacred to me. Let your hands pass through the Fire—once for each angle of my Shining

Trapezohedron. Speak again that great Key which suspends the barrier between Hell and Earth, that I may bear witness to that which you undertake in my name.

Receive now my tribute. Our pact shall be consumed in the Flame, and with this act I release you from your bond with me. . . .

By my will, Anton Szandor LaVey, you are divest of your human substance and become in your own Self a Daimon."

Aquino says that the Church of Satan stopped promoting a literal Devil because "media distortion would have lumped us together with the nut elements, and our access to serious channels of communication would have been seriously impaired." It was always understood, however, in the higher councils, that Satan really did exist, not just as a psychological archetype but as "an essential, intelligent entity," a divine being that allows man to stand against nature and the will of God.

In order to deal with the spreading popularity of the Church of Satan, LaVey had set up a formal examining process, which he used to ordain new members of the priesthood. Some of LaVey's Hollywood friends, such as Jayne Mansfield, were awarded priesthood status without having to pass any tests, as was LaVey's chauffeur. Sammy Davis, Jr., was made an honorary warlock in the second degree. That rankled some of the membership. Then, in 1975, LaVey made the controversial decision to sell degrees in the priesthood. Aquino says he begged LaVey to reconsider. "In my letter of resignation, I said essentially that the Church of Satan is not the same thing as the Church of Anton LaVey. Those priesthoods are not yours to sell." In Aquino's opinion, LaVey was turning his back on Satan. The church split over the issue. "Virtually the entire nationwide priesthood resigned en masse," Aquino claims. Some of LaVey's former priests joined Aquino's competing organization, the Temple of Set. LaVey himself lapsed into the bitter retreat from which he has never emerged. "That's when he said, 'I don't believe in the Devil,' " says Aquino.

"It was not a schism, it was a drop in the bucket," LaVey says of his break with Aquino. "He took twenty-eight people with him and started spreading rumors that the Church of Satan was defunct and that he had divine word from the Man Downstairs to take over."

◆

Karla LaVey is a real-estate broker in Marin County and an occasional lecturer on witchcraft. She has her father's dark features and India-ink hair, and a tolerant, amused look in her eye. I noticed that she and her father do not hug; in fact, I realized I hadn't seen him touch anyone at all, with the exception of our first handshake. "My father gravitates to this room," she said fondly as we entered her study. "It's cold and dark and it has spiders." Like her father, Karla is a collector. She has covered her walls with vintage rock-and-roll posters and various funky movie artifacts, such as a costume worn by Debbie Reynolds in *How the West Was Won*.

"I'm going to have to bequeath my underwear collection to you," her father said.

"He has girdles and corsets of all the major stars," Karla informed me. He got them from the MGM costume department.

"Lana Turner, Elizabeth Taylor, Cyd Charisse, Greer Garson—all the MGM greats," said LaVey. "I have them in plastic neatly labeled in suitcases. You can learn a lot about the personal habits of the stars by examining their underwear."

There was a piano in Karla's living room. It was there mainly for her father's use. While Karla was mixing me a martini, I impulsively sat down and began playing a few tunes. LaVey sat in an armchair nearby and watched with focused intensity. I played "Lover Man," "My Romance," "Love for Sale." I have a limited repertoire.

"Those are my songs," said LaVey. "They're on my list."

"I know."

Indeed, certain shared similarities had drawn me to LaVey and had frightened me at the same time. I realized that what he represented evoked a powerful correspondence in me. The mood he lives in, which is compounded of nostalgia and comic-book Nietzscheanism, was part of my nature as well. Having grown up in the snooty, pious, sanctimonious, and sanitized precincts of middle-class Dallas, I had developed an attraction for the obscene and the bizarre. I wanted to look closely at the places in life that society had declared off-limits. In this manner, I identified with LaVey—in fact, it was exactly my own interest in the forbidden that had drawn me to him in the first place. The difference between us was that this was only a part of me and it was all of him. He had refined himself into an archetype. He was, it seemed to me, the last great romantic.

He became cheerful, and when I finished he rearranged the same tunes and mischievously played them against a march beat. "It sounds like the Soviet national anthem," he observed.

At dinner, Karla reminisced about her childhood in the notorious black house. "I've always been conspicuous," she said. "Like, my teachers would tell us to write a story about our pets, and I would write about my pet tarantula and the leopard that slept in my bed."

"You were quite an introspective little girl," LaVey said.

"Then my parents got a divorce," Karla continued. She was nine. Although the court awarded custody to Anton's mother, Gertrude, in practice that meant that Karla stayed with her father. "That was about the same time we got the lion. The other kids called me 'the lion girl.' But then Jayne Mansfield would come to visit and they would all want to come over."

"Karla and Zeena grew up in such bizarre, outré circumstances," LaVey commented.

"We really were like the Addams Family," Karla agreed.

It was a colorful life, but sometimes a dangerous one. Crank phone calls and threats were a constant nuisance. Once Karla was shot at by a classmate. On another occasion Zeena came home from school to find a Jesus freak sitting on the front steps with a meat cleaver in his hands.

Both girls grew up feeling ambivalent about women. "To be honest, I never thought of myself as a woman," Karla said. She always considered herself "in between" genders. Zeena told me that while she felt "very cared for, very loved" as a child, "I would not live like my mother lived." It was common knowledge that Anton had numerous affairs, and some of his mistresses virtually lived in the house. "It was almost like Mormonism," Zeena had said. "My mother was so busy she viewed it as a relief. Some of the mistresses I really liked. Oftentimes they were my baby-sitters."

When Zeena was thirteen she discovered she was pregnant. "My parents were ecstatic," she remembered. "Actually, I was a little surprised by their reaction. They were so excited they were going to be grandparents." They all rejected the idea of abortion. "That was just an example of how my parents raised me. They were more open and honest. There was never any deceit." They named the baby Stanton, which was Anton's real middle name.

While Karla and her father ordered their meal, poor Blanche dabbed at her nose with a Kleenex.

"They've really got the dial turned up this week," LaVey said sympathetically. Barton nodded.

I asked what they meant.

"There's a war on," said LaVey, "a Third World War, a silent, invisible war that is being fought without slings or bows or nuclear weaponry.

The point of the war is economic stability or recovery, and setting up a new structure conducive to economic needs."

"Who's in control?" I asked.

"You mean what powers?" said LaVey.

"I mean, who's giving Blanche a cold?"

"The old guard is waiting till it's safe to make the big change," said LaVey. He went on vaguely about pioneers breaking through with independent movies and small presses, softening up the consumer market. "Then the established troops can move in, Gulf and Western and so on."

"How are they giving Blanche a cold?"

"You mean what is the warfare agent?" asked LaVey. "More than likely it's a satellite or an earth-grounded microwave dish. Or it could be droplets seeded in the atmosphere punctuated by pollution caused by catalytic converters in cars." He began raving about how the Geneva Conventions should have stopped this sort of thing years ago. "If anything happens to me because I'm talking too much—well, I've got my own trump card. I've got my little black boxes. If anything happens to me, all hell breaks loose."

As LaVey thoughtfully chewed his lamb chops, I wondered if for the first time I had seen past the artifice, the bluster, the role playing, to the madness at the center.

◆

"Yeah, I knew LaVey back in the early fifties," says a retired San Francisco police inspector with the improbable name of Jack Webb. "He was an outstanding pianist locally." Webb used to hear him play at the Lost Weekend, and during breaks the two would chat about magic and the occult. Webb was impressed. "One night I said off the cuff, 'Tony, with all your ideas you ought to start your own church.' "

The seed of that idea fruited in 1966 when LaVey ceremonially shaved his head and ordained the beginning of the Age of Satan. It was April 30—Walpurgisnacht, the highest holiday of the satanic calendar.

Now it was another Walpurgisnacht, more than two decades later, and LaVey was in a reflective mood. "I try to minimize it, but deep down inside I can't. It's still a meaningful anniversary," he said as we sat in his favorite neighborhood French restaurant. The chef noticed him as he entered and sent out a tray with a glass of Dubonnet on the rocks for each of us—LaVey's only alcoholic indulgence. "Life everlasting, world without end," LaVey said in a sardonic toast.

He had thought, he said, that his little church would be a covert activity. "I had no idea it would snowball in a year's time. I was stunned when everything happened so fast." The publicity explosion began with a satanic wedding. LaVey performed the rites in his parlor, joining John Raymond, a former writer for the *Christian Science Monitor*, and Judith Case, the daughter of a Republican stalwart in New York. With all the television cameras trying to crowd into the parlor, the ceremony had to be repeated five times for the press. A photograph of the couple, with LaVey standing beside them in his black cape and horned cowl, and a naked redhead draped across the mantel as an altar, was carried in magazines and newspapers all across the world.

Barbara McNair, the black actress and singer, attended the ceremony. That began a correspondence between LaVey and Hollywood that would add luster and credibility to LaVey's organization. Among the many stars LaVey has claimed as friends over the years are Kim Novak, Christopher Lee, Laurence Harvey, and Keenan Wynn. LaVey has served as a consultant on a number of different films—notably the stylishly kitsch *The Abominable Dr. Phibes* (1971) and *Dr. Phibes Rises Again* (1972), in which Vincent Price plays the vengeful magician Dr. Anton Phibes, a character LaVey says was based on him. Phibes is an organist and ex-vaudevillian who builds a clockwork band of robot musicians to accompany his moody performances. In 1968 LaVey worked with director Roman Polanski on the production of *Rosemary's Baby*, which LaVey proclaimed "the best paid commercial for Satanism since the Inquisition." It is often said that LaVey himself played the serpentine devil who rapes and impregnates Mia Farrow. In the movie, one can only see the amber eyes of Satan, and it's difficult to tell whether they belong to LaVey. A few weeks after the movie finished shooting, Polanski's wife and unborn child were murdered by the Manson family.

LaVey's most notable conquest in Hollywood, however, was Jayne Mansfield. "I remember Jayne, all right," Jack Webb told me. In the early days of the church, Webb used to drop by for some of the rituals, along with several other San Francisco cops. "She was lying naked on Tony's grand piano. I'll never forget that sight." Mansfield already had made a reputation in Hollywood for her vigorous sexual appetites. "She liked to be humiliated," LaVey says. "She longed for a stern master." He claims Mansfield sought him out after reading a newspaper article about him. She wanted LaVey to put a curse on her Italian husband, with whom she was involved in a custody dispute. Soon after that, she became a priestess in the Church of Satan. She even posed for publicity photos with LaVey, kneeling at his feet as he administered a chalice of some magical liquid. When she went on a tour of Vietnam to visit the troops, says LaVey, she shocked her military escorts by asking for a satanic religious service. Satanism seemed to strike some deep chord inside her. She called it "Kahlil Gibran with balls."

For his part, LaVey responded to what he saw as a kindred spirit. "She never let down, not even in private. I could see a lot of myself in that," he admits. "Perhaps she feared that people wouldn't love her without the image."

Once, Mansfield's son Zoltan (coincidentally the same name as that of LaVey's former pet leopard) was mauled by a lion in a private zoo, called Jungleland, north of Los Angeles. The lion was on a tether, but the child came too close, and suddenly the cat had the boy's head in his jaws. The zookeepers pried the child loose and drove him to a hospital. He had a fractured skull and a ruptured spleen. "Jayne called several times when he was in critical condition," LaVey recalls. She pleaded with LaVey to work some magic to save her son. "I was very sincere in those days," says LaVey. He drove through a rainstorm across the Golden Gate Bridge to Mount Tamalpais, the highest point in the Bay Area, and performed a ritual, invoking the many names of the dark powers. "The following day Jayne called and said her son was out of danger. He did recover miraculously."

Mansfield herself had a rendezvous with tragedy, however, and her death would become a major element in the LaVey legend. Sam Brody, her attorney, agent, and frustrated suitor, was jealous of LaVey's relationship with his client. LaVey felt likewise. "I don't know why attorneys have that effect on me—to the point that I have no choice but to say, 'Look, you don't know who you're dealing with.'" One night Brody mischievously lit a pair of black candles on LaVey's altar. "Mr. LaVey was furious with Sam," Mansfield told her friend and biographer, May Mann. "He proclaimed, 'You are cursed by the Devil. You will be killed in one year!'" A few months later, on June 29, 1967, Mansfield and Brody were riding on U.S. 90 near New Orleans when their driver rear-ended a tank truck that was spraying for mosquitoes. Brody and Mansfield were both killed instantly—the actress was actually decapitated in the accident.

LaVey says that he had been looking through his scrapbook that night when he noticed that in clipping an article about himself placing flowers on Marilyn Monroe's grave, he inadvertently had cut into a picture of

Mansfield on the next page and had lopped off her head. Then the phone rang. It was an AP reporter with the tragic news.

He puts a lot of weight on such coincidences. Walpurgisnacht, for instance, is the birthdate of television at the New York World's Fair in 1939 ("What a satanic bomb that proved to be!"). It is the day Hitler committed suicide in 1945. The day LaVey's lion, Togare, died in 1981. Just this very afternoon, Barton was reading through a Mansfield biography and observed that the date of Jayne's first studio tryout was April 30, 1954. "Things are always turning up like that," LaVey said, unsurprised, as we examined our menus. "It's the little things that are the big things. Luck and coincidence are key."

When he conjures, he believes he is sending out a vibratory signal to the universe, tapping into a force that is like electricity, "unexplained, but not unexplainable." "I have seen people who've thrown in their lot with me soar, and then people who try to discredit me, their lives just fall apart. I believe you reap what you sow. You know, they talk so much about that thing with Jayne—it was truly the last straw when I confronted Brody and spoke the words. There was no way that could not have had some effect.

"I really do believe in magic," he continued. "Every act is a magical act. I don't think I should do this or do that. I just do what comes naturally. Generally speaking, the magician should be in harmony with the is-to-be, or what is to be called forth. I can't be pretentious enough to say that I'm going to make something happen, unless somebody backs me into a corner and I feel fear, like I did with Sam Brody, and then I have amassed so much adrenal energy I can force the cards a bit."

"Can you show me some of your magic?" I asked.

"I couldn't perform magic to satisfy your need to witness," he said. "If someone comes to me wanting to be fooled, I'll go along with that. Expectancy is one of the primary ingredients in stage magic. But the kind of magic you're talking about is not based on sitting around in an expectant state but something genuinely, inexplicably surprising. I'd feel stupid boasting that I'm a great magician. Others might say it, but I'd rather let the record speak for itself."

He was beginning to turn melancholy. "Deep down, I still have an urge to put on the paraphernalia and go through a ritual," he admitted. But that is behind him now. He hasn't performed a black mass in twenty years.

He was talking now with his eyes closed. It was a peculiar affectation, one that hinted of his great need to live in his own world, to shut out the intrusions of reality and stay locked inside his head with his own dark imagination. He said he expects society naturally to stratify itself, with satanists rising to the top to inherit the earth, a process he says is happening faster than he could have predicted. But until that day comes, he has chosen the strategy of abdication. "I have decided to withdraw, to give up my citizenship in the human race."

Later, I learned that earlier that same evening LaVey's younger daughter, Zeena, had chosen this special day to renounce her father. "I officially and ritually ended my positions as Church of Satan representative-defender and daughter of Anton LaVey," she declared in a letter to Michael Aquino. "While I have no regrets in my battle with the forces of ignorance, and my own unswerving dedication to *my* religion has only grown, I could no longer defend such an ungrateful and unworthy individual as the so-called Black Pope." She complained that her father "was filled, and still is, with petty jealous criticism of my efforts. This was easy for him to do from the safe vantage point of the comfortable and risk-free easy chair we know he has lived in for decades."

LaVey's duck arrived, baked in a currant sauce. This seemed to revive him. He started railing against the popular notion that satanists are child murderers or that they sacrifice animals—practices he has always preached against. In any case, he is opposed to the graffiti, the discord, the assault on public order. "The police force has to take care of people without conscience. In fact, there's very little conscience left. I'm not advocating a benign police state, exactly, but there's a need for certain elements of control. There has to be tyranny. If you don't want to call it tyranny, call it rational stratification. The alternative is chaos and anarchy, savage and bestial. If this sounds fascistic, so be it."

"He loves Disneyland," Barton added. "That's been a real trial balloon for a lot of this—the incorporation of androids, a private enclave with a self-contained justice system, its own private police force. It's a good example of capitalism at its peak."

Something had been bothering me, and this mention of Disneyland brought it to life. It was the sense that under all this brooding philosophy there was a man who was fundamentally harmless. Of course, that was the very thing LaVey feared the most. Where was all the sin? Where was the ribaldry? Where was the dangerous action? From my two weeks of observation, Anton LaVey lived a life more circumscribed and reflective than that of a Benedictine monk.

This observation put him on the defensive. "I'm just as ribald as I used to be," he said, "but I have to be more careful now. Security isn't what it used to be."

But what were his indulgences? So far all I had noticed were his single glass of Dubonnet in the evening and a single daily Excedrin, which he takes instead of coffee for "a little lift."

"I would like to indulge more," he admitted. "If I were unencumbered, I would. My vice now is to wake up in the morning feeling halfway decent."

What about sex?

"I've been around women all my life. It takes more than a lot of nude female bodies to move me now. I'd rather be reading an old book. I don't want to say I'm too old to cut the mustard, but if the battle's raging and shells are coming through the window, the stress level rises, and it does tend to dampen one's ardor. These guys that go around saying their pilot light's out—maybe they're concerned about their health—they're going to get pretty limp. The demoralization factor has to be considered rather . . ." He groped in the air for a word.

"Inhibiting?" asked Barton.

"Inhibiting," LaVey agreed.

No liquor, no tobacco, no drugs, no sex, no black masses, no baby sacrifices—what vice or indulgence was left for a satanist to set himself apart from the common herd?

"What if they kill people?" LaVey said.

"Do you kill people?"

He looked up and smiled. The waiter had just arrived with a healthy slice of mud pie.

◆

"I don't want the legend to disappear," LaVey told me anxiously in our last conversation, after I confronted him with the many inconsistencies in his story. "I like your family," he said ominously on the phone. "Was that your little girl I was speaking to? I would hate to see ill come to you or your family. I mean this very sincerely. Scoffing doesn't do any good—" He was especially offended that I had tracked down his eighty-seven-year-old father in an effort to verify some of the details of LaVey's early life. "I'd rather have my background shrouded in mystery. Eventually you want to be recognized for what you are now."

It is a theme he has sounded many times before. "I don't want to give anyone the satisfaction that they have me all figured out," he says in Barton's biography. "If people only knew. I've always loved that ubiquitous Johnson-Smith Company ad copy, 'Imagine the expression on their faces . . . !' That's a kind of leitmotif that has tempted me into most of the heinous, evil, or disreputable things I've ever done. Just imagine people's reaction if they ever found out. But they won't. It began in mystery. I want it to end that way."

Will Campbell: A Prophet in His Own Country

"I had meant to time the closing of the door with a subtle emission of a fart," my guru said as he shut the door to his room at the Holiday Inn in Oxford, Mississippi. "Evidently, my timing was off."

He was being "Will Campbell" today. You could tell by his outfit—his cheap black preaching suit and the wide-brimmed Amish hat that capped a freckled dome and a riotously unbarbered fringe of gray hair. On his feet were a pair of rather pricey alligator boots, which were given to him by his closest friend, the country songwriter and singer Tom T. Hall. In one hand, Campbell carried his staff—a handcarved cherry-wood cane—and in the other, a plastic glass to spit tobacco in. A maid in the parking lot gave him the sideways sizing-up such a metaphorically mixed outfit demanded.

As a matter of fact, I was a little suspicious as well. Who was this Will Campbell anyway? Some called him the conscience of the South, a white Martin Luther King, and yet he is one of the most profane and wickedly funny men I've ever known. Considered by many to be among the most radical thinkers in America, he is seen by others as little more than a whiskey-swilling gadfly and spiritual provocateur. A poor son of the Mississippi soil who studied theology at Yale, Campbell returned home to become a legend in the civil rights movement, then alienated many of his fervent admirers by turning his ministry to the Ku Klux Klan. He ministers to the poor, the dispossessed, and the unknown, but he is idolized by the rich, the powerful, and the famous. His life and work are studied in colleges and seminaries across the country; he is a subject of endless speculation among the clergy of many faiths; he has been compared on occasion to Jeremiah or Hosea and even has been called a modern-day Jesus, and yet Campbell himself admits that "in all these years, I can't point out one thing I've actually, personally accomplished." He is a preacher without a church, a Southern Baptist who is detested by the leaders of his own congregation. He is, in short, an assemblage of rude contradictions, a man not easily loved or understood but impossible to dismiss.

At this particular moment the Sage of the South had hold of a plastic dry-cleaning bag, about five feet long. He knocked on the door next to his and handed it to the man who answered—Campbell's biographer, Tom Connelly, a distinguished Civil War historian from the University of South Carolina.

"Connelly, I want you to dispose of this for me," Campbell said imperiously.

"What is it?" the white-haired professor inquired.

"What the hell do you think? It's one of my condoms. I think it's time we started practicing safe sex."

I had followed Will Campbell to Oxford because for twenty years he has been an unresolved enigma in my life, since the day he wandered into my office at the *Race Relations Reporter* in Nashville, Tennessee. It was my first day on the job. Campbell doffed his Amish sombrero and said he needed a haircut. I had no idea that one of the most controversial figures in the civil rights movement, which was supposed to be my beat, had just plopped himself into my office chair. Such was my confusion that I wasn't certain whether cutting hair was a part of my job description. Of course, as soon as he took off his hat, I could see that nature already had done most of the work.

Now I see that initial meeting as a characteristic Campbell gesture: intimate, surprising, presumptive, somewhat self-serving, and enduringly memorable. I knew instantly that I would never forget him, even though I didn't yet know who he was. But I soon found out, and like many young writers in the South at that time, I made a point of knowing Will Campbell. I idolized him for having been right at a time when being right was dangerous. He had been the only white man at the creation of Martin Luther King's Southern Christian Leadership Conference in 1957; later that same year, in Little Rock, Arkansas, he had walked hand in hand with the nine black children through the cordon of National Guardsmen and the raging mob in that first, failed attempt to desegregate Central

High. Wherever the races came into conflict, Campbell was quietly there, counseling the demonstrators at the lunch counter sit-ins, ministering to the Freedom Riders, consoling the mothers of the children murdered in the Birmingham, Alabama, church bombings, forever moving through the turbulent South with a small leather suitcase, a bottle of his sour mash "medicine," and his old Gibson guitar hung over his shoulder. "He was a walking nerve center," recalls author David Halberstam, who was a young reporter in Mississippi when he first noticed the slightly built white man always on the edge of events, at the shoulders of black leaders and white power brokers, whispering his message of radical change but also of the power of love, forgiveness, and reconciliation. "He was enormously important, but so deft and nimble that the re-actionaries never caught on to him," Halberstam told me. "His fingers were everywhere, but when you looked around—there were no finger-prints. He was the Invisible Man." Gradually, legends grew up around Campbell, concerning his vast influence, his talent for being in a dozen places at once, and his unconventional, unchurched religious beliefs. The main plank in his theological platform was "We're all bastards, but God loves us anyway." This single, radicalizing axiom would lead Campbell to begin his solitary and often misunderstood ministry to the Ku Klux Klan.

"I have seen and known the resentment of the racist, his hostility, his frustration, his need for someone upon whom to lay blame and to punish," Campbell wrote in his first book, *Race and the Renewal of the Church*. He continued:

I know he is mistaken, misguided, and willfully disobedient, but somehow I am not able to distinguish between him and myself. My sins may not be his, but they are no less real and no less heinous. Perhaps I have been too close to this man. Perhaps if I had not heard his anguished cry when the rains didn't come in time to save his cotton, if I had not felt the severity of his economic deprivation, if I had not looked upon his agony on Christmas Eve while I, his six-year-old child, feigning sleep, waited for a Santa who would never come; if I had not been one of him through these gales of tragedy, I would be able to condemn him without hesitation. If I had not shared his plight; if I had not lived with him in an atmosphere of suspicion, distrust, ignorance, misinformation, and nefarious political leadership, surely my heart would break less when I see him fomenting mob violence in front of *his* schoolhouse and *his* church house. Perhaps I would not pity him as much if I were not from his loins. But pity him I do.

But the church must not pity the racist. It must love and redeem him. It must somehow set him free.

Therefore, in 1969, on the night before Bob Jones, the Grand Dragon of the North Carolina KKK, was to enter the federal prison in Danbury, Connecticut, for contempt of Congress (he had refused to turn over the Klan membership lists), Campbell was there in the Dragon's Den to celebrate communion with a bottle of bourbon. He helped children of Klan families get scholarships to college. Later, Campbell talked with James Earl Ray, the man who murdered his friend Martin Luther King. When people asked if he really expected to save the souls of such men, Campbell allowed that that would be presumptuous. "They might, however, save mine."

He managed to further infuriate or scandalize many of his supporters by his insistent attacks on institutions—notably, the church, foundations, academia, and government, which together employed practically all of his liberal friends—and by his inflammatory statements about the true equality of the races. "If I live to be as old as my father is now, I expect to see black people killing white people for the same reason that white people have killed black people," Campbell said, or attempted to say, at the 1963 National Conference on Religion and Race in Chicago. That part of his speech was censored, but extensively reported in the press, along with the remark "With the emerging powers being primarily of the darker races, I expect to see little white children marched into the gas chambers, clutching their little dolls to their breasts in Auschwitz fashion at the hands of black Eichmanns." Such statements confounded nearly everyone in the movement; Campbell got the reputation of being a kind of intellectual porcupine that no one sought to embrace.

I did not know Campbell well during my tenure in Nashville—I was a little awed and afraid of him as well—and after I left there in 1971, I saw him only once more, performing a wedding in Atlanta. Back then, I thought that Campbell had the moral authority to become the spiritual voice of our time; but as the civil rights movement faded from public consciousness (and from my own), Campbell's legend faded as well. Through mutual friends, I kept up with his peregrinations through the still-seething South. I heard about his ongoing campaign against the death penalty. I also knew that he had been taken up by the country music establishment in Nashville as an unofficial chaplain. He made a literary splash in 1977 with the appearance of his extraordinary memoir, *Brother to a Dragonfly*, about his relationship with his doomed elder brother, which was nominated for the National Book Award. His subsequent books and novels received less attention. I assumed that whatever Campbell had meant to me twenty years before had been a part of an ancient reality; perhaps he had just been a creature of a particular historical moment, and now his time had passed. When Doug Marlette, the Pulitzer prize–winning cartoonist for New York *Newsday*, appropriated the Campbell persona for a character named Reverend Will B. Dunn in his cartoon strip "Kudzu," it seemed to me that the culture had absorbed even this most indigestible morsel and rolled on.

And yet there remained in my mind a suspicion that Will Campbell was the closest approximation of a saint that I had ever met. I suppose I knew from the moment I trimmed his hair that one day I would have to find out whether this man was a modern prophet or, as I feared, just a windy old fart who had managed to create a myth about himself. I realized that part of my anxiety was my own fear of destroying him. But there was another fear, which was more complex and even more daunting—that he would endure my scrutiny and prove to be a true spiritual genius. In that case, what was I to do? How would my life have to change? Could I come so close to Campbell without being drawn into his orbit and being forced to accept the truth of his experience? The stakes were too high, and I think Campbell knew it. He had been elusive and discouraging when I proposed to write about him. From the start there had been this tacit understanding that we would have to be careful around each other. I might poke a hole in his legend, and he might make me a Christian; in either case, the damage to our self-esteem would be hard to bear.

◆

Campbell had ridden into Oxford this spring morning in 1990, along with Tom T. Hall, author Alex Haley, and half a dozen other eminent writers, poets, and scholars who form a southern literary gang informally known as the Brotherhood. They all had come down from Nashville on Hall's tour bus, which was graced with a portrait of Hall's idol, General George Patton. This evening members of the Brotherhood were scheduled to read and perform at a benefit for the Mississippi branch of the American Civil Liberties Union.

"Tom, we're gonna run out to the campus before the show," Campbell called out to Hall, who is a burly man with massive features and intelligent gray-blue eyes that seem about to pop out of their sockets from the stress of containing his tireless mental combustion.

"Suppose I came along," said Hall.

"Well, come on, then."

We rode past the courthouse square through the picturesque Old South neighborhoods toward the stately campus of the University of Mississippi. The dogwood and the azaleas were blooming in an absurd, almost morbid abundance, like some metastasizing floral cell; indeed, the whole of Oxford had the gussied-up, sanctimonious, perfumed air of a high-class funeral parlor. Adding to this atmosphere of cordial necrophilia was the eternal presence of "Mr. Bill"—Oxford's ubiquitous ghost, William Faulkner.

The friendship between Hall and Campbell began fifteen years ago, at a publishing party for one of Hall's several books. "I thought he was a colorful character, with his hat and his cane, and I was told he was quite literate," Hall had told me earlier, "so I wanted to meet him. I remember the first question I ever asked him. I said, 'Reverend Campbell, being a man of the world, what do you see out there?' And he looked at me with an alarmed expression and said, 'I'm not a man of the world.' That's the kind of answers I've been getting ever since."

It was here in Oxford that the Campbell myth began. "I came out here to be university chaplain in 1954, about three months after the Supreme Court decision outlawing segregation in public education," Campbell said as we swung onto the campus. "I thought at the time that I would spend the rest of my life in Oxford. I guess I lasted a little over two years."

Here, in the white-hot center of resistance to integration, Campbell discovered himself as that most despised creature of the southern racial landscape, the nigger lover. His early efforts to integrate Ole Miss would culminate in 1956 with the admission of James Meredith, a black Air Force veteran. "Didn't I hear that Meredith was working for Jesse Helms?" Hall asked as we surveyed the grounds where the bloody riots surrounding the integration of Ole Miss occurred. (Meredith was then serving on the staff of the conservative North Carolina senator as an adviser.) Campbell laughed. "Yep, I guess if folks had known how it was going to turn out, they wouldn't have raised such a ruckus."

Because he was a preacher, Campbell may have been spared some of the physical punishment inflicted on white integrationists, although the message was delivered to him quite pointedly after he was observed playing Ping-Pong with a black minister at the YMCA. Several days later, Campbell found his lawn covered with Ping-Pong balls painted half white and half black. The dean of student personnel told him that he would have to consider where he was, and to "adjust" his thinking accordingly.

"And then, by God, we were having a reception for new students, right here on the back gallery," Campbell said as he led us outside the antebellum building that had once housed his office (many years before, it had been a Confederate hospital). "The dean was present. One of the assistant chaplains pulled me aside and said, 'Will, I think somebody put something in the punch.' I went over and looked in the punch bowl, and sure enough, there were two human turds covered with what appeared to be powdered sugar. I said to the dean that I find it rather difficult to adjust to fecal punch."

Campbell was subdued on the ride back to the motel. This retracing of his early days had left him curiously empty. It was as if he had left some part of himself behind. When we got back to the Holiday Inn, the other members of the Brotherhood were all gathered in a single room drinking whiskey and watching a basketball game. "Where've you guys been?" one of them hollered.

Tom T. poured a drink. "Aw, we went out to see where Will Campbell's buried," he said.

Campbell chuckled, but the gibe stung. He soon excused himself and retreated to his room.

That evening at the ACLU fundraiser, which was held in a blues club called the Oxford Alley, Hall tried to redeem himself with his friend by introducing Campbell as "our best chance for a clear conscience." Campbell was mischievously wearing a tie with a yellow thunderbolt, which had been the insignia of the National States Rights Party, an old white racist organization, but his audience was too young to catch this subversive gesture. He proceeded to make a speech about why all Baptists should be members of the ACLU. It had to do with early Baptists in America who were influential in establishing our civil liberties: in particular, Roger Williams, founder not only of the Rhode Island colony but also of the Baptist Church in America; Isaac Backus, a Baptist preacher who lobbied for constitutional guarantees of civil and religious liberties; and John Leland, an abolitionist and friend of Thomas Jefferson, who was instrumental in adding the First Amendment constitutional guarantees of freedom of speech and religion. Campbell's talk that evening would later be the subject of several angry letters to the editor of the local paper by conservative Baptists, who had strong feelings of antipathy toward the ACLU, no matter what Campbell said about the Baptist legacy.

After the rally there was a reception at the home of Dean Faulkner Wells, William Faulkner's niece. I was told more than once that Mr. Bill had written half of *Absalom, Absalom* "right here on the kitchen table," which at this moment was covered with mixers and peanuts. In the living room, Hall had consented to sing some of his tunes. He was in the middle of "Old Dogs, Children and Watermelon Wine" when Willie Morris, the resident heir apparent to the Faulkner legacy, appeared with his latest woman on his arm.

Morris, best known for his poignant and amusing 1967 memoir, *North Toward Home*, and for his turbulent years as editor-in-chief of *Harper's*, had sunk into semiobscurity in the last couple of decades. He was in a feisty but maudlin mood, which seems to be the effect that liquor has on him; and as Hall tried to sing, Morris loudly held court—this was *his* territory, after all. Finally Hall set his guitar aside. He had been looking forward to meeting the author; in fact he had read most of Morris's work. But now Hall looked peeved and dismayed as Morris launched into some unfocused tale about an Ole Miss halfback whom he was attempting to lionize for *Esquire* magazine.

A few drinks further, it occurred to Morris that he and his companion ought to get married. As this thought unfolded and grew grander, he speculated that Campbell might marry them *right now*. "Hell, Will, I know you don't require a license. All you need is a community of friends, and here—" Morris said, sweeping the room in an expansive gesture "—we are."

"Why, that's a wonderful idea," said Hall delightedly, and everyone seemed to agree. This sudden consensus caught Campbell off guard. "There ain't many things I take seriously," he said, "but two younguns gettin' married is one of them." He proposed that Morris give the matter a little more thought.

"Now, Will, this is your field," Hall conceded, "but why can't we marry these people tonight?"

Morris himself already seemed to be having second thoughts. He began recounting, for my benefit, the night he met Will Campbell. "We were all in Hattiesburg, Mississippi," he said in the broad tones of a man about to recite an epic poem. The rest of the partygoers stood rapt. "I didn't know what I was up to at the time. My mama had died, my daddy had died, my pore ole dog was gettin' old—"

"We love this story and it beats the hell out of gettin' married," Hall interrupted sourly.

"—my best friend, Jim Jones, died *in my arms*, and I just broke up with my Jewish girlfriend, so I came down to Hattiesburg and checked in to the Holiday Inn to write about Mississippi."

"Will, dammit!" said Hall. "You know how short life is! They're obviously in love and want to *get married*."

"Then the phone rang in my room," Morris continued, "and this voice says, 'Willie, this is Will Campbell. I'm down here in room one forty-two. . . .' "

It turned out to be an inconsequential story, and as Morris embroidered the details, Hall wandered into the kitchen to mix another drink. A few moments later Campbell came in and pulled him aside and chewed him out. "Marriage is one institution—maybe the only one—that must be treated with dignity and respect and utmost seriousness," Campbell said sternly. "I will not have you frolicking with people's lives for your own amusement."

Hall was chastened but still disappointed that Campbell wouldn't go ahead and perform the ceremony. "They love each other, Will—what else do you require?"

"My *requirement*?" asked Campbell. "Well, for one thing, I require that the groom be able to stand up."

Campbell went back to the party with a fresh glass of bourbon. Hall watched him go with a complicated look in his eye—which he then turned on me.

"I know what you're up to, Larry," he said.

"What am I up to, Tom?" I said, humoring him, but knowing that one had to keep alert around Hall. Like his friend Campbell, Hall has a taste for dangerous discourse.

"All these religious people you're writing about?" he asked rhetorically. "I see what you've got in mind. You think you can start your own religion. You have that quality. It's a blessing and a curse." He paused and looked at me with his huge, now rather red although still intensely concentrated eyes. "But there's a gap in you. You can start your own religion, but you could never lead it. Too bad for you it doesn't ever work out that way."

Hall patted me on the shoulder and went back toward the living room, leaving me standing at Mr. Bill's table, staring at the peanuts and potato chips. I felt surprised and even staggered by what he had said. Was that what I was up to? I had told myself, when I began this quest, that I just wanted to find something worth believing, but now I could see through

Hall's eyes that this whole pursuit had been a way of measuring myself against religious leaders. I remembered the sensation I had experienced in the First Methodist Church in Dallas when I imagined standing in the pulpit where Walker Railey had stood and Bishop Goodrich before him. It had been only a passing fantasy, I had thought, and yet it had been a powerful one—I could physically feel myself standing there, grasping the lectern, draped in the holy cloth. Yes, I had wanted that, I now had to admit; I had wanted to be the anointed one, the one who had the message, who had looked inside himself and found the answer and now brought it forth to the hungry masses. That is why I chose to write not about religion but about religious leaders—it was not just their beliefs I was drawn to but their *roles*. Is that what Hall had meant when he said I had "that quality"? Did he mean that he could see me as a spiritual leader? Or did he simply mean that I had the quality of wanting to be something that I really wasn't—that I was just a pretender to the pulpit?

I thought about the people I had written about so far. Railey, Swaggart, O'Hair, LaVey—hadn't there been with all of them an element of competitiveness on my part, a bit of looking down my nose at them, as if I might have done better? But was that all there was to it? Because that is a feature of nearly every relationship a journalist enters into; he is always making sly comparisons with himself. No, there was more here than the mixture of smugness and envy that a reporter might feel around a politician or an athlete. There was savage, unfulfilled longing. This must have been the source of that rage that I discovered in myself when I entered the church in Dallas, a rage that I had carried in different degrees throughout my life. Oh, the yearning, the aching, famished *need* to believe! That was what powered me as I ransacked other people's beliefs, looking for something I could swallow, something nonabsurd, something *believable* to believe. But there had never been anything there that I could accept, no coat of faith that was tailored for me.

And how cruelly perceptive of Hall to see that gap inside me, which would envy spiritual leaders, and which would even labor to bring them down, but which prevented me from ever actually taking their place. I could only destroy; I couldn't proclaim my own beliefs or finally even know them. In that moment I felt ashamed, but also released. I had not even realized that I was protecting this secret ambition. Now that it was discovered and at the same moment blasted by Hall's insight, it was as if I had been shaken out of a trance. At least I knew now what I was up to.

◆

Campbell calls himself a "bootleg preacher," which in his lexicon means that he conducts his ministry outside the traditional church. For him, the church is a human institution, not a divine one, and such creations are inherently evil. "*No* institution can be trusted, including the institutional church," he says. "They're all after our souls—*all* of them." What institutions actually institute, he contends, "is inhumanity, by advancing the illusion that form is substance, the means are the meaning, doing is being, procedure is redemption—and so they can only further dehumanize relations between those they were instituted to reconcile." The church, in Campbell's opinion, is the most pernicious institution of all. "It was a cop-out from the outset. You build an institutional church for one reason: in order to provide a buffer against radical discipleship."

In 1981 Campbell was invited to make a speech at New York's prestigious and historic Riverside Church on the subject of what role the church might play in improving race relations in the city—a matter of profound interest at Riverside, which is situated on the edge of Harlem. Campbell climbed into the nine-ton pulpit of handcarved limestone. He stood there dwarfed by the towering nave and the gleaming organ pipes like the captain of a mighty vessel addressing his trusting crew. "I've been invited to enough of these affairs by now to know what you mean," Campbell began in his Mississippi drawl, which he probably exaggerated, given the setting. "What you mean is 'How can we improve race relations in New York City—'" and at this point he paused significantly, casting his eye over the magnificent stained glass, the opulent icons, the velvet-padded mahogany pews, all paid for with Rockefeller millions—"'and *keep all this!*'" His own modest solution was to hold a giant auction, give the proceeds to the poor, and disperse the congregation to evangelize the world in the name of Jesus. "Surprisingly," he says, "they did not act on my proposal."

Until the mid-seventies, Campbell was supported by a highly informal organization called the Committee of Southern Churchmen, whose main reason for existence was to shelter Campbell from starvation. Since then he's made his living from writing and farming and lecturing (he speaks frequently at universities and religious gatherings). Having turned sixty-five in 1989, he draws social security. Although he will not serve on juries, Campbell does vote (he's a liberal Democrat) and pay his taxes. So one could not say that he is entirely independent of the grip of institutions himself.

"Institutions are inevitable, I know that," he says. "What I'm saying is, let's not worship the institution. They are all basically self-loving and self-perpetuating. They are trying to make you over into their own image—it doesn't matter if it's Yale or Bob Jones University. They all have a line. What I try to say is that I may be working *within* this particular institution, *but I don't trust you.* Anyway, that's my story, and I'm sticking to it."

He regards his loathing for institutions as a feature of his Baptist heritage. Once, when he was going through a metal detector at the Dallas–Fort Worth airport, the security guard made him go back through the line and put his cane through the X-ray machine, even though Campbell had not set off the alarm. Campbell did so, but then crawled on his hands and knees through the metal detector, while the crowd hissed at the security guard. Then he stood and danced off, twirling his cane. The point he was trying to make, he says, is that "we live in a technological concentration camp. That was just my way of saying I am not a robot. It is also about being a Baptist. We are a movement that was built on what it means to be free."

"Bull," says his wife, Brenda, when Campbell tells this story. "I don't know any other Baptists like that."

He does not like to be called "Reverend Campbell" because "it sounds condescending and a bit imperialistic." "Some people call me a counselor," Campbell says, "but it's such an arrogant concept—like I can do something better for you than you can do for yourself. I'm not a reverend, and I'm not a counselor. I'm just a preacher." Even the word "ministry" gives him trouble. "I don't really have a *ministry*," he says, holding the word at arm's length. "I have a *life*."

From the beginning Brenda has handled the family finances, doling out a meager allowance to her husband, who believes that money is "evil." Campbell's attitude toward money has been a subject of frustration to his friends. John Egerton, a Nashville writer and a former colleague of mine at the *Race Relations Reporter*, has taken to booking Campbell's speeches and making his airline reservations after learning that Campbell often failed to charge for his services and would never bother to shop for a discounted ticket. Campbell once told Tom T. Hall that the William Morris Agency had called and guaranteed that they could quadruple his speaking fees. "What's wrong with that?" Hall asked, annoyed that Campbell would reject such an offer when he was constantly on the margin of need. "I don't know," said Campbell. "I guess it's just tacky to say that I'll come speak to you about Jesus for a thousand bucks. Besides, I don't think Amos would have let the William Morris Agency book him into Judea."

"I thought it was the *love* of money that was supposed to be evil," I said to Campbell, "not money itself."

"I know that's what the Bible says," said Campbell, "but I do think that evil is a greater problem for wealthy people. Now, the opposite is not true—I don't think the poor are virtuous. I know plenty of poor folks who'd blow your sweetbreads right through your earlobes."

When he is not on the road giving a speech or marrying and burying, Campbell spends his days on his forty-acre farm outside Mount Juliet, Tennessee, planting tomatoes and hot peppers, or sitting in the log-cabin office behind his house, pecking out sermons and books on his Tandy computer. Should someone come to visit, Campbell will pull up a couple of rocking chairs in front of his wood stove, whittle on a stick, and occasionally spit into the flames. "I never do anything big," he says. "It's a series of little things, like helping people to read, holding a man's hand who's dying, singing a few songs to a fellow who's about to go to jail." Each year hundreds of people seek him out. They may be famous singers fighting a drug problem, ex-cons just off the road gang, young couples trying to reconcile a failing marriage; somehow they all find their way to the little cabin behind the apple tree in the hollow of the Stones River valley, where Campbell conducts his business of "just trying to survive as a human being."

"Will sorta ambles around, so sometimes you forget he's at work," Hall had warned me. "I recall when a couple of students from a seminary came down and spent a whole day asking Will all sorts of questions. Then when they got ready to leave, one of them said, 'By the way, Reverend Campbell, what do you *do?*' 'Oh, nothing,' he said. But here he had been counseling them all day long, and it didn't even dawn on them that *this was what he did.*"

To those inside the glassy walls of foundations or the ivory towers of academia, Campbell is a pesky, elusive gadfly constantly dodging the nets with which they try to capture him—and then categorize him and file him away. In a story often told about Campbell, he was at a university seminar where a professor of theology with a long cigarette holder in his hand kept eyeing him intently. As Campbell spoke, the theologian would puff on his cigarette and shake his head. "But what's your actual *business*, Reverend Campbell?" he would ask. "What do you actually believe in?" Finally Campbell erupted, "Look, I've been trying to tell you, I believe in Jesus, dammit—*Jesus*! That through the saving grace of his sacrifice on the cross, we all have been redeemed and made brothers to each other. So if we accept this gift, we're free, there ain't no need to hate anymore. Getting the word around about that is my business, Professor."

He cannot even pass a ringing public phone in an airport without answering it. "Because it might be someone in trouble?" I prompted. "Oh, no!" Campbell replied. "Might be someone I want to talk to."

Who he does not want to talk to are the innumerable acolytes who show up on his doorstep with a copy of one of his books in hand, saying they want to sit at his knee. "Well, tough shit," Campbell tells them. "I don't want any disciples. I'm trying to *be* a disciple. I look back and see a bunch of people following me and I fall to pieces."

"Which is," Campbell told his biographer, Tom Connelly, "the distinction between being a guru or cult figure and not being one of those things. The guru says, 'Yes, come on down. We have this program and we'll put you to work.' I've never done that. It's dangerous. Soon you start believing that shit."

Once a priest in New Jersey phoned Campbell and said he wanted to come down south and join Campbell's ministry because he felt called to do something important with his life.

"Where are you now?" Campbell asked.

"I'm at a pay phone in Newark," the priest replied.

"Is it one of those glass booths?"

"Yes, it is," said the puzzled priest.

"Are there any people out there, or are the streets deserted?"

"There are lots of people."

"Well, son," said Campbell, "*that's your ministry*. Now go to it."

Campbell never keeps correspondence or papers of the sort biographers and university collections hunger for. His former secretary Andy Lipscomb once discovered a pile of Campbell's sermons moldering in the compost heap. When he reproved his boss for destroying such valuable records, Campbell observed that "bullshit makes the cabbage grow."

He will not be lionized. Sometimes he purposely subverts himself, as at Duke University, where he was appointed "theologian in residence" for part of a term. To many of the students and faculty there, Campbell was virtually a mythic hero, and yet when he gave his main address in

Page Auditorium, he suddenly folded up his speech after two pages, said "That's it," and walked off the podium—leaving many of his supporters wondering why he had bothered to come. Doug Marlette had a similar experience when he was a Nieman Fellow at Harvard and invited Campbell to speak to the other fellows. "They didn't get him at all, and Will didn't bother to explain himself," says Marlette. "He was excruciatingly inappropriate."

Other times Campbell will be so incendiary he almost invites people to loathe him. He has on more than one occasion told a university audience that "this institution right here"—meaning Ohio State or Georgia Tech or whatever school he happens to be visiting—"has contributed, wittingly or not, to incomparably more bloodshed and misery, done more to maim and murder, than the whole lot of poor old country boys in sheets holding cross burnings in rented cow pastures. Now, the Klan may be more bigoted than the 'children of light,' but they're not more racist. Racism is in the structures, the system in which we are all bound up. We're all basically of a Klan mentality when it comes to our own structures and our own institutions."

Although he had grown up with a calling to be a preacher, and had gone to Yale to polish his theology, Campbell claims he was not really a Christian until his friend Jonathan Daniel was murdered in 1966. Daniel was a young theology student from the Episcopal Theological Seminary in Cambridge, Massachusetts, who had gone down to Lowndes County, Alabama, to register blacks to vote. He had walked into a country store with a white priest and two black friends, and when he came outside with a Moon Pie and a soda pop, he was summarily shotgunned by a sheriff's deputy named Thomas Coleman. Campbell got the news of Daniel's death while he was visiting his friend P. D. East, the colorful and defiant editor of the Petal, Mississippi, newspaper called the *Petal Paper*. East was a cynic who liked to call the Church "the Easter chicken." Years before, he had badgered Campbell into giving him a definition of the Christian message in ten words or less. " 'We're all bastards but God loves us anyway,' " East recalled Campbell saying. "Let's see if your definition of faith can stand the test. Was Jonathan a bastard?"

Campbell was still in shock, furious at the injustice and deeply grieving for his friend. It seemed cruel of East to make this occasion a test of faith. Mainly to get East to shut up, Campbell admitted that Jonathan was a bastard.

"Is Thomas a bastard?" East asked.

It was easy enough to agree to that.

Then East pulled his chair around, put his bony hand on Campbell's knee, and, staring directly into Campbell's glistening eyes, whispered, "Which one of these two bastards do you think God loves the most?"

It was the turning point of Campbell's life. "Suddenly everything became clear," he recalls in *Brother to a Dragonfly*. "I walked across the room and opened the blind, staring directly into the glare of the street light. And I began to whimper. But the crying was interspersed with laughter."

He was laughing at himself: "at twenty years of a ministry which had become, without my realizing it, a ministry of liberal sophistication. An attempted negation of Jesus, [a ministry] of human engineering, of riding the coattails of Caesar . . . of looking to government to make and verify and authenticate our morality, of worshiping at the shrine of enlightenment and academia, of making an idol of the Supreme Court, a theology of law and order and of denying not only the Faith I professed to hold but my history and my people—the Thomas Colemans."

At that moment Campbell became a convert to the doctrine of unmerited grace; that is, that the rain of forgiveness falls on the deserving and the undeserving alike. Salvation does not depend on our own goodness but on God's forgiveness. Later, when an all-white jury acquitted Coleman, Campbell endorsed the verdict. "Jonathan can never have died in vain, because he loved his killer," Campbell expained in an article that enraged many:

> And since he loved his murderer, his death is its own meaning. And what it means is that Tom Coleman, this man who pulled the trigger, is forgiven. If Jonathan forgives him, then it is not for me to cry for his blood, his execution. Any act on my part which is even akin to "avenging" Jonathan's death is sacrilege. . . . For when Thomas killed Jonathan, he committed a crime against the State. When Thomas killed Jonathan, he committed a crime against God. The strange, near maddening thing about this case is that both the offended parties have rendered the same verdict—not for the same reasons, not in the same way, but the verdict is the same—acquittal.

"A whole bunch of my civil rights friends came to me and said, 'Good God, Campbell, you stupid idiot, you can't go saying things like that to a bunch of rednecks. Man, that just gives them *license*,'" Campbell later recalled. "But of course, I told 'em, that's not true. What the jury told Tom Coleman was, 'You are forgiven. Go thou and kill again, if you want.' But what the gospel says, and what we are obliged to say, is, 'Your sins are already forgiven you, brother. Go thou and kill no more.' That's the difference, and it's all the difference in the world."

"What I like about Will," says the black scholar and writer Julius Lester, a longtime Campbell watcher, "is that he does not divide the world into us versus them. It's that quality that enables him to really startle people. His whole object is to affect the soul of the other, and he does that better and more directly than anyone I've ever seen."

A hazardous example of that occurred during the sixties at a radical student forum in Atlanta. Campbell simply announced: "My name is Will Campbell. I'm a Baptist preacher. I'm a native of Mississippi. And I'm pro-Klansman because I'm pro–human being. Now, that's my speech. If anyone has any questions I will be glad to answer them." Pandemonium followed. "I had intended to start a dialogue," Campbell recalls. "I had not intended to start a riot." He might have explained to his audience that "pro-Klans*man*" did not mean the same as "pro-Klan" in his vocabulary, the one having to do with the individual, the other with ideology. The blacks in the audience stormed out en masse, followed by half the whites. Those who remained were so abusive Campbell was genuinely frightened. Half an hour later, when the crowd finally settled down enough for Campbell to speak again, he pointed out that just four words, "pro-Klansman Mississippi Baptist preacher," coupled with his own whiteness, had turned the students into everything they thought the Klan to be—hostile, frustrated, angry, violent, and irrational.

Why does he do this? Why will he deliberately puncture the esteem people feel for him and even court their hatred, rather than accept the love and admiration and even the idolatry that attends even the most ordinary preacher in the high-steepled church? It would have taken very little for Campbell to become a media saint or a TV evangelist on the order of Swaggart or Falwell, the "electronic soul molesters," as Campbell calls them. He had tasted that power as a young man, still in his teens, at Louisiana College, a Baptist Academy in Pineville, when he and his future wife, Brenda Fisher, traveled through the Catholic parishes in a rattletrap mission bus, stopping at every crossroads hamlet, where Brenda would pump out "Bringing in the Sheaves" on the field organ while Campbell delivered the searing message of fundamentalist Christianity. "Yeah, I used to be a street-corner preacher," he says about that period, "with my Bible in one hand and a microphone in the other. There was a great sense of power. My voice would be booming out through four loudspeakers, and I'd be strutting around, swishing the microphone cord. One time the power went off and I just kept on preaching; I couldn't stop—it was a form of homiletic masturbation."

He did have his own church once, in Taylor, a mill town in north Louisiana, right after he graduated from Yale. Those rough edges of the budding young evangelist had been polished smooth from three years in the Ivy League. He came back to the South with certain eastern habits of dress—white buck shoes and a tweed cap—smoking a calabash pipe and getting around town on a ten-speed bike. He had studied under Reinhold Niebuhr and Liston Pope, two of the great Christian thinkers of the time. Campbell was twenty-six years old, and he intended to bring enlightenment to these poor backwoods Baptists. He soon learned that his fine education hadn't taught him everything he needed to know—for example, how to run a vacation Bible school. Moreover, he soon came to cross-purposes with the first family of the church, the family that owned the paper mill, when he lent his support to a labor strike in nearby Elizabeth. And yet the traditional order was so much in control that Campbell was never seen as a threat, even when he preached about civil rights. "I wouldn't have survived there," Campbell acknowledges. "They thought it was cute when I talked about race." The atmosphere of repression was so overpowering that Campbell began to realize that his nervous system couldn't take it. "I think I was already beginning to see that the only way you teach anybody is by precept and example. What you say up there in the pulpit, that's probably *the* poorest way to communicate with a congregation."

He left Taylor for Ole Miss. He had already decided that he would be a Baptist preacher in the South for the rest of his life, but never again would he be a Southern Baptist preacher. From that day, his alienation from his denomination, the largest Protestant body in America, has only grown more intense and bitter, as his church leaders have purged the liberals and anyone with less than strictly fundamentalist views from the seminaries and positions of power. When I asked Campbell why he stayed a Baptist, when he so profoundly disagreed with so many things his church has come to stand for, he said, "I don't know. I tried being an Episcopalian. I came within five steps of being a Methodist—I took Methodist polity at Yale and I was going to be ordained in the Methodist church. I took the exam and was the last one in line to go through the door for ordination, but just before I went in I turned around and got on a train and went back to New Haven. I guess it's just a disease. It gets in your genes and you can't shrug it off." He had grown up Baptist, was baptized at the age of seven and ordained as a minister at sixteen. His father was a Baptist deacon for more than sixty years. Later, in researching the history of the Baptist movement, Campbell discovered its connection with the Anabaptists of the sixteenth century (precursors of the Amish and Mennonite sects), "a stubborn little band of left-wingers," as Campbell calls them, who refused to baptize infants or serve on juries or defend themselves or their country. For these offenses, they were brutally persecuted. Campbell's Amish hat is a gesture in the direction of the Anabaptist tradition, which the Southern Baptist Convention has so completely renounced. "I discovered that the Baptist heritage is a glorious one," Campbell says. "I'm depressed because that's gone. It ain't ever coming back."

He carries the loss with him in his perpetual isolation from his peers, who for their part have never really known what to do with Campbell anyway. A few years ago he was invited to Austin, Texas, to speak at the investiture of a young Baptist minister. The passage Campbell chose to speak on was drawn from the Olivet discourse in Matthew 25, in which Jesus greets those who will enter heaven with the statement: "Come, you blessed of my Father, inherit the kingdom prepared for you from the foundation of the world; for I was hungry, and you gave me meat; I was thirsty, and you gave me drink; I was a stranger, and you took me in; naked, and you clothed me; I was sick, and you visited me; I was in prison, and you came unto me." And the righteous respond that he is mistaken, that they have done none of those things for their master. Jesus explains: "Inasmuch as you have done it unto one of the least of these my brethren, you have done it unto me." The question Campbell posed to his audience that morning was "Who are the least of these?" It was a question every person has to answer for himself, so Campbell cast back over his own life for an answer. Were the least of these the poor, bigoted dirt farmers he grew up with in southern Mississippi? No, it was easy to forgive people who were not responsible for their benighted condition. Was it the angry mob in Little Rock who screamed and spat upon the little black girl whose hand Campbell held as he walked through the cordon of National Guardsmen? No, they were only misguided and misled. Was it the Klan leader . . . ? He continued in this vein, wrapping his audience in a rhetorical cocoon, mystifying and tantalizing them, and at the same time making them feel good about themselves, letting them warm themselves in the glow of forgiveness as they assented, step by step, to Campbell's parable. "No, the least of these," he finally said, when he had them completely bound and gagged in the Christian tradition, "are you, my fellow Southern Baptist ministers. You are the only group I feel superior to. Jesus died for this: so that I may be reconciled unto you."

◆

It was Saturday night at Gass's Store, a roadside juke joint in Mount Juliet, a couple of miles from Campbell's farm. The house band was playing some standard country tunes. Kitty Wells's pretty granddaughter was on the drums. This is as close to being Campbell's church as any place is likely to be. There is a strong sense of community and tradition in this dark little nightery with its neon icons in the names of Miller and Bud. "Will married nearly half the people in this room," his wife, Brenda, remarked as we sat down. "Some he had to marry several times."

After we ordered our pizza, Campbell went over to talk with a neighbor, a genial ex-con with a drinking problem, and Brenda asked me to dance. She was an elegant two-stepper, and she expertly guided me around the tiny dance floor, while her husband hung out in a booth talking with various confederates and joshing with the waitresses. All along I had wondered how he kept it up, this lonely performance of his life, this one-man passion play. Now, as I stood in his place in his wife's strong arms, I realized that Brenda was his secret. They have a charming, teasing relationship, which has survived more than four decades of marriage, the raising of three children, and an endless stream of needy and troubled people at their door, but which is based in part on the fiction that Brenda dominates Will. Whenever people ask, "How is Brenda?" Campbell is likely to tell them that she's as mean as always. Friends say that Brenda is the one person Campbell is truly afraid of; in fact, early in their marriage it was rumored that Campbell was henpecked. The preacher in the little church he grew up in was so concerned that he held special prayers for their marriage. "I went from being henpecked to being a liberated husband in a single generation," Campbell jokes. Each complains loudly about the other's driving habits: Will is the tortoise and Brenda the hare in this long-standing tirade. Each had made a point of asking me to drive.

Campbell comes to Gass's nearly every Saturday that he's in town to listen to the music and mix with his congregation. He also hopes to be called on to sing from time to time. "Sure, I wanted to be a country singer—long before I ever decided to be a preacher," Campbell has admitted. "My first guitar was nothing more than a piece of wire tied to a milk safe; I would strum it and release tension on the wire to change sounds. Then when I was about twelve, my daddy traded a pig and got me a Hawaiian guitar. The trouble was, nobody in our community had ever seen one like that and I never learned to play it." He had grown up listening to the gospel sounds of the church and the Delta blues of the field hands. When he got the offer to go to work for the National Council of Churches as a roving representative and eye on the South during the civil rights movement, Campbell took the opportunity to set up his office in Nashville, home of the Grand Ole Opry.

In 1969 an unknown songwriter and former Rhodes Scholar named Kris Kristofferson arrived in Nashville and rented a room in a slum house on Music Row. The city was just then turning into the Hollywood of the music industry. The tenements with fifty-dollar-a-month rooms like the one Kristofferson was living in would soon be razed for the glassy recording studios and the gaudy museums the stars would build for themselves. But that was in the glittering future. In the meantime Kristofferson was tending bar at the Tally Ho Lounge and taking out the trash at Columbia Studios and filling up the pages of a looseleaf notebook with unheard songs such as "Me and Bobby McGee" and "Sunday Morning Coming Down."

One afternoon a friend, songwriter Vince Matthews, introduced him to the fellow in the office next door, a skinny preacher with fawn-colored eyes that appeared (once one had located them behind the thick, cheap lenses) wan and well used, like the eyes of a bookworm or a very old man. He had a sensual crooked mouth that was full of mischief and comedy in some lights and defiant and even cruel in others. It wasn't more than a few minutes after they met that guitars were produced, and Campbell played a song he'd written about a friend of his youth, a twelve-year-old black field hand named Leon, who slept in the smokehouse and was paid five dollars a month to work on the Campbell farm. Campbell had given his boyhood friend the pet name "Brother Mother." The song is about their reunion many years later, when they accidentally find each other in a northern city and discover that the gulf that separates them now is too wide for friendship.

> *Hello, Brother Mother, friend of mine,*
> *Ain't seen you in such a long, long time.*
> *But I know where you been*
> *'Cause it's all a case of skin,*
> *So hello, Brother Mother, friend of mine.*

After the song, Matthews mentioned that Campbell was a sometime preacher to the Klan. Kristofferson was dumbfounded. "Well, Preacher, I guess I misunderstood the words to your song," he said to Campbell. "Mister Kristofferson, you have the reputation of being an educated man," Campbell replied. "Do you know of anyone who *needs* ministering more than the Klan?"

Kristofferson would spend many more hours in Campbell's office. He borrowed money occasionally, and at one point offered to sell 50 percent of his future earnings to Campbell for five thousand dollars. "Not wanting to offend his medicated sensibilities, I changed the subject," Campbell recalls. "Besides, any future earnings for him seemed rather remote at the time."

Their friendship drew Campbell deeper into the world of country music. He maintains that "country music is people music—honest, liberal —it's the only true American art form. It is also theologically sound." The music lets Campbell touch on the shameful and frequently violent sides of human nature. The songs he chooses to sing speak of the hurt and hopelessness of a lonely woman alcoholic, or an anguished father waiting for his son to come home from the war in a box, or a murderous lover in jail. Each of them testifies to Campbell's central message, which he finds in 2 Corinthians, chapter 5: "God was in Christ, reconciling the world unto himself, no longer holding men's misdeeds against them, and has committed to us this word of reconciliation. Therefore we pray you in Christ's stead, be reconciled."

"*Reconciliation!*" Campbell will thunder whenever he reads this passage. "Reconciliation to our *own natures*—it's a hard idea to accept, and that's why the gospel is a whole lot more drastic than most folks have ever dreamed. Our trespasses are not held against us, we're *already forgiven!* Don't you see how that liberates us all? Black, white, Kluxer, preacher, banker, teamster, murderer, chairman of General Motors, head of the Ford Foundation—we're *all* bastards, but God loves us anyway."

This message has a special appeal for the "outlaw" element of country music—Willie Nelson, Johnny Cash, and particularly Waylon Jennings. "I'm really antipreacher," says Jennings, who grew up in the Church of Christ and once aspired to be a preacher himself. "But Will Campbell is one of the few people in the world I believe to be completely sincere. If you want to talk about an outlaw, there's the man. He doesn't take what anybody says—he goes and finds out for himself. As best I can figure, Will Campbell is exactly what the Bible tells us to be."

Jennings and his wife, singer and songwriter Jessi Colter, met Campbell at the wedding of a friend. It was the usual eccentric Campbell ceremony, held on this occasion in his office in Mount Juliet. In one corner was the woodburning stove. Books were scattered on a shelf and piled on the floor in disorder. There was an old Olympia manual typewriter on a butcher block that was supported by a milk jug. On the wall behind the barber chair Colter was sitting in was a three-headed china doll. "I was immediately taken by this place," Colter recalls. "It was very humble, very authentic. There was a pot of beans on the kettle. Then this man appeared who looked like something out of the eighteenth century."

The wedding began abruptly with Campbell's having the couple sign the marriage certificate. "Now, what we have done has nothing to do with Christian marriage," said Campbell. "It is no more than a legal contract between you and the state that gives you the right to sue one another if you should ever desire to do so." He tossed the contract aside. "Now, Mr. Caesar," he said in a contemptuous voice, "we have rendered unto you the things that are yours. At this point, the *wedding* begins."

Campbell spoke quite personally about the two people—the problems they had had in the past, the ones they would likely have to face in the future, and the endless need for forgiveness any such relationship demands. At moments he was so intimate that Colter could feel herself flushing. "The words he said went deep inside me," she recalls. "The whole experience bonded everybody together. And I was very much drawn to Will. I felt no pressure, no condemnation in his presence. He's far more of a force than what you'd call a force of personality or charisma. Of course, I couldn't have said any of this at the time. I was working in a far place, spiritually."

Campbell remembered the beautiful woman in the barber chair, dressed, he thought at the time, like a jezebel. After that first meeting, he made a point whenever he was around her of treating her with extravagant gentility, like a Victorian lady. He became an object of fascination to her. "Each thing I learned about him seemed just another wonderful trait. Here in this world, going at the speed of light, was this man who worked his own land, raised his own food, ground his own meal. He would come by to see us on his way to visit someone on death row, or perhaps he'd just come back from some community where they were handling snakes. The next thing I'd hear he'd be lecturing at Vanderbilt. He was a prince of the unexpected."

When others would talk about Campbell's drinking or chewing or cussing, it would seem they were talking about someone else. He kept those parts hidden from her. She had known him for years before she learned, secondhand, that he was a singer and a picker himself and that the song he performed more often than any other was one of her own haunting compositions, this healing ballad:

> *Storms never last, do they baby?*
> *Bad times all pass with the wind.*
> *Your hand in mine steals the thunder,*
> *Your love makes the sun want to shine.*

When Tom Connelly's biography, *Will Campbell and the Soul of the South*, appeared, Colter read it eagerly, although she was shocked by the profanity Connelly attributed to Campbell. "You don't talk like that!" she complained to Campbell. "No, sugar, I don't," Campbell responded. "The man's a goddamned liar."

He holds on to his shadow. It protects him from the temptation of becoming what others want from him, which is to be perfect. His vices are a shield against piousness. They keep him human. They are a way of reminding himself and everyone else that he's no better than the next fellow, despite his spotty famousness and the adoration of many important friends. Over the years Campbell's eclectic circle has included novelists Walker Percy and Robert Penn Warren, psychiatrist and Harvard scholar Robert Coles, the Trappist monk and mystic Thomas Merton, comedian Dick Gregory, and writer Studs Terkel, not to mention his many acquaintances in the music industry and politics and his comrades in the civil rights movement. His own ambivalence toward fame is reflected in his treatment of other celebrities. At times he can be the most cloying fan imaginable. "I always thought there was something odd about this kind of groupiness Will manifests," says Doug Marlette, "like when he talks about Waylon Jennings in such reverential tones. It seemed odd to me for him to be treating these people like gods. The only thing I could figure was that he wanted to be treated that way himself." And yet when Campbell really is admired and sought after, he turns prickly and peculiar. When novelist Pat Conroy came to pay homage, for instance, Campbell put him up in the Dolan House, a primitive little guest cottage on his land, but neglected to tell him how to turn on the heat. "I froze my ass off," Conroy recalls. "It's like you have to pass a country-boy test with Will before he'll accept you." On another occasion, the governor of Tennessee (later President Bush's secretary of education), Lamar Alexander, telephoned to express his admiration for Campbell's writing and invited

Mr. and Mrs. Campbell to spend the night in the mansion and talk about literature. Campbell said he was too busy to drive into town, but if the governor wanted to come out to the farm, he reckoned he could put him up. The governor did come out to Mount Juliet. What Alexander remembers about that visit is that Campbell and another minister friend "spent the entire afternoon making a list of the most despised people in the country, people nobody else would touch with a ten-foot pole, and then they were going to go see them." Dick Cavett, another fan, asked Campbell to appear on his television show. Campbell had watched and admired Cavett, and readily agreed to come to New Orleans, where the program was taped; and yet throughout the interview he persisted in calling his host "David."

Is there anger there, toward people more famous than himself? Is there some sense of frustration with himself that he chooses to live in partial withdrawal from the world, denying himself that which he craves and could easily have—celebrity, the glorification of the world? One senses the longing and the anger of the reformed addict for the object of his addiction. But there is another side of Campbell that prefers the company of simple people, like his neighbors here in Gass's Store. He is drawn to extremes: the very famous and the utterly notorious, on the one hand; and the poor, the neglected, the downtrodden, on the other. The bourgeoisie doesn't capture his attention.

In the early eighties, Campbell's finances, always precarious, suffered from a drought of speaking fees and book advances and the additional burden of caring for a woman who had come to him when she was dying of cancer. He finally asked Waylon Jennings for a job. Jennings put him to work as a roadie. "After two days on the tour bus, unable to figure out exactly what job he had given me, I discovered that I was the one who turned the microwave oven on and off; in other words, I was the cook," says Campbell. The band took to calling him Hop Sing, after the cook on "Bonanza," and at the end of each trip every member of the crew would donate a small bag of marijuana for Campbell to give to the dying woman living in the Dolan House. It helped her keep the nausea down during her chemotherapy.

By then Jessi Colter had become a devout charismatic Christian. She and Campbell were having a kind of affair of the spirit. Jennings, on the other hand, had become remote and inscrutable, trapped in a narcotic inner circus that no one else could enter. Colter was frantic about the state of her husband's soul. She asked Campbell to speak to him.

The story Campbell tells about what followed frankly puzzles me. I'm uncertain whether the point he makes is as significant as he seems to think it is, or if he inadvertently reveals a part of himself that is star-struck and vacuous. "About two o'clock in the morning on the way from Columbia, South Carolina, to Tampa, I decided to try it," Campbell relates in one of his sermons. " 'Waylon, what do you believe?' I asked, almost tentatively. 'Yeah,' he said. Way down in his throat. Like he sings.

"Now, when you're riding a stagecoach from Columbia to Tampa at two in the morning, conversations need not be rushed. There was a long pause. 'Yeah?' I finally muttered. 'Just what the hell is that supposed to mean?'

"Apparently he saw no need to hurry the matter along either. As the bus rolled on down America's highway, into the night, we sat in contemplative silence. Then he said, 'Uh-huh.'

"Looking back, I suppose that was one of the most profound affirmations of faith I ever heard."

After Brenda and I finished dancing, Campbell came back to the table for a bite of the now-cold pizza. Just then the heavy-lidded bandleader stepped up to the microphone. "Friends and neighbors, you all know Preacher Campbell," he said. "Let's give him a hand and see if he'll bless us with a song."

Campbell popped eagerly onto the stage. The band struck up "Rednecks, White Socks, and Blue Ribbon Beer," which has become an anthem for Campbell whenever he is in Gass's. I had seen him sing many times before, in his kitchen, hugging his old Gibson in his lap, or in a church when he had some theological point to make and a song just seemed to say it better. On those occasions Campbell had a sly, apologetic, and in some respects passive way of delivering the music. His baritone voice is true but thin and wavery; here at Gass's, however, standing under the spotlight, with the microphone in his hand, there was a surprising transformation. He let loose something raw and confident and exceedingly indulgent. "No, we don't fit in with that white-collar crowd," Campbell sang, as the crowd whooped with identification:

> *We're a little too rowdy and a little too loud*
> *But there's no place that I'd rather be than right here*
> *With my red neck, white socks, and Blue Ribbon beer.*

At last, for about five minutes in this shadowy saloon in the middle of a Tennessee nowhere, on a Saturday night in the Church of Miller Lite, Zen Master Campbell was giving the people what they wanted to hear.

✦

"I'm not very old, but I have seen a lot of changes," said Campbell's ninety-one-year-old father, Lee Campbell.

"Me too, Daddy." Campbell was sitting on the screened porch of the white frame cottage he grew up in, outside Liberty, Mississippi, staring at the passing pulpwood trucks on Highway 24. Mr. Lee, as everyone called Campbell's father, was in apparent good health, and yet he would be dead within a few months of this visit. It was the last good time they had together.

In this house, when Campbell was five years old, he got pneumonia. He wasn't expected to live—he had never been a healthy child—and his brother actually dug a grave for him in the yard. But when the fever passed and the child survived, it was seen as a sign. After that, says Campbell, it was always assumed that he had been given to the Lord.

When Mr. Lee finished dressing, we went to visit some of Campbell's kinfolk and see the sights. This piney woods region of Amite County is sacred ground for Campbell. Here on the road to Aunt Dolly's house was a place where trees don't grow. Once a schoolhouse stood here. That's where they found the body of Noon Wells, a black man murdered by two jealous husbands. There's another bare spot, where Lee Campbell's oldest brother, Uncle Jessie, was shot in the leg by a crazed storekeeper. The gangrene from the wound finally killed him. Now the store is gone as well. In this climate human constructions are quickly folded back into nature, but the memories persist.

We drove past abandoned homesteads with the martin-house gourds still hanging above the untended, riotous gardens. Many of the people Campbell grew up with are gone; only the old folks stay. This part of Mississippi was once ruled by the Choctaws and the Chickasaws, who ceded it in the Fort Adams Treaty of 1801. There are still some Choctaws around, and lately Campbell has been studying their language. "I first learned to drive on this road," Campbell said as he steered the subcompact rental car down the two-lane hardtop. "I was about fourteen, and I was driving along with my arm hanging out and speeding, whereupon I cleaned out this ditch with Daddy's Ford." Mr. Lee laughed at the memory. "Daddy didn't ever say a word," Campbell recalled, "just that we might as well go on up to the house and eat supper and come on back tomorrow with the chain."

This place has marked him. He carries Mississippi around with him like the long, pallid scar of the rat bite on his index finger. I realized as we drove through the second-growth pine trees that Campbell wanted me to understand this about him.

"Over there's where Mama and Aunt Dolly saw Lum Cleveland and his wife, Aunt Stump, get killed by their son-in-law, Allen Westbrook," said Campbell, indicating a weedy field. There were ghosts all around.

"I saw Allen Westbrook hanged at the Liberty courthouse," added Mr. Lee. "I never want to see anything like that again."

We crossed the east fork of the Amite River—a negligible stream that can be hopped over at nearly any spot. There was one sluggish, muddy swell under a stand of sweet gum trees where a couple of black men in overalls had stopped to fish. "There it is," said Campbell, "the Glory Hole. I was baptized right here on a Sunday morning in June of 1931." Across the creek was the East Fork Baptist Church, once a simple frame building constructed of longleaf yellow pine in 1887, which has since been handsomely bricked over. One of Campbell's earliest memories is of the Ku Klux Klan marching into the middle of a service and presenting the pulpit with a new Bible. Later, when he preached his first sermon in that same pulpit at the age of sixteen and read from that Bible, he could feel the raised letters of the KKK embossed on the back cover. Mr. Lee began to recount his son's first sermon and how Will had written it out and nailed it to a plow handle, then spent weeks delivering it to the rear end of a horse as he tilled the fields. "After that," Campbell remembered, "I was a full-fledged preacher, entitled to buy a Coca-Cola at a clergy discount."

Actually, that was not his first sermon; his preaching career had begun a few months before, at the rehearsal for high school graduation exercises. Someone was playing "Follow the Gleam" on the piano as the graduating seniors filed in down the aisle, singing, and found their places among the folding chairs. While this was going on, Campbell made his way to the dais and plopped himself down in the oversized chair reserved for the preacher. "It was a holy position and I felt presumptuous and insecure sitting there," Campbell has written.

> I had borrowed from Holland Anderson, one of our classmates, his big, black hat, looking like those worn by Italian priests and it, two sizes too large, covered my head and ears. When the class finished the singing of "Follow the Gleam," they were supposed to sit down. At the precise moment

they sat, like a jack-in-the-box, I stood up, placing my hands firmly on the pulpit and looking down at them in judgmental fashion. I had intended to be cute, but not funny. At least not as funny as it apparently was. As they roared with laughter my ears burned with embarrassment. And yet I was more than pleased that I had made them laugh. I glanced quickly in the direction of the principal and his wife. I feared I had committed an act of sacrilege. But they were bursting with uncontrollable guffaws. I was a hit! There was no stopping me then.

There has always been this side of Campbell's ministry, the outrageous clown in the silly black hat, who likes to shock people, who punctures the sanctimonious moment with some nicely timed foolishness. It is no wonder that he is a fan of cartoonists—and vice versa. That association began in 1976, on a similar trip to Campbell's home ground. Jimmy Carter had just received the Democratic nomination for president, which occasioned an inebriated conversation between Jules Feiffer, the playwright and *Village Voice* cartoonist, and Mike Peters, who draws for the editorial page of the Dayton *Daily News*. The two decided that before they could decipher Carter, they first would have to understand the South, which was terra incognita for both of them. They arranged for Doug Marlette, who was at that time drawing for the Charlotte, North Carolina, *Observer*, to set up the tour.

"We were told our first stop would be at the farm of some saint called Will Campbell," Feiffer recalls. "Doug described him as a white hero of the civil rights movement. So we drove out to Mount Juliet, but instead of a saint, we met this rather grumpy, quite unfriendly, truly unpleasant man." To Marlette's alarm, Campbell couldn't seem to get Feiffer's name right. He kept calling him "Fizer." "Damn it, Will, it's *Feiffer*," Marlette would say, citing Feiffer's books and plays, which should have been familiar even to a backwoods know-nothing like Campbell. Campbell merely shrugged and pretended to be contrite.

They were all sitting on the porch eating boiled peanuts when Feiffer asked Campbell if he was "born again" like Jimmy Carter. Campbell acknowledged that he was. "By the way, Mr. Fizer," Campbell continued, apropos of nothing, "how's Kate?" Before Feiffer could ask his host how he came to know the name of his eldest daughter, Campbell was called away to the phone. When he returned, he offhandedly asked how Susan was doing. "How the hell do you know the name of my girlfriend?" Feiffer asked in astonishment. "Here you can't even get my name right, but you seem to have a complete dossier on my life."

"Why, that's one of the features of being born again," Campbell informed him. "You get so you know all about folks."

It was late in the evening, after many songs and more than a little local moonshine, before a thoroughly spooked Jules Feiffer realized that Campbell had followed his life and work avidly since his first book. "I had to pass the Campbell test of fire," Feiffer says now. "He's just not going to have people come down from New York and expect to cash in on their reputations. You have to prove yourself first."

By then Campbell had seized control of their itinerary. "It was the Will Campbell Memorial Tour," says Feiffer, "during which we learned nothing about the South and everything about Will." They drove down to Oxford to see the site of the fecal-punch episode, then wandered into the Delta, visiting civil rights leaders and good ole boys and wealthy plantation owners and famous writers—Campbell knew everybody, from Compsons to Snopeses, and those he hadn't met yet he quickly folded into his vast network. Finally they came to the old Campbell homestead on Highway 24. "Why, you two look just alike!" Campbell's mother observed when Feiffer and her son entered the house. Both men were dismayed. Feiffer promptly started growing a beard.

Naturally, the cartoonists were struck by the "Will Campbell" persona, a caricature that came and went depending on the whim of its master. "I found it unpleasant," says Marlette, who is a Southerner himself and had once been a Campbell acolyte. "It's a great self-parody—this preacher who doesn't like to be bothered, who doesn't care for people, who dresses in this cartoon outfit. At the same time there's this bizarre anti-intellectualism that is so southern and so unattractive."

Feiffer, on the other hand, was in love. "Here I am, a Judeo-atheist, buddying up to a Baptist anarchist," he recalls delightedly. "When you're alone with Will and he's just being Will, you get into the most complicated, thrilling conversations. There's a cool distance but also a great deal of sweetness there." At the same time, Feiffer also saw "Will Campbell" as being more like a character in a novel than a creature of real life. "He will oppose the image of a bourbon-swilling, expectorating-in-a-Coke-bottle character with the cane and the hat—but you don't come by that stuff by accident. I think he prefers the mythologizing because it keeps you from getting at the truth. The truth for him is too personal, and he's too vulnerable. It's almost as if he has to put on a persona in order to be real."

Perhaps the mask has grown onto the face, so it's no longer possible to see who the real Will Campbell is. He hides that part of himself even from those who are closest to him. "Sometimes it's hard for me to separate him from the legend," says Penny Campbell, a lesbian-rights and political activist in Nashville and the eldest of Campbell's three children. "I wish he could let that persona down with his family, but a lot of times he doesn't do that. He's just not able to carry on an intimate conversation with his children. It's painful sometimes."

It's painful for Campbell, too. The gulf he creates between himself and others is almost too great for him to bear. "When I went to first grade, my father stood outside the window the entire morning," Penny says, "and when he took me to college, my mother said he cried the whole way home. But I never knew about this. I always saw him as someone who could stop a conversation with a single cutting sentence."

Campbell has spent his life spiritually mothering others, and yet there is an immense unconsoled sadness inside him. It is as if healing the world were a way of healing himself. I had learned enough about him now to understand where some of this sadness came from. His own mother was an unapproachable, unhappy woman afflicted with imaginary illnesses, who sometimes ran off into the woods to hide from her family. His older brother and childhood hero, Joe, died of a heart attack brought on by years of drug abuse. Because of who he was and what he believed, Campbell himself had endured many years of loathing on the part of people whom he grew up with and loved.

I could see that behind the priest and the prophet and the religious clown—behind "Will Campbell"—there was a hurting child, a small, sickly, almost unnoticed boy who had been made special only because he had been given to God. That had been his destiny since the age of five, a decision made for him by his neurotic mother. And what would be the greatest tragedy imaginable for such a person, what would cause him to erect this extraordinary public façade? "I think when you get to the bottom of Will Campbell," says his friend Tom T. Hall, "what you're going to find is a Jesus-loving agnostic."

After we visited his relatives and the old East Fork Baptist Church, we drove up to the cemetery, which sits on the highest spot in the county. Campbell's people are buried here; in a few months, his father would be as well. The plastic flowers on the tombstones were shaded by giant oaks and sycamores. Campbell's first job had been to tend this plot; he received fifteen dollars a month from the East Fork Cemetery Association for cutting the grass and weeding. At the end of the summer, when he had amassed the sum of forty-five dollars, he left Mississippi. In many respects he has been trying to get home ever since.

There is a song Campbell wrote at three o'clock one morning in the early sixties when he was riding back to Nashville under cover of darkness, still in exile from the people he loved and the place he came from, longing for the reconciliation he so often preaches. He called the song "Mississippi Magic." It is a story of his own death. That is the day he will finally be loved and accepted again by the people who raised him. They will come for miles around to the old Hartmann Funeral Home in McComb City, to stand around his coffin and say, "Ole Will was a good ole boy, he just had some crazy ideas. . . ."

> *Then that Mississippi madness, be Mississippi magic again.*
> *Yeah, that Mississippi madness, be Mississippi magic again.*
> *'Fore we was born we was all kin,*
> *When we dead we'll be kinfolks again.*

"Is this where you're going to be buried?" I asked him, as we sat in the car looking at the plots.

"Yep."

"Where, exactly?"

"Well, I'm not gonna show you that. You're just gonna have to find it yourself someday."

He was trying to push me away. I knew he was feeling crowded by me, by my constant cross-examination and microscopic inspection of the details of his existence. I would not want someone like me going through my life with the same remorseless curiosity, holding me to account for everything I have said or done, noting with a cold eye all my habits and flaws. It would not be just the inadequacy of my life but the emptiness of the observer's that would appall me—that he would be so flexible and unresistant as to be able to pour himself into my mold. That had always been my greatest talent as a reporter and my biggest failing as a human being: I could be anybody. I wondered if this was why Campbell clung so desperately to the "Will Campbell" persona. Without his eccentric clothes and colorful vices and the mask of self-assurance that he always wore, he could be like me. He could be anybody, too.

◆

That evening Campbell, Mr. Lee, and I rode over to the attractive little planters' town of Centreville, in neighboring Wilkinson County, where

Campbell was to speak and read from his work at the public library. Mississippi has a tradition of venerating its writers, no matter what their views, and Campbell's established literary reputation has gone a long way toward rehabilitating him in the minds of people who otherwise wouldn't have much to do with him. "It's always good to come home," Campbell began, then stopped himself. "Well, it wasn't *always* good to come home, but it is now." Perhaps he was remembering the death threats that pursued him in the past, when he had to sneak in and out of the state. "Daddy and I were driving around all day, visiting kinfolks and friends, and I suddenly realized what the central theme of every book I have ever written has been about. It occurred to me, really for the first time, that everything I have ever written has really been about community—what it means to live *in community*, to be a part of a neighborhood. If my life has been about a single thing, it has been a diligent search for a sense of place.

"It also dawned on me that it's not easy to make a speech to home folks. They know who you are. You can't fool 'em. So I had this little talk with myself. Kinfolks: who are they? Those that borned you and nurtured you. Taught you your ABCs. Brought blackberry juice to your bed when you were sick. Told you first about Mr. Jesus. Don't go over there and say harsh things to them, I told myself. That's your people, boy. You're going *home*—place, kin, blood, Jesus sounds. So what do you say, little country boy from the piney woods, who left fifty years ago with a suit of clothes and forty-five dollars in his pocket that he had made working that summer in the East Fork cemetery? Don't go talking to them about Faulkner and Welty and Richard Wright and Willie Morris. They know of Nobels and Pulitzers, depressions and riots, of saints and of sinners from their midst; they know as well as you the thin line between the two. They've heard all this many times, boy. They want to hear something fresh, something new, something powerful and profound— something maybe they've never heard before. Just tell 'em, just tell 'em that you love 'em, boy, and that you hope that they are glad that you are of them. That's all you need to say."

It was an uncharacteristically sweet and sentimental speech. It made me realize once again the anguish of separation that Campbell feels. He talks about family, community, neighborhood, and yet he is the one who can never really come home. He holds on to his roots as if he were about to blow away in the wind of anonymity. No wonder it is the central theme of his life.

This was an interesting paradox. Campbell has always set himself apart from others. He must have known early in life that he was a spiritual genius, and he had a sense of his own dangerousness. If he gave in to his own yearning for love, if he allowed himself to court the masses and bathe in their adoration, he might destroy the people he was closest to. And certainly love of that sort could cripple him: if he consented to be who the hungry public wanted him to be, he would no longer be a prophet. He could have been a towering figure, a Billy Graham or a Swaggart, perhaps someone even greater in public esteem, but he would have failed in his mission. He would have become answerable to public opinion, not to Jesus. And so as much as he longs for it, he holds love at a distance—because loving too close means conforming, and that is something he will not do. He will be who he is, even if that means standing alone. Even if that means, in some martyred fashion, being a fraud.

There is a shocking passage in *Brother to a Dragonfly* that I have always admired. I think it is the bravest thing I have ever read. It begins with the coming of the dummylines, as the railroad spurs were called, which were laid down in the primeval Mississippi forests to speed the harvest of longleaf pines—towering trees with needles eighteen inches long and trunks so big that two men couldn't reach around them. World War I had created a demand for timber, and within a few years all those great trees were gone, leaving only the stumps in the ground, which people used for kindling, and the memories and legends of the great virgin forest. After that, the respect and sense of mystery people had for the land changed, turning coarse and mercenary. Soon they found a market even for the stumps and taproots, which were dynamited out of the ground. Eventually the great trees were replaced with crops of slash and loblolly pines, second-growth timber that was never meant to grow tall and mighty, only straight and fast. It was into these ruined woods that Campbell's hero, his brother Joe, led him. They were young boys, not yet in their teens.

> Joe explained what we were going to do and I was scared. But he instructed and assured me. He stationed me on the side of the old levee and said for me to wait there, that he would be back directly. I had not known this feeling before, this willingness and unwillingness, hesitation and eagerness, prurient steam extending and expanding tiny veins and tissues, lust and passion not even words yet. I was only imagining what we were about. But he returned, as he had promised, leading a gentle and pubescent bovine, and suddenly I knew it all. He turned his head away from where I stood,

whistling, humming and then mumbling words of a tune, casual and discreet, leaving me to cumbrous instinct.

Going into the forest I had been as the forest itself had been when the dummyline came. And leaving now as the forest had been left when the dummyline was gone.

There is a lot to learn about Campbell in this passage: his mystical identification with the land, his adoration of his brother, his preacherly skill in finding redemptive meaning in the often shocking details of life. But of course what arrests the reader in this unflinching confession is the display of vulnerability, which one might almost describe as ruthless. How can he do this to himself? Of course, bestiality is the constant slur on the reputations of shepherds and farm boys, but how like Campbell to purposely stigmatize himself, to direct the blow of condemnation upon his own shoulders.

In fact, as I considered this story more carefully, I began to doubt it ever happened. The passage is too literary, for one thing, and Campbell himself was probably not mature enough at the time to accomplish a sexual act. Whether it happened or not, the impulse to admit it reveals his intention to take the sins of his kinfolk as his own. He will not escape them. He will not transcend his own people. This is his way of loving.

◆

"It always bothered me that I didn't get arrested," Campbell admitted as he looked out at the audience of mostly young, mostly black students who had come to see their counterparts of thirty years ago, the veterans of the 1960 Nashville sit-ins, who had assembled for a reunion at American Baptist College.

In the civil rights movement, the Nashville students became known as the most disciplined and persistent nonviolent student group in the South. They were the core of the Freedom Riders. They were in Birmingham, Albany, and Selma—the signal battles of the movement. Out of this extraordinary group came Diane Nash, John Lewis, Bernard LaFayette, Jr., Marion Barry, and Cordell Reagon, who all became leaders of the Student Nonviolent Coordinating Committee; and C. T. Vivian and James Bevel, who were on the staff of Martin Luther King's Southern Christian Leadership Conference. They made Nashville a synonym for nonviolent direct action. These veterans were mostly gray-haired and portly, joking about their bifocals and waistlines as they bumped into each other in the lobby. Bernard LaFayette, who had been an undergraduate at the Baptist college that was putting on the conference, was now its vice-president, and he raced around with a cellular phone and an anxious expression on his face. James Lawson, Jr., an old friend of Campbell's, had been the one to train the Nashville students in nonviolent resistance, which he had learned while studying in India in the fifties. He was currently the white-haired pastor of the Holman United Methodist Church in Los Angeles. (A small detail about this fascinating man, who had been a close friend of Martin Luther King's, is that he performed the prison wedding ceremony for King's slayer, James Earl Ray.) John Lewis had been a seventeen-year-old farm boy from rural Alabama, arriving in Nashville with fifty dollars and his grandfather's trunk. He soon found himself arrested as a leader of the sit-ins. He would be arrested forty-three more times, and beaten savagely on many occasions. These days he is a balding congressman from Atlanta, who arrived at the reunion wearing a camel-hair overcoat and already demonstrating the stolidity of a man who will one day be in bronze.

Many of them were bloodied in that first snowy morning at the Nashville Woolworth's, when the police made the cynical decision to withdraw and leave the situation in the control of the white mob that had come to heckle and throw food on the demonstrators. The scene quickly went out of control. "There were actually two lunch counters, one upstairs and one downstairs," Campbell explained. "The situation was that the students would file in from Kelly Miller Smith's church [the First Baptist Church, Capitol Hill] and request to be served. Of course they would be arrested. But as soon as that group was carted off, here came another. You see, we had a lookout, so there was a continuous stream, wave after wave. This patrolman at the scene turned to me and said, 'Where in the hell are all these niggers comin' from?' " Campbell chuckled. His own role had been as counselor to the students, a spy on the establishment, and an undercover observer in case he was needed to testify in court. He never claimed to be a hero of the movement or even a civil rights activist; he was always "just a Christian minister" who was demonstrating his faith.

"At the downstairs lunch counter, the hecklers picked up the pace," Campbell continued. "They began putting out cigarettes on the backs of the demonstrators. I watched one young man cry out, 'You black bitch, take this!' as he spat on a young girl. Folks just laughed and clapped as that big wad of spit slowly slid down her spine. Then, out of the crowd came this small, elderly white woman, who was holding an egg poacher in her hand. She walked right up to that young man and said, 'I have a grandson about your age. How would you feel if that were your sister?' He dropped his head and drifted away. Then this big ole boy came up holding a glass of what he said was battery acid and stood there with it poised above this girl's head. The same old white woman gathered this fellow in her arms and cried, 'Why? Why? Why? My God, why?' He looked down at her and turned beet red. This whole scene was completely chaotic and went on for about forty-five minutes, as this old lady with an egg poacher in her hand would take them on one by one, single-handedly controlling the mob.

"Upstairs, the situation was worse, even rougher. It was a smaller lunch counter, and all the students sitting in were male. One of them was obviously about to break—he was a big fellow, his fist was clenching, and the veins in his neck were standing out. The mob was trying to jerk him off the stool. Then in comes this group with a character they called Ole Green Hat—he had on a kind of Robin Hood hat with a peacock feather sticking out of it, and a Jerusalem cross around his neck. Ole Green Hat singled out this one student who was about to crack. He punched him in the kidneys and got him around the neck and finally succeeded in pulling him off the stool and then jerked him to the floor. The student tried to crawl toward the stairs, but Green Hat was kicking and screaming obscenities. Suddenly I heard this *whiiit!* and I saw that Green Hat had a switchblade. At that very moment a new face appeared out of the crowd, a well-dressed young white student that we would probably call a preppie these days. I had never seen him before, but as Green Hat lunged with the knife, this young collegian hit him with a powerful blow to the face, knocking him to the floor. 'If you touch him one more time, I'll stomp the piss out of you!' he cried. Ole Green Hat and his crowd beat a hasty retreat.

"I have given that day a great deal of thought. There in the course of one hour, a little elderly woman who embodied the spirit of nonviolence single-handedly prevented loss of life, and a preppie young man with fast fists flying also prevented violence. I would not presume to judge who was doing the will of God on that snowy February afternoon."

Another Campbell challenge, this time to the moral primacy of non-violence, in one of its sanctuaries.

Few of the students in the audience knew who Campbell was or really what to make of him. After all these years, he was still a creature of the margins, still an anomaly as a white man from Mississippi involved in race relations. "How I became involved in this," Campbell said in response to a question, "is that I was born and reared the son of a yeoman farmer. We worked the land ourselves. We were white and therefore prejudiced. I remember at the age of five about a dozen of us were playing on my grandpa Bunt's porch and we hollered at a black man who was going down the road. The man's name was John Walker. He had recently been beaten by a group of white men for stealing a sack of roasting-ear corn. 'Hey, nigger . . . hey, nigger,' we cried. We saw no harm in taunting him. But apparently Grandpa did. He pulled us aside and said that there were no more niggers. 'Yessir, Grandpa, there's still niggers,' we protested. 'We just saw one go down the road. John Walker's a nigger.' 'No, hon, he's a colored man,' Grandpa said. 'He's not a nigger and he's not a boy.' We continued to protest. Finally Grandpa said, 'Hon, there ain't any more niggers. All the niggers are dead. All that's left now is colored people.'

"I don't know why that made such a deep impression on me, just a little shirt-tailed boy at the time. I don't know why it affected me and not my brothers and cousins who were all there, some of whom stayed on and maybe joined the Klan or the White Citizens Council.

"Later, during the war"—Campbell was a surgical assistant in the Army during World War II, serving in the South Pacific—"I had another conversion experience. One night I was awakened at midnight to do surgery on a native lad from Saipan who had a ruptured kidney. I asked what had happened to him, and I was told that he had dropped an ashtray. For this crime, his white master had kicked him until his kidney burst.

"One other thing that turned my head around about race during that time was a brief novel about Reconstruction, which was by Howard Fast. It was called *Freedom Road*, and I checked it out of the Armed Forces library. After I read that, I knew that my life would never be the same, and that the tragedy of the South would occupy the remainder of my days."

The following Sunday of the sit-in reunion there was a memorial service at the First Baptist Church at Capitol Hill for its revered former pastor, Kelly Miller Smith, who died in 1984. Campbell had been close to Smith and had once belonged to this church. We arrived and were shown into a special room for dignitaries of the movement. As a reporter, I'm often allowed into places where I otherwise wouldn't belong, and I felt privileged to be here. Many of these people were heroes of mine, and this church had been the spiritual center of the Nashville movement. I spoke to John Lewis, whose head still bears the scars of the billy clubs. I had worked in his first political campaign years before, and it was a joy for me when he finally got elected. "I remember Will," Lewis recalled. "I guess the first time I met him was thirty years ago this month. He was one of the few white adult religious leaders who was supporting the efforts of the students. And on that Saturday morning, February the twenty-seventh, in the old church—this church, but the former building, up on the hill—he had gotten word that on this particular morning that we would go down to the city and that the local law enforcement people were going to allow people to beat us up, and then they were going to arrest us. He was informing us of that fact. One thing about Will, he always had pretty good information. He didn't try to discourage us from going; he didn't encourage us to go. He was just laying it out for us, sitting with the students. He was always there when we needed somebody. He was a counselor to us, a minister to the movement. But he has also been able to reach out to forces in the white community that would have strong differences with us."

"What did people in the movement think about his ministering to the Klan?" I asked.

"I don't think they had any ill feeling about it," Lewis replied, "because they knew Will, they knew his own commitment and dedication to the goals of the movement. They felt that if anyone could maybe change these guys and reach some of them, he could. That's what the movement was all about. It was not to destroy anyone. It was to redeem, to save, to convert. It was to change people's attitudes, their positions, their hearts. That's what Dr. King spoke of—redeeming the soul of America, creating the beloved community."

Lewis and Campbell did not always agree during those days. At one of the strategy sessions held at this church, Kelly Miller Smith brought Campbell in to discuss the violence surrounding the picketing of Nashville movie theaters that refused to admit blacks. Night after night James Bevel had been dispatching demonstrators to stand outside the theaters, and the mob reaction had become riotous. The picketers were being mauled and stoned. The standoff between Campbell and Lewis is recounted in Taylor Branch's *Parting the Waters*, the first volume of his *America in the King Years*:

Painfully, Smith, Campbell, and the other adults recommended . . . that the picketing be suspended in favor of negotiations. As James Bevel and other articulate students debated the proposal, John Lewis sat stoically in a corner. Whenever asked a question, he ignored the fine points of whatever theory was being put forward and said simply, "We're gonna march tonight."

Theologian Campbell, who was deeply preoccupied with the question of whether the demonstrators would bear responsibility for provoking the violence inflicted upon them, had known Lewis from the previous year's sit-ins as an unpolished student who stuttered badly. Finally, exasperated by the deference the monosyllabic Lewis seemed to command from the other students, Campbell lost his patience. "You know there's very apt to be violence, serious violence, tonight if there's another demonstration," he said sharply to Lewis. "And I can only conclude that it's just a matter of pride with you. And bullheadedness. You're refusing to agree with us because of your own pride and your own sin."

The room went silent under the sting of Campbell's rebuke. Lewis smiled warmly at Campbell, as though taking pity on him. "Okay, I'm a sinner," he replied softly. "We're gonna march."

Campbell found no words to engage such directness.

Now Campbell was across the room chatting with a tall, bald white man with large glasses. "Jim, you look a sight better than you did the last time I saw you," Campbell said. He was talking to Jim Zwerg, a former exchange student at Fisk, now an affable IBM executive. It took a moment for me to recognize his face from the old photographs of the Freedom Riders. "This man was beat up worse than any person I ever saw who still survived," Campbell said by way of introduction. I could remember now the photos of Zwerg in the Montgomery, Alabama, Greyhound station. Both he and Lewis had been beaten unconscious by a white mob, as had John Seigenthaler, who was then Robert Kennedy's administrative assistant in the Justice Department and later was editor of the Nashville *Tennessean* and *USA Today*. Zwerg had been repeatedly struck with lead pipes and baseball bats, and his teeth were methodically broken with a Coke bottle. "I was lucky," Zwerg told us. "I was knocked unconscious early, so my body relaxed." The morning after that gruesome episode, Campbell visited Zwerg in the Catholic hospital, Saint Jude, the only place in the city that agreed to treat him. That same day Zwerg told reporters, "We will continue our journey, one way or another. We are prepared to die."

What a long time ago that had been, I thought as I sat in the sanctuary listening to Zwerg preach on love. His text came from the thirteenth chapter of 1 Corinthians, where Paul says, "Love rejoices not in iniquity, but in truth; love bears all things, believes all things, hopes for all things, endures all things. Love never fails." "It was a blessing in my life," Zwerg said, "to be touched by people." His voice choking, he spoke in earnest, unpretentious language about the force of love in his life. Tears were flowing all around me, and I stiffened. Oh, I remembered this old dream of the beloved community. I felt my own eyes clouding up as Zwerg spoke about the power of dynamic love. So many times, when I had covered the last days of this movement, I had wanted to be inside it, not outside as I always seemed to be. I knew even then that what separated me from being a part of this larger life was faith—faith in myself, faith that I knew what was right, faith that I would have the courage to act.

I stole a glance at Campbell and he looked lost in thought. He contends that he was never surprised by the failure of the civil rights movement to create a utopia of racial harmony and brotherly love, but then he will complain that American society was better—more humane, more loving, less violent—before integration than it is now. He has often said it would have been better had the Supreme Court not ruled favorably on school desegregation in 1954, because it would have been left up to the individual Christian to resolve, and not the government. "We would have been forced to say 'Thus saith the Lord!' not 'Thus saith the law!'" I didn't agree. I saw the same violence and the racial distrust, but I had never believed in the beloved community in the grand way these people once did. To me the architecture of laws enacted in my lifetime was a profound and heroic accomplishment. It had made us a more just society. And if it had not yet led us to a promised land, just the fact that blacks and whites could sit together in church and pour out their souls—the way Zwerg was doing, as the audience called to him, "Tell it, Jim, go on and tell it again"— this was a sort of miracle, this was the beloved community, however small it might seem to those who had fought so hard for it. And I had to say that I was grateful for the beautiful thing their faith had made.

At the end, as we crossed arms and joined hands and sang that old song "We Shall Overcome," by now so hackneyed and disregarded, but resurrected once more as a salute to the spirit of those who were now gone, I felt something breaking inside me.

◆

Campbell's office was surrounded by bird feeders and daffodils and various metal constructions of his own creation. There is an old manifold and some rocker arms from an Allis-Chalmers C-model tractor which he welded together in the form of a cross. He slyly calls the piece *The General Confession*, because of a phrase he ran across in the 1928 Book of Common Prayer: "We acknowledge our *manifold* sins and wickedness." There is a giant earth auger studded with various drill bits called *Babel Tower*. Out back is *The Pool of Siloam*, an old sugar pot that serves as his baptismal font. It is filled with goldfish.

"Hey, bud," he said as I came in. He was sitting in front of the fire, whittling a stick of white pine.

"Something Tom T. told me has been troubling me," I said as I sat down. "He told me you were a Jesus-loving agnostic."

"Well, I can see where he would say that, maybe half kidding and half serious. We got into this discussion pretty good one night. I was quoting Edith Hamilton in that book of hers on the founding of the early church, *Witness to the Truth*, where she's talking about the development of creeds and theologies. Her point was that you couldn't build a church by Jesus' way of doing things. It just could not be done, because he didn't have any *system*. He didn't say you had to do this, don't do that, believe this, don't believe that—he didn't really have a theology. Hamilton says something like: 'The fathers of the church were good men, often saintly men, who cared enough for Christ to die for him. *But they did not trust him*. They could not trust the safety of his church to his way of doing things. So they set out to make the church safe in their own way. Creeds and theologies protected it from individual vagaries; riches and power against outside attacks. So the church was safe. Life means danger. The more the church was hedged about with confessions of faith and defended by the mighty of the Earth, the feebler its life grew.' I believe that. I think she's on to something. The institutional church has been a cop-out from the beginning. The church fathers thought in order to preserve their man they loved so much they would have to build a big institution to contain him. What they did, in effect, was to construct a buffer against radical discipleship. Jesus was not a churchgoer! He was outside all institutions! That's what got him in so much trouble in the first place. And yet somehow we've constructed this fraud about Christianity, that it is about building budgets and altar guilds and decision cards. That ain't what Jesus died for! Every step the church has taken away from the catacombs to the brush arbors to these magnificent brick edifices has been a step away from his example."

"Do you think the church is evil?"

"No, I don't think it's *evil*—that's a strong word. I think the church is in the same position as the rich young ruler who came to Jesus and said, 'I want to follow you.' And what did Jesus tell him? He said first he would have to give away his worldly possessions. Lord have mercy! If the institutional church would have a garage sale we could eliminate poverty overnight! But obviously, they ain't about to do that. No, the evil that the church does comes out of this confusion between belief and faith. Belief is not faith. Belief is passive. You don't have to *do* anything to believe. Even the devils believe—and tremble. All these inquisitions and holy wars that the church has engaged in over the years are about *belief*. 'Do you believe that a fish swallowed a man and that Jonah lived in the whale's belly for three days? If so, you go to heaven. If not, we burn your ass.' They don't condemn people for living unethically. They condemn them for believing or thinking incorrectly. The problem with emphasizing belief is that it leaves no room for discipleship. Discipleship is the struggle to be like Christ. Even though I know I can't be like Christ, I'm expected to try. But if you make what I *believe* the issue, then I'm off the hook. That kind of theology has nothing to do with faith. Faith is active. Faith implies doubt instead of certitude. Like Edith Hamilton says, when faith is supported by facts or logic, it ceases to be faith."

His mention of the Jonah story reminded me of an episode his daughter Penny had told me. It was a scene in the Campbell kitchen in which Will was arguing that the Bible stories were literally true—in particular, that Jonah lived in the belly of the whale for three days. Whereupon Brenda rolled her eyes and said, "Yeah, and I guess you believe in the virgin birth, too."

Campbell laughed when I repeated this story. "That sounds like Brenda, all right," he agreed.

I could sense he was avoiding this line of questioning. "But do you believe that?" I asked him.

"To me, it's irrelevant. For all I know, that's just the way it happened—but that is not the point. I don't know and I don't *need* to know."

"Can a person have faith without believing anything?"

"Yeah, I think you can. If by 'belief' you mean 'certainty.' Certitude leaves no room for faith. You can have faith on the basis of what you *suspect*, 'cause you don't really *know*. The only definition that I can find of faith in the New Testament is in Hebrews, where it says that 'faith is the substance of things hoped for, the evidence of things not seen.' It is going out—like Abraham—going out, by faith, not knowing where he went. Consider the apostle Paul, who was plagued with the thought at the end of his ministry that he might have missed the way himself. Even Jesus pleaded for the passing of the bitter cup, asking if there were not some other way. They all had doubts and questions. There are a lot of people who don't believe that Jesus Christ was God incarnate that come nearer to living as he lived, because Jesus himself wasn't a religious person. Hell, he was really the first agnostic. When he cried out, 'My God, my God, why have you forsaken me?'—if that's not the cry of an agnostic, I don't know what is. He's saying, 'Father, they just nailed my ass to the cross—where the hell are you?' "

Campbell had never had a religious conversion, or at least never admitted to one. Once, when he had an operation on his colon, he died for about three minutes on the operating table, but he did not have the afterlife experience so many report. He had simply been dead. So where did his faith come from? What did he really believe? I thought about a passage in a book by John Egerton, in which Campbell is quoted as saying, "I believe in God, and I believe Christ is God—though it's not necessary for me to accept the divinity of Christ in order to believe in God." "Do you accept the divinity of Christ?" I asked.

Campbell groaned and cut a slice of Red Ox tobacco from what looked like a moldering length of smoked sausage. "We'd have to talk about what you mean by 'divinity of Christ.' And I'm not saying that we're all little Christs or, you know, that we're all little gods. God is God is God—period. Or maybe exclamation point. You know, the Anabaptists had trouble with the Trinity. Again, they didn't believe correctly, so they were put in tow sacks and drowned in the Amstel River."

"Why do I think you're evading my question?"

"Well, if you're going to press me for a yes-or-no answer, then I would say yes, but if you're going to press me to define Father, Son, and Holy Ghost in some neat little formula that people repeat every Sunday, then I will say 'Excuse me.' " He punctuated his point by spitting into the fire.

This conversation was beginning to infuriate me. "You can answer however you want!" I told him. "I just want to understand what you think about the divinity of Christ, if there is such a thing, and what it means to you."

"Well, what it means to me is that God revealed himself, herself, whatever, in the person of Jesus in a way that he has never revealed himself in anyone else. If you want to go from that to some elaborate doctrine of the Trinity, I'm not going to quarrel with you, I'm just not going to ring the tambourine for you."

"Will, why are you avoiding me? You make it sound like I'm asking for a loyalty oath or something."

"That's because you haven't been paying attention!" Campbell said irritably. "It all hangs on this question of faith and belief. If I go too far in responding to these questions, I'd be saying 'Yes, I believe! Yes, I believe!' I choose not to talk about it because it doesn't matter what Will Campbell believes. It defeats the notion that what is ultimately important is faith! Discipleship is more important than theology! So why do I need to answer that question? What business is it of yours?"

But of course that was exactly my business. The whole object of my enterprise, as I had been made to discover, was to find out why people believed what they believed—and then reject it. My method had been to connect their beliefs to their biographies, and thereby dismiss each person's conclusions about belief as mere pathology. Campbell was frustrating this process with that damnable White Rabbit act of his. He would not let me into his closet of beliefs. I think what frightened me is the possibility that he was no more a believer than I was. I half hoped that he really did believe that Jonah lived in the belly of the whale. That would put him safely out of reach. He would be harmless then, because I certainly couldn't accept that.

I had been telling myself that I was looking for something to believe in. I thought if I could find it, my restless life would have purpose and I would be consoled. Hadn't I, by now, at least proved this much to myself—that *nobody knows anything*? The truth was that I relied on my own disbelief. I counted on it as a reason to avoid living what Campbell would call a life of faith or discipleship. If I didn't believe, then why bother? But obviously there was something calling to me. I had wanted to find a new way to live my life. I thought I wanted a system of belief that would give structure and meaning and, I suppose, hope to my existence; but at the same time I knew I didn't really want that. The demands upon my life, the compromises that belief would bring, frightened me. And so I held it apart—held myself apart as the kind of person who can't believe.

Now, I was beginning to see Campbell as that same kind of person. Of course, I couldn't know; he wouldn't let me in on the truth of what he did and did not believe. But the challenge he was presenting was that I could live a life of faith without belief. I could live as if there were meaning, as if there were hope—but without the consolation of believing it. Frankly, this seemed to me as much a curse as a blessing.

I had gone as far as I could go with my guru. I had set out to see who he really was and whether I could accept his teachings—or anyone's. I had tried as much as possible to pry off his mask of authority and to see the person inside—the flawed, insecure, fallible, often foolish person who was no better than I. And I had seen that person or at least caught a glimpse of him. He seemed to me like a deer I had once come upon in the woods, who had given me a brief, direct look, passing some piece of obscure intelligence between us, and then had fled into the cover. But I had seen him, nonetheless.

And somewhere in the process of deeply seeing Campbell, I had come to love him. To me, this was the strongest argument for the existence of divinity, this encounter with the majesty and nobility of another human being, no matter how deeply buried under the layers of failure and insecurity. That moment of contact and recognition that I call love is the gateway to higher feelings, whatever they are called. Perhaps this was as much religion as I could ever achieve or accept. Love opens a door. Where it leads, I don't know.

"One last question," I said. "What is the meaning of life?"

Campbell laughed. "How the hell do I know?" he said. "Go ask God —he started it."

Matthew Fox Rolls Away the Stone

For several weeks before meeting Father Matthew Fox I had a persistent fantasy. I was inside a darkened chamber with a group of naked people. I don't know how I knew they were naked except for the fact that I was. In this darkness voices arose. People were speaking deeply from their hearts. Never had I felt so close to the souls of others. Was this some sort of new encounter group? It felt almost like an afterlife experience— not a single universal consciousness but a heaven of opened-up spirits pouring out narratives of love and truth.

I spoke to several friends about this fantasy—I'm not sure why, nor do I know what prompted me to imagine it in the first place. As it happens, this fantasy was a premonition of an actual experience, which would be very affecting to me. It was also, I realized, a metaphor for the life of Matt Fox. It wasn't until I got to this place I had been imagining, which turned out to be a remote New Age community on the northern shore of Scotland called Findhorn, in a sweat lodge with twenty ghostly Europeans, that I finally began to understand Fox's ongoing war with the Vatican, his intense but suppressed sexuality, his craving for experience, his longing for spiritual union, his doomed mission to rescue Christianity from the deadly polarity of fundamentalism and secularism, and finally his own divided loyalty between the ancient traditions of his faith and the lure of the New Age. Was he a Catholic priest or a transcendental guru? Even Fox wouldn't discover the answer until we arrived in Findhorn.

Fox, who is fifty-two, is a spare, angular man with a heavy Irish jaw and a large beaked nose. His hair is a white mop, except for his eyebrows, which are tangles of sandy blond. Boyish, amusing, overflowing with curiosity and mental energy, Fox nonetheless has a flinty remoteness about him that bespeaks a life that was meant to be lived alone, in exile or rebellion. For millions of alienated Catholics and seekers of many other religious traditions, Fox has become a hero and a symbol of intellectual freedom. For them, his decade-long struggle with the Vatican over the soul of Catholicism mirrors their own attempts to find a spiritual harbor in the modern world. At a time when the church is threatening to break apart over critical issues such as celibacy and abortion, Fox represents a hugely attractive alternative. Some have called him a new Martin Luther. "He's going to be right up there with the greats like Galileo that the church has persecuted," one ex-monk told me. Fox himself, with heedless immodesty, rolls out the names of Thomas Aquinas, Meister Eckhart, Teresa of Ávila, and John of the Cross, who were all condemned in their time. "One might even get the impression from a litany such as this," Fox said when he was silenced in 1988, "that the Roman Catholic church's track record on silencing its most prophetic voices is not impressive."

Actually, it was astounding that Fox was still a part of the church at all, after publicly denouncing it as a dysfunctional family and complaining of its "creeping fascism." He has launched a theological assault against some of Christianity's most cherished dogmas, in particular the doctrine of original sin. "In religion we have been operating under the model that humanity, and especially sinful humanity, was the center of the spiritual universe," Fox wrote in his eleventh book, *Original Blessing*. "This is not so. The universe itself, blessed and graced, is the proper starting point for spirituality. Original blessing is prior to any sin, original or less than original." He attacked what he calls the "fall/redemption" model of salvation, which views passion as a curse and human beings as wretched sinners; instead, Fox offered a "creation-centered" model that sees passion as a blessing and humanity as divine. The patriarchy of the old model is replaced in the new by an exuberant feminism. "What does God do all day?" Fox asked cheerfully. "She enjoys Herself!" The old ideas of sin and repentance give way to creativity and transformation. Instead of trying to stay in control, we should practice letting go, allowing ourselves to participate in the natural ecstasies of the universe—including sexual pleasures. "Biblical spirituality cannot tolerate this put-down of the blessing that sexuality and lovemaking are by veiled references to original sin," Fox wrote. "The sooner the churches put distance between themselves and Augustine's . . . put-down of women and sexuality, the sooner original sin will find its proper and very minor role in theology."

To some, the preaching of this juicy Dominican priest sounds like a giddy New Age wish list. The confounding feature of Fox's thinking, however, is that it is anchored in the church's own neglected mystical traditions, in particular the teachings of Meister Eckhart, an early-fourteenth-century Dominican; Hildegard of Bingen, a twelfth-century Benedictine abbess; and the most famous Dominican of all, Thomas Aquinas. He has written books about all three, in which he finds historical grounding for his own beliefs. "Matt Fox in historical costume," complained his critics, but the committee of three Dominican theologians that the Vatican convened to review Fox's work found no heresy; instead, they commended Fox's "hard work and creativity." However, under continuous pressure from Cardinal Joseph Ratzinger, the Vatican's doctrinal watchdog, the Dominican office in Rome finally ordered Fox not to preach, speak, or publish for a year. That was clearly a compromise. Ratzinger had been pressing "the more basic question of whether Father Fox should be permitted to publish at all."

When his year of silence ended in 1989, Fox resumed his vigorous schedule of writing and speaking and teaching at his Institute in Culture and Creation Spirituality at Oakland's Holy   College. He was certainly not subdued by the experience; indeed, the sanctions did little more than magnify his renown and make him appear a martyr to free thought. Since then, the Vatican has demanded that Fox stop his frontal attacks on church doctrine and resign as head of his institute. Fox's immediate superior in the Dominican order—his provincial, Father Donald Goergen—repeatedly demanded that Fox return to live in a monastery within the Chicago province. In accordance with the rules of the order, the third time Fox disobeyed his superior, Goergen submitted a request to the master of the order asking for Fox's dismissal. The Vatican has not, at this writing, responded. That happened in August 1992.

I met Goergen in 1991, when he came to Oakland to interview the ICCS faculty and to confront his wayward priest. In Goergen's opinion, it is not Fox's philosophy that keeps him in trouble with the official church hierarchy but his hotheaded personality. "Someone in the order might say that only a certain amount of obnoxiousness is tolerable," he observed. Goergen was also concerned about Fox's need to flaunt what he calls the "deep ecumenism" of his staff: on his faculty there was a Jewish Sufi, a Nigerian drummer, a Yoruba priestess, a Zen master, and of course the infamous witch Starhawk, who was the focus of much of the Vatican's ire. Cardinal Ratzinger had declared in 1987 that the witch would have to go; but on that matter, as with everything else, Fox had proved inflexible and combative. "I find the rancor toward witches unbelievable," Fox wrote in his public response to Ratzinger, "as if Christians, in killing anywhere from three hundred thousand to three million through the centuries, have not had enough of witch hunts." Four years after Ratzinger's order, Starhawk was still on the ICCS faculty.

Goergen's visit coincided with the publication of Fox's fourteenth book, *Creation Spirituality*, a brief outline of his theology that sold twenty-five thousand copies in its first month of publication. The gymnasium at Holy Names College was crowded with about five hundred admirers who came to purchase the book and to hear Fox speak. Many of them were former Catholics who were themselves alienated from the official church because of its positions on abortion or homosexuality or the role of women in the clergy. For them, Fox was as much a political hero as a spiritual leader. Some envision Fox as a force in creating a Catholic church of the Americas, free of Roman dominion. There were others—Catholics, Jews, Protestants—who were searching for some new way of fitting religion into their lives. They were drawn to Fox because he offered them a radically modern cosmology, one that drew from the latest conclusions of science but also from the ancient insights of medieval mystics and shamans of many different traditions. For them, these spiritual drifters, Fox was a ringmaster of this whole tumultuous circus of belief. They filled the ranks of folding chairs and leaned against the wall under the upraised basketball goals.

"During the sabbatical that the Vatican so graciously granted me," Fox began ironically, as the audience tittered, "one of my learning experiences was to visit the Amazon, where Bishop Pedro Casaládaliga—a wonderful man, a poet and a mystic who has also been silenced by the Vatican—works with the Amazon Indians and with the rain forest people defending the forest. And while I was there, a young Jesuit priest said to me, 'I've been living with these Indians for three years, I've learned their language, I live just like them, but I have one problem. I don't know what to teach them.' And I said to him, 'But what are they teaching you?' Immediately he answered, 'Joy. They experience more joy in a day than my people do in a year.'

"Joy is the ground of being human. Thomas Aquinas said, 'Joy is a human's noblest act.' Permission to get in touch with our joy—we have a right to it, we have a need for it, it is the basis of everything that follows. . . ."

It was the usual bravura Matthew Fox performance: sweeping, ecstatic, political, impetuous, learned but in an offbeat fashion (who else would ever think to quote Aquinas on joy?), and deeply appealing to the audience. . . . But was it Catholic? Was it Christian? Was it even religious? Or was it just a feel-good New Age spiel tailored to make the yuppies feel better about themselves, a designer theology for the millennium— God Lite for the free-floating middle class?

◆

"Matt's going out now," Fox was telling his dog. "Tristan stays home and does his work."

As usual, Fox was wearing a plaid shirt and jeans. He put on a jacket and a scarf against the chill Oakland spring morning, and a sporty driving cap. It was Palm Sunday and he was going to Mass.

Tristan, a white spitz with intense black eyes, has been Fox's companion for nearly sixteen years. He stood on the landing of the staircase with a morose expression on his face—a long-suffering, unsurprised, spousal look.

"We'll walk later," Fox promised his dog, noting the reproach.

Fox's life as a Dominican priest has been an ongoing, steadily intensifying struggle with the teachings and the politics of the official church. At first, as Father Goergen remarked to me, it had been unclear exactly what "Matt's project" was. Fox had been a brilliant student at the Aquinas Institute in Dubuque, Iowa, and later at the Institut Catholique in Paris, graduating summa cum laude (the most distinguished student since the controversial Swiss theologian Hans Küng, who has also been disciplined). But that early promise led to confusion as Fox's books began to appear, with titles such as *On Becoming a Musical, Mystical Bear: Spirituality American Style* and *Whee! We, Wee All the Way Home: A Guide to Sensual, Prophetic Spirituality*. In both cases, the titles came from dreams Fox had, one about a dancing bear and the other about the three little pigs. Already in those early works Fox was asking the questions that would form the basis of his thinking: What is the relation between mysticism and the struggle for social justice? What is prayer? He derided the habitual Catholic obsession with sex and sin, preferring to speak of God as a pleasure seeker and Jesus as an earthly sensualist. And there were as well the then-subtle attacks on some of the stalwarts of the church, particularly Saint Augustine, the author of the church's doctrine of original sin.

Although Fox developed quickly as a popular writer, he was not yet taken seriously by the Catholic hierarchy. "I decided years ago that I was going to write for the people, not for academic theologians," Fox later explained. "Even though I had the credentials, it's not where the action is. I had an intuition that mysticism would catch on, that it would change the church and society."

"What did you mean when you said, 'Tristan does his work'?" I asked when Fox got into the car. "Oh," he said, and laughed nervously, "did I say that?" His relationship to his dog is a subject of amusement and conjecture among colleagues and critics alike. ("We have meetings at Matt's house all the time," says Victor Lewis, a member of the ICCS staff, "and Matt pays as much respect to his dog as to anyone else in the room. It's very powerful to watch.") In his lectures, Fox sometimes refers to Tristan as his "spiritual director," and it is uncertain exactly what he means by this. ("How seriously can we take a book that lists Tristan, a dog, in the acknowledgments?" scoffed a reviewer of Fox's book *Illuminations of Hildegard of Bingen*.) "Well, you see, all creatures work in the universe," Fox explained as we drove into downtown Oakland. "Every galaxy is working, every star is working, all the grasses, the whales, the dogs, the animals, they're all doing their work. The only ones who are 'out of work' are humans! We've invented it! We invented unemployment. The problem with our species is that we don't know who we are yet. Whereas Tristan is a dog—and he's good at it! He's close to the earth, he knows he's interdependent with it. He's kinda proud just to be here. These are all lessons he teaches me."

"What's his 'work'?"

"His work is to hang around the house and sniff."

As we entered the Cathedral of Saint Francis de Sales, we were given palm fronds to signify the entry of Jesus into Jerusalem on the last week of his life. About forty other worshipers were present on this Lenten Sunday. It was a common scene in every city in the country. Although the number of Catholics in America is growing (largely because of the influx of Hispanic immigrants), many of the churches are virtually empty. Catholicism is dying from the inside out. For more than a generation the church has been drained of priests and nuns as the people who make up the celibate core of Catholicism have come to different conclusions about the church's position on birth control, the role of women in the clergy, the salvation of homosexuals, and the need for their own sexual abstinence. Laypeople now run many of the parishes because there are not enough priests. The number of nuns has fallen by a third in the last twenty years, from 153,000 to little more than 100,000 today—and many of those, perhaps the majority, are elderly or retired. More ominous for the future of the church is the fact that for the past thirty years the number of seminarians has been dropping by 50 percent every decade. In 1965, when Fox was in seminary, there were 48,992 young men aspiring to be either diocesan or religious priests. Today that number is fewer than 7,000. At that rate, Catholicism may soon be as dead in America as it is in Europe.

Fox seemed a bit embarrassed by the elderly priest who was leading the Mass. "I hope this guy doesn't put you to sleep," he said. Fox personally doesn't like to perform many of the rites of a priest—for instance, he does not hear confession ("I don't do windows," he sniffs) or perform weddings ("I *hate* weddings"). "The whole priest thing was never a big part of my identity," he admits. "I can't stand being called 'Father.' " He reminded me of Will Campbell in his reluctance to assume authority and in his distrust of the church. He criticizes the church for failing in its main mission, which is to allow people to experience the sacredness of their own lives through ritual. "The churches have tried taming our bodies and putting us in pews," he declares. "I say that until we unscrew those pews, we're not going to have genuine ritual in the church, just a lot of snoring." As I sat with him in the partly filled church, I thought what an odd battle this was, between a church that appears willing to die rather than change and a radical, sometimes arrogant prophet of transformation who doesn't seem to value the basic structures and beliefs that the church is built upon.

After the reading of the Passion story, the old priest gave a short and to my Protestant ear rather un-Catholic sermon on human nature. "We're neither saints nor sinners, but we're invited into the world to see it as God sees it," the priest said. There was a nudge in my side. "I think he's been reading my stuff," Fox said proudly.

What is important to Fox is the tradition of his order. He has often stressed the "intensely Dominican" nature of his work. The Dominicans, also known as the Order of Preachers, were founded by a son of the Spanish nobility, Domingo de Guzmán, later canonized as Saint Dominic. In the early thirteenth century, Dominic led a small band of barefoot evangelists to convert the heretics and pagans of southern France. Like the Franciscans, Carmelites, and Augustinians, who came into existence at about the same time, the Dominicans were mendicant friars who modeled their lives on the rule of Saint Augustine. Neither parish priests nor contemplatives, the Dominicans are *preachers*, Fox points out, "and preachers are concerned with *metanoia*, or conversion of lifestyles." However, the Dominicans have also been known throughout their history as ferocious defenders of orthodoxy; indeed, in the fifteenth century they were entrusted with the prosecution of the Inquisition, a fact that Fox relishes. He frequently points out that the office of his main antagonist, Cardinal Ratzinger, which is now called the Congregation of the Doctrine of Faith, was formerly known as the Holy Office of the Inquisition. Irony is Father Fox's favorite flavor.

"I had a strange dream last night," said Fox as we came out of the church. "A priest came to me and said, 'Matt, you're just as pure as any other Dominican.'"

"Did you think you weren't?"

"Not really—it's just . . ." Fox fell silent for a moment. "This is not my idea of warfare. A nine-year siege. I guess patience is not my long suit."

◆

"No, no, no! A celibate doesn't live apart from sexuality!" Fox was complaining as we sat in his living room drinking tea. He lives in a two-story shingled house on a hillside in Oakland. It is spartanly furnished and is given over largely to his office and cluttered library, where he does most of his work. Although Fox's books have sold nearly half a million copies in the United States alone, he gets by on his $28,000 teaching salary, 20 percent of which is returned to the Dominican order. His book profits are plowed back into the Friends of Creation Spirituality, Inc., which supports Fox's institute and publishes *Creation Spirituality* magazine. Fox also started Bear & Co., a publishing house in Santa Fe that printed several of his earlier books. On the couch was a volume of Aquinas's biblical commentaries; Fox's latest project was a "dialogue" between himself and Aquinas, which has required him to spend many hours translating closely spaced Latin text, an especially trying task for him. Since childhood, Fox has had a "lazy" left eye, and over the years it has become more difficult for him to read or to focus on his computer screen. Threading a needle is quite beyond him. Because of that, Fox leaves the holes in his pockets unmended. When he goes out, he wraps his keys and his coins in handkerchiefs to keep them from falling out of his pants.

"Celibacy is not about being neutered," Fox was saying. "It's not about being neutral. It's really nothing more than sexual fasting. People think of it as a kind of purgation, but it's really about *awakening* the senses—" He suddenly broke off, noticing that Tristan had begun to take an amorous interest in my leg. "Tristan, stop that!"

"I still don't understand the appeal of living a celibate life," I said.

"It's a warrior thing—it takes that kind of energy. We're actually wrestling with the demons of loneliness. On the other hand, I do think in our generation a call to chastity is very rare, and frankly I don't recommend to healthy young men that they go into the priesthood as it is currently constituted. You realize that celibacy was invented by the Council of Trent in the sixteenth century because the priests were illiterate and the church wanted to teach them to read [aided by the discipline of abstinence]. I believe," he continued dryly, "that it is currently at the end of its usefulness."

Christianity has always had a conflict with sexuality. Jesus scandalized many of his followers by befriending prostitutes and defending adulterers while at the same time attacking the hallowed institution of marriage. In Luke, Jesus tells the Sadducees, "The children of this world marry, and are given in marriage. But they which shall be accounted worthy to obtain that world, and the resurrection from the dead, neither marry, nor are given in marriage" (Luke 20:34–35). To be a Christian, Jesus preached, one had to be willing to turn away from one's own family: "If any man come to me, and hate not his father, and mother, and wife, and children, and brethren, and sisters, yea, and his own life also, he cannot be my disciple" (Luke 14:26). The idea of celibacy, which seems to be implicit in such statements and by his own example, is extended by his foremost apostle, Paul, who wrote to the Corinthians that "he that is unmarried careth for the things that belong to the Lord, how he may please the Lord: But he that is married careth for the things that are of the world, how he may please his wife. There is a difference also between a wife and a virgin. The unmarried woman careth for the things of the Lord, that she may be holy both in body and in spirit: but she that is married careth for the things of the world, how she may please her husband" (1 Corinthians 7:32–34). Still, the notion of sexuality as being sinful in and of itself, without regard to circumstance, is not scriptural.

It was a fourth-century North African priest named Aurelius Augustinus, the most influential thinker of the early church, whose philosophy made sexuality the centerpiece of man's sinful nature. As a young man,

Saint Augustine was beset with perhaps more than the usual adolescent sexual longings ("I was tossed and spilled, floundering in the broiling sea of my fornication"), which his adulterous father encouraged. He later moved to Carthage ("a hissing cauldron of lust"), where he fathered a child by his mistress and fell under the spell of the Manichees. This Persian sect believed there were two equal, independent forces in the universe, God and Satan, which represent Good and Evil, Light and Darkness. Certain features of Manichean dualism would always remain in Augustine's thinking: for instance, among the elect, the Manichees abominated intercourse because physical generation served the dark side of man's nature. Later, Augustine would reject the Manichean heresy when he converted to Catholicism, but he was still left with the problem of evil in a world that was created by a single, all-powerful, beneficent being. Augustine resolved this dilemma through his theology of original sin.

Although Augustine did not invent the idea of original sin—that all humanity is fallen because of the first sin of Adam and Eve—he made sexuality into the agent of transmission of that sinfulness, literally through the semen itself. That mankind is a slave of sexual desire is sufficient evidence to demonstrate the profound connection between sin and sex, Augustine reasoned; and the obvious fact that we can be aroused even against our will means that sinfulness is already inside us, woven inextricably into our fallen natures. In Augustine's radical reformulation of the Christian message, man is therefore in bondage to his own corrupt nature, and only God's grace can save him. Indeed, this doctrine calls into question the whole notion of free will. It is this philosophy that would become the target of Fox's revisionist theology.

"I don't deny the doctrine of original sin," Fox said as he rocked in his chair. "I just think it should be placed on a back burner. It's part of our anthropocentric way of looking at the universe—the typical hubris of the human species. The fact is that original sin has been preceded by eighteen billion years of blessing! And how religion can leave that out is truly amazing. To teach people, especially the oppressed or those who feel oppressed—women in a patriarchal culture, or gays in a homophobic culture, or blacks in a racist culture—to teach them all about original sin is to reinforce their own self-doubts and despair. It builds up internalized suppression. So it is a political tool.

"In many ways, Western churches built their paradigm around this ideal. It's a very peculiar thing. You have to ask why, and then you realize that it served political interests. The key to Augustine is that he came along at the same time as the church inherited the empire. So original sin ideology is an empire ideology—it divides and conquers.

"What's weird is that the church has never actually defined what original sin is. It's like having a skeleton in your closet. I propose that the sin behind sin is dualism. It's our species' temptation to think in either-ors. You have to be either male or female, saved or unsaved. It's us versus them, soul versus body, matter versus spirit! That just doesn't wash in today's cosmology or physics. When Einstein said E equals MC squared, it's about the *convertibility* of matter and energy. It's nondualistic! The whole ecology issue is about this! Are we *masters* of nature? Or are we *interdependent* with nature?

"This is the basis of Aquinas's big fight with the Augustinians. Aquinas talks about *consubstantiality*—in other words, the equality of soul and body. He says the soul is more like God *in the body* than not in the body. No wonder they condemned him three times before they canonized him. Tristan! Leave Larry alone!"

I asked why, if original sin had nothing to do with sexuality, there was a need for priestly celibacy.

"Well, first of all, there is no *need* for celibacy. Celibacy should be an option. But it's about our folly, it's about being able to laugh at our sexuality. A celibate is someone who's all dressed up with no place to go. And I think in our culture that's very important, because we put so much weight on sexuality. As a result, we've removed *play* from our sexual lives. If you talk to any native people, sexuality is something they laugh at. The word for 'making love' in Inuit, the Eskimo language, is 'to make laughter together.' I think the West could use a heavy dose of that theology.

"Another category, when we talk about celibacy, is the prophetic dimension. I would define the celibate as one who stands by the sexually oppressed. I think in our culture there's a lot of sexual oppression that we're denying. I mean, look at advertising. You're always seeing the—what should I say?—sexually successful. A lot of that is illusion, but who are the people who do not have perfectly satisfying sexual lives? Let's name them: the poor, sick people, prisoners, homosexuals, single people, divorced people, many married people—there's a lot of suffering and pain around sexuality. I think standing by the sexually oppressed is a useful and therefore prophetic thing to do, but the ideology of celibacy has gotten wrapped up in the hatred of the body. To consider sexuality strictly as a problem of sinfulness is an insult to creation."

As a young Dominican priest, wearing at that time the dresslike habit of the order, Fox was often looked at askance. "It sensitized me to the projections and judgments that go on about sexuality." Being a handsome young blond, blue-eyed celibate, especially during his three years in Paris, gave him plenty to think about. "I had a lot of interesting offers," he admits. But the sexual revolutions of the sixties, says Fox, "did not stop at the monastery door. Some of the greatest monks and priests also had relationships. Remember that, except perhaps for John, all of the disciples of Jesus were married. And of course, Jesus himself was certainly a fully sexual human being."

"In what sense?"

"He was as biologically developed as any other human being. He had energy, he had vitality, he had passion—that's all sexual energy. As to whom he made love with, or if he did, we don't know, but I feel this: because he was Jewish, I don't know how he could be celibate. Celibacy is not a part of the Jewish tradition." Fox took another sip of tea and looked off at an angle, presenting his sharp profile. He put his index finger to his lips, a gesture I learned to recognize as indicating second thoughts or self-censorship. But he evidently dismissed them. "My own theory," he said, "it's just a theory, is that Jesus was a widower."

"A *widower*? Why?"

"Because of his feminism! It must have come from the influence of a very strong wife. Obviously he knew a lot about women, and they were attracted to him, not just sexually but politically. He broke all the taboos toward women in his culture, and I think it had a lot to do with his crucifixion."

Fox's controversial writings about sex form a part of the church's brief against him. "If I were asked to name in one word the message I have received from my religion regarding sexuality," Fox writes in *The Coming of the Cosmic Christ*, "I would answer: *regret*. I believe that the Western church . . . basically regrets the fact that we are sexual, sensual creatures." In Fox's theology, eros and even lust are celebrated. "Lust is a great, awesome, and wonderful beast, a stallion that can run away with people, driving them mad, jealous, or cynical, or deadening their souls if ignored," he writes. "Yet once bridled, it ushers in to lover and progeny alike all the promise of the universe, all the beauty of cosmic history, earthly, sexual adventure. . . . Two people riding the great horse of lust can indeed ride more deeply and swiftly into one another's souls."

That certainly doesn't sound like the work of a celibate. Once before, when a reporter caught him off guard by asking Fox if he was still leading a celibate life, he replied, "I try. Most of the time." Now he simply says: "I don't write about what I haven't experienced. I've got to save *something* for my autobiography. Tristan, get down!" Fox looked at me apologetically. "There's some neighbor dog in heat and it's got Tristan all excited. Honestly, sixteen years old! You'd think he'd be over that."

◆

"At the heart of Matt's theology is the story of his life," says Father Daniel Morrissey, a priest at the Columbia University Medical School, who happens to teach a course called "Theology as Autobiography." Morrissey has known Fox since he was a newspaper carrier in Madison, Wisconsin. Back then his name was Timothy James Fox. "I have often thought that people who speak against Matt in his own order, they see the critic who is able to answer back smartly, they see the invincible theological superstar, who's able to publish his own magazine and run his own institute; they don't realize Matt's vulnerability," says Morrissey. "They don't see the little Timmy Fox inside."

Tim, the fourth of seven children—the "neurotic middle," as he calls it—was born on December 21, 1940. "That's on the cusp of Sagittarius and Capricorn," Fox points out, "with Gemini as my rising sign. That fits my life story, because Geminis are intellectual and Sagittarians are always getting into trouble."

Fox's father, George, had been a great collegiate football player (he was on the same all-American team as Vince Lombardi) and became the assistant coach at the University of Wisconsin. George Fox was a powerful, dominating, sometimes wrathful personality, who had been raised by Augustinian priests from the first grade all the way through Villanova University. His rage went back to the slums of Chicago and the chaotic, abusive family he had had to support even as a child. In George Fox's opinion, the priests had saved his life, and he repaid them by being a militantly pious Catholic to the end of his life. "He could never see the gray," says his widow. "With him it was always black or white."

The well of anger inside him was hard to control. When he reprimanded his children, he often spoke from notes, so that he could keep his emotions in check. If one of the kids failed to kneel properly during Mass, their father would force them to kneel at home for the rest of the afternoon. He raised his children with a game plan. All nine family members were expected at the table at every meal, and each plate was to be licked clean at the end. (Tim learned to hide the food he didn't like in his cheeks and spit it out afterward.) The really important thing in life, according to George Fox, was dying well, and that could only be accomplished by living a blameless life.

Tim's mother, Beatrice, is of Jewish and English background. She was brought up a liberal Episcopalian. A former journalist, she is still a strong-willed, independent personality. "She was quite a liberated woman for her time," says Fox. "She had seven kids in eleven years, but every day she would take two hours off for herself. She had a sense of her own dignity as a woman." Beatrice eventually converted to Catholicism, but she kept her distance. "She was always much more worldly than my father," recalls her eldest daughter, Terry Draper. "She didn't like the ritual and the phoniness of the Catholic church. She believed that if you're going to be religious, you don't just mumble the rosary. She was always involved in the community. In many ways, Matt fashioned his themes around mother's philosophy."

The church, however, was always at the center of the children's lives. Tim and his younger brother, Mike, operated a newsstand outside the main cathedral in Madison from 4:30 a.m. until after the 12:15 p.m. Mass. They would sell five hundred to seven hundred papers a morning. "Back then, everyone went to church," Fox recalls. "Sometimes there'd be seven masses in a morning. I'd go in and hear seven sermons. I learned something about how *not* to preach." He was a critic from the very start.

And yet church remained a place of mystery. "The Mass was still in Latin; there were Gregorian chants, which were very powerful, the smell of incense and burning beeswax candles, the darkness; it was a complete right-brain experience. Also, as a religion, we had all these extremists—hermits, monks, parents with twenty-four children. For me, Catholicism is the Middle Ages."

Fox was an altar boy and a Boy Scout, but this shell of orthodoxy disguised a rebel and a mystic. "One cannot speak of growing up in Wisconsin without acknowledging the Native American spirit that still wafts through the land and its lakes and trees. That spirit was part of the air I breathed and it influenced my dreamlife as well." In the midst of his crowded family, he sought time alone, amusing himself with his ro-mantic imagination. He says he later recognized the mysterious dreams of his youth as Indian visions.

Every once in a while he would stumble upon something so astonishing, so revealing of a great spiritual territory he longed to explore, such as the first time he heard Beethoven's Symphony No. 7 or read Tolstoy's *War and Peace*, which he says "blew my soul wide open." He wanted to live a life that would provide him that same sense of aesthetic fullness.

The university atmosphere provided a constant air of intellectual challenge. George Fox enjoyed the stimulation and made sure that his children were exposed to a wide range of personalities, from boxing coaches to history professors. Over the years, as the older children left to go to college, their beds would be filled by exchange students. "At various times I shared the third floor of our large, eight-bedroom home with a Singh from India, a failed bullfighter from Venezuela, a communist from Yugoslavia, a champion national athlete from Sweden, and an Australian architect—to name just a few," Fox recollects. Young Tim swam in a constant flow of ideas and personalities. "That became a part of my spirituality," he says. "I get high on ideas."

In the late forties and early fifties the country was in the midst of a polio epidemic, which killed or crippled thousands of children every year. Jonas Salk had not yet developed his miraculous vaccine. The disease would sweep through communities without warning, then just as quickly disappear. The summer it hit Madison an eleven-year-old child in Fox's neighborhood died overnight; the onset was that sudden. But the epidemic passed through, and everyone in the Fox household was safe.

Later that summer they traveled to Warren, Pennsylvania, to visit Beatrice's kinfolk. The family stayed with friends, who quietly informed George and Beatrice that there had been a case of polio next door—did they still want to stay? They stayed ten days. As soon as they left for the drive home, Tim began to get a headache. By the time they got back to Madison he had to be taken to the hospital. The family held a vigil in the waiting room, knowing that it was polio, knowing that even if Tim survived the critical first hours, he might be crippled for life, or worse—paralyzed, perhaps confined to an iron lung like so many victims of that epidemic.

He did survive, but his legs were gone, and the doctors weren't certain if they would ever come back. At the time, just having his life was enough. Tim had come so close to death that something changed inside him. "Apparently, he made a pact, a promise to God," says his sister Terry, "that if he spared him he would devote his life to understanding God and doing good work."

Still, the loss of his legs was hard to bear. He had always known that he wasn't his father's favorite child. George would frequently praise the athletic accomplishments of Tim's older brothers, both of whom had been all-state football players. Even though Tim had always been slight, he had that same ferocious competitiveness, and until then he had expected to follow in his brothers' footsteps, despite his father's complaints that he was too skinny and didn't try hard enough. Now that prospect was lost. "It was a time of deep 'letting go,' and I decided that if my legs were to return to me I would not waste my life or my legs," Fox has written.

Twelve-year-old Tim stayed in the hospital for most of a year, isolated from other children, including his brothers and sisters, who could speak to him only through the windows. When he thinks back on that time now, Fox recalls the story of twelve-year-old Jesus getting lost in the temple. Jesus was missing for three days. When his anguished parents finally discovered him conversing with the learned elders, Jesus reproved them for their worry, telling them that he had "been about his father's business." That struck a chord with Fox, who was consciously seeking a new father figure, a "cosmic father" who would help him discover his reason for being in the world.

His parents struggled with the question of whether to tell Tim he had polio. For months they had danced around the word, realizing that Tim had already seen a friend die of the disease. Finally George confronted his son with the truth. "I know," said Tim when his father told him. "I heard you talking on the phone three months ago." His father was stunned. It was years later that Beatrice told her son that he had changed his father's life in that instant. "Up to then, he admired only physical courage," she told him, "because that was his life—the body, football, physical courage. But he found in you a moral courage at the age of twelve that he had never experienced before. He wasn't the same toward you after that."

During that time a Dominican brother came to visit. "[Tim] was a very fragile child, thin but high-spirited. He had that spark in his eyes," remembers Tom Able, who was called Brother Martin then. He is now a family therapist in Baton Rouge. Without playmates, Tim was thrown on his own resources, and he was always grateful when Brother Martin appeared. The two would have long and intimate discussions about books and ideas. "Psychological theory indicates that whenever a child has a serious illness and is separated from his peers even for a few months, something happens to them," says Able. "If he has a balanced psyche, he can make a healthy adjustment and let that whole right side of the brain develop through reading and reflecting. It can be a very maturing experience." As the year passed, Tim became a different person, more inward, and although he was never a somber personality, there was a searching and serious side to his nature that his family had never seen before. When he was younger, he had had the reputation of being something of an attention-grabbing pest. Now that he was so much alone, with neither the competition of six brothers and sisters nor the comfort of his parents' care, a new Tim Fox was unfolding.

Brother Martin acted as a midwife to the birth of this new personality. Although Tim had always had an easy relationship with the clergy, Brother Martin came along at a moment when Tim had already made a pledge to serve God and also at time when he was looking for another kind of man to model himself upon. This gentle man in skirts was a striking counterpoint to Tim's vigorous, angry father, but he was also a man whom George Fox respected and, indeed, even revered. Slowly, the call of Tim's vocation began to let itself be known.

Six months after his illness struck, Tim regained the use of his legs. He was "filled with gratitude—not just for the 'miracle' of my legs being healed, but rather gratitude for *having legs at all*." But although he was healed, Tim Fox walked out of the hospital a different person; everyone could see it. There was a brusque and impatient side to him now; he had his sights set, and he was not going to be sidetracked or delayed. Months of solitude had forged him into a solitary personality. When his family went away for the summer, to a cottage on the Wisconsin River, Tim would walk briskly four miles every morning to Mass at a rural church, then linger in intense, prolonged talks with the parish priest. The family soon came to accept that Tim had made a choice about his life, although that wasn't always so clear to him. "I never felt I had a lighted path," he says now. "For me, life is messier than that. But in retrospect, it's easy to see a providential line." Even when he made his decision, he withheld the information from the one person who would have been the most interested—his father.

The Dominicans ran a summer camp in upstate Michigan for boys like Tim who wanted to sample community life. He was drawn especially to the sense of male companionship that was made so much more powerful by the utter absence of women. The camp was beautiful, but also rigorous. Tim never complained; he seemed to flourish in spartan environments, like a plant that prospers in rocky soil. He formally joined the Dominicans at the age of nineteen, breaking his girlfriend's heart. At that time the rule of the order was that a novice had to leave his home and his family and never return. He wasn't even allowed to go to his sister's wedding. It was a firm and perhaps cruel way of breaking old bonds, of declaring that Dominicans were his family now.

Once again Tim was confined and set apart from the people he loved. His first year was spent at a Dominican farm in Winona, Minnesota, set upon a rise called Stockton Hill, overlooking the Mississippi River. There was a moving ritual upon his arrival at the novitiate, in which his old self was buried and his new self was reborn and renamed. "In the world, you were known as Timothy. Now you will be known as Matthew," the brothers said as they clothed him in the order's distinctive three-piece white habit with a belt tied around the waist. Attached to the belt was a wooden rosary. What Fox remembers most about this ceremony is the smell of the coarse habit: it was like a field of wheat.

Many of the novices hated being stuck on a farm in the middle of nowhere, but Fox loved that year. It was spiritual boot camp and he was an eager recruit. He was awakened every morning at five. The days were filled with chanting and chores, prayer and meditation. "They were not conscious about what they were doing. This was tradition by osmosis. We were celibate because Dominicans have always been celibate. We don't eat meat at this time of year, and we fast at this time of the year—they didn't have any reasons for any of this. I think that's why I eventually decided to get my doctorate in spirituality: I wanted to understand the rationale for all this. What I eventually realized is that these were ancient tricks to get the right brain going, you see? To get mysticism going."

The young men were also introduced to the heroes of the Dominican past—in particular, to Thomas Aquinas. Although the bane of so many Catholic theologians because of his relentless categorizing and his faith in pure reason, Aquinas was a powerful lure to the newly minted Matthew. Despite the dry formality of Aquinas's prose and the remorseless symmetry of his arguments, Fox was drawn to the Aquinas who declared that the essence of philosophy is wonder, as opposed to Descartes, who believed that philosophy arises from doubt. In twelve years of training, however, Fox never heard the name of Meister Eckhart, the great Dominican mystic whose masterful sermons in the common speech (rather than Latin) were instrumental in creating German as a modern literary language. Many years later, when he finally read Eckhart's work for himself, Fox would be stunned to find entire sentences that he himself had already written in his own books. In Eckhart he would find a creation-centered ancestor in his own tradition—but it was a tradition the Dominicans had rejected.

"What they also didn't teach us was about the Inquisition," Fox recalls with a laugh, "in which the Dominicans were very much involved, or about Tetzel, a Dominican friar who was selling indulgences during Martin Luther's time. The Dominicans, like any other human enterprise, also have a real shadow side."

At the end of that first year, Fox went to the Aquinas Institute in Dubuque with forty other potential brothers. They formed a strong bond; they played sports and went to ball games, ate every meal together, argued endlessly, prayed morning and evening; it was an ecstatic time in Fox's life. "Mystical experiences abounded," he recalls. Occasionally his family traveled to Iowa to visit Matt in the seminary. "It was another world," remembers Terry, "so strict, so rigorous and disciplined, so ascetic and bare—and he was just a kid. It was like he was locked in a dungeon, although he seemed content. You see your brother wearing white, living that life, you realize he's special, you revere him a little bit, but I would cry. I thought he had given up the ghost. And then all these gorgeous young celibate men would fill up the church and chant. I'd think, 'What a waste!' But such beautiful chanting! The tears just wouldn't stop."

There were tears in his father's eyes as well. To have a son become a priest! That had been the road not taken in George Fox's life. Despite his great physical power, he knew that he did not have the emotional or spiritual strength to live the life his son had chosen. He was the only one in the family really enthusiastic about Tim's vocation. Beatrice worried about the great sacrifices her son would have to make—most poignantly, children of his own—but George would remember the humble Augustinians who had saved him from a life of sin and crime. With Tim's vows, George felt that an old debt had been paid.

Like so many to come, he misgauged his son's ambition.

The more deeply this young novice was initiated into the life of the order, the more he came into contact with its shadow. One day his novice master mutely handed him a new book on religious life by an Italian cardinal. Fox turned to the chapter on celibacy, where he read that the main question a celibate had to ask was whether he was permitted to wash his sexual parts while taking a shower. "In retrospect I see that moment as my first awareness of the immense importance that *culture* plays in spirituality," Fox writes. " 'I am an American and not an Italian,' I said to myself as I held the book over my wastebasket. 'My questions are different.' "

Fox began reading Heidegger, and he had such mystical experiences that he considered becoming a contemplative. His provincial was appalled when Fox told him he was going to spend the summer in a colony of hermits on Victoria Island, off the coast of British Columbia. (Actually, the idea had been suggested by Fox's confessor, who was at a loss to understand his mystical outbursts.) "Don't tell anybody about this or you'll never be ordained," the provincial warned. It was a highly romantic summer. Fox lived in a candle-lit hut with a mattress on the floor. There were snakes everywhere; but, strangely enough, they didn't seem as bothersome as they might have been. The other hermits were not allowed to speak to each other, but the young visitor fell outside the ban on social intercourse, and the bearded, unwashed hermits would seize the opportunity to chat or send him off to borrow a cup of powdered milk from someone they couldn't otherwise communicate with. A part of Fox could easily sink into this life of pure ascetic mysticism, but there was another part that could not forget, even here, that there was evil in the world. He believed that Christianity had a prophetic role to be fulfilled, and he wanted to be involved in the struggle for justice. Somehow, he knew, he would have to craft a life that combined these two passionate halves of himself, the mystic and the prophet. On the very last day of his summer, he went down to the river with a bar of soap and took his only bath. He laughed and sang, enjoying the sound of his own voice. "I had psychologically risked the priesthood and let go," he recalls. "Like Meister Eckhart talks about living without a why. I just wanted to live." He says he ran on the energy of that summer for the next twenty years.

In May 1967 he graduated from the Aquinas Institute and took his final vows. He was a priest at last—although that had never really been his goal. "It was a search for the spirit," he says. "I just wanted to learn to say 'Thank you.'" Now he was looking for a way to continue his studies in mysticism and spirituality. "Not many people were writing about mysticism then," he says. "Thomas Merton was, so I wrote him and asked where was the best place to study spirituality." Merton, a Trappist monk and a widely read author, responded four days later. "I'm glad you are going to work on spiritual theology," Merton wrote. "The prejudice in some Catholic quarters is a bit strange, when outside the church there is such an intense and ill regulated hunger for and curiosity about spiritual experience (what with LSD and all that). I do think we are lying down on the job when we leave others to investigate mysticism while we concentrate on more 'practical' things. What people want of us, after all, is the way to God." As for Merton's suggestions about schools: "The first place that comes to my mind is the Institut Catholique in Paris."

Fox's Dominican superiors weren't pleased. "They kicked and screamed. They had never sent anyone to Paris who ever came back," Fox says. Of course for a young man who had lived a semicloistered life for the past nine years, Paris was an intellectual banquet. The air was fragrant with art and music and especially politics. It was in France that Fox realized how much he loved excitement and intrigue and endless delicious political arguments. He arrived in Paris in 1967 just as the student movement was heating up (it would boil over into the streets the following spring), and "all of Europe was up for grabs." France felt like the center of the world then. Sartre and Beauvoir could still be spotted sipping espresso at Café Deux Magots. There was a heady sense of being on the edge of profound change, while at the same time being a part of a deep historical tradition.

The Cato, as the French called the Institut Catholique, was black with coal tar and seven centuries of history. "It looked," says Father Morrissey, who shared an apartment with Fox, "like a public high school in Harlem." Oddly enough, for a school renowned for its intellectual rigor, the courtyard was adorned with a statue of Saint Thérèse, the "Little Flower," a Carmelite nun remembered for her simple piety, her spirituality, and her nervous disorders. "It would be like having a statue of Charles Schulz in Harvard Square," says Morrissey.

If he breathed deeply, Fox would inhale the same molecules that had been breathed by his Dominican ancestors Albert the Great, Thomas Aquinas, and Meister Eckhart, who had studied or taught here hundreds of years before. More recently Pierre Teilhard de Chardin, the mystical Jesuit paleontologist and an immediate progenitor of creation spirituality, had also taught at the Cato; but the Jesuits exiled him to China and forbade him to publish during his lifetime. Many of the faculty members had struggled heroically against church doctrine, risking their professions and reputations in the belief that the church itself was in need of redemption.

One of these men was M. D. Chenu, a big, warmhearted Frenchman with bushy eyebrows and a lively gaze, who became Fox's mentor and in many respects a model for the kind of priest he himself would become. Chenu had been silenced because of his involvement with the worker-priest movement in the forties, when the clergy went into the factories and the construction sites in order to join forces with the alienated proletariat. It was a grand experiment that was twice condemned by the

Vatican because of its political overtones. Finally Pope John XXIII brought Chenu back after twelve years of silence and made him an important adviser during the Second Vatican Council, which shook the Catholic world with its reforms in liturgy and social policy. Chenu was a Dominican who was profoundly engaged in the political struggles of the day; but he was also a mystic, and it was Chenu who first introduced Fox to the creation tradition. "It was because of him that I remained a Dominican," Fox has written of his relationship with Father Chenu. "I saw in him a genuine integration of the prophet as mystic in action and of the theologian as prophet—not as a tenured professor in a comfortable seminary." During the *événements* of May 1968—the student riots that would bring down the de Gaulle government—Chenu turned his own classes out into the streets. "We have been talking of twelfth-century history," he told them. "Here's your chance to *make* history. Go out and join the revolution."

Fox and Morrissey were living at the time in the home of a Mme de Campeau, a former aristocrat who had lost her wealth but had clung to her pretensions. She was an Integrist, part of the old-guard Catholic resistance to change. "First they took away our king and now they're taking away our faith," she would complain. Naturally, the May riots had the landlady in knots. One morning she saw a procession of students carrying a red banner, and she suddenly panicked. "They're coming to chop off our heads! Father, please," she said to Fox, "will you hear my confession?" Fox cringed. Even then he detested hearing confessions, but a priest is never supposed to reject such a request. "One moment, madame," he said politely, as he opened the window and hollered at the top of his lungs, *"Vive la révolution!"* Then he turned to his landlady. "Now, madame, your confession?" She fled in horror.

The young Dominicans in Europe decided they needed a revolution in their own order to match the one that was taking place in the streets. They met in Trier, Germany, near Luxembourg. Fox presented a paper and found himself elected their spokesperson. "Matt, this is your finest hour," a friend told him. Back in Chicago, however, the news was received rather differently. His infuriated provincial ordered Fox home at once. Some of Fox's friends managed to mollify the hierarchy, but in many respects the die was cast. From this point on Fox would always be seen—and would see himself—as a frontier thinker and a rebellious outsider, the Dominicans' own prodigal son.

Fox returned to his studies, grateful to still be in Europe. He finally finished his thesis at a farm in the Basque country. It was an examination of American religion and culture as revealed through the medium of *Time* magazine, which was George Fox's favorite reading matter. The morning he typed the last page, some friends picked him up to go on vacation in Spain. The radio was playing a new song by the Beatles, "Let It Be." His life seemed so full, so complete, but at the same moment the life he had known was at an end.

For the first time in his life, at the age of thirty, Fox was no longer a student. He was given a teaching post at the Aquinas Institute, back in Dubuque. It was suddenly a very long way from Paris. He was dismayed to discover that in the three years he had been away many of his classmates and most of his friends had left the priesthood. Never had he felt more lonely in his calling. Also, he realized he was under scrutiny because of his political activity. He made a decision to lie low and steer clear of controversy. Two months after school started, however, the prior—the school administrator—came to Fox and said it was time for him to lead the community Mass. The subject he chose to preach on was "What Celibacy Is Not."

That was a crystallizing moment in Fox's life and his relationship to his order. After the sermon, in which he spoke about the need of the church to awaken the erotic sense of playfulness and wonder in the universe and not try to suppress it by spreading fear of human sexuality, he returned to his room to find several dozen students lined up at his door. Some of them were in tears. "No one had ever spoken to them in language like this, in terms they could understand," Fox recalls. "Of course, I became an immediate threat to the priests in the house."

One of those students was an affable young Dominican brother named Brendan Doyle. He was a popular singer, an Irish tenor, and a composer. He and Fox quickly became friends. They would spend the next fifteen years living together.

Not long after that sermon, there was an election for vice-prior, an office that is supposed to be chosen jointly by the students and the faculty. Fox was the popular candidate, but six weeks passed after the election with no word on the outcome of the contest. Finally, he went to the prior and was told that while he had gotten nearly all of the sixty student votes, he had received none from the fifteen faculty members. "We cassated the vote," the prior told him, meaning that the faculty had simply overruled the will of the students. Learning of this, a number of students actually left the order in dismay. "There was much hurt," remembers Don

Goergen, who was himself a novice in Dubuque at the time, "much frustration and pain." Fox himself felt so spurned that he considered leaving as well. He actually did move to Chicago and commuted back and forth to Dubuque to finish out his teaching commitment. The fact that Doyle went with him added to the feeling of loss and betrayal on the part of those who remained.

The following year, 1972, he and Doyle moved to Boston. They rented a beach house in the off-season in Marshfield, down the coast, and scratched out a meager living while Fox taught a single course for a thousand dollars at a Catholic women's college and Doyle made a little money playing music in bars. Fox was still anguishing over whether to stay in the order. It certainly didn't seem that the Dominicans wanted him to stay. "One thing that went through my mind is, 'You've got a doctorate in spirituality—what are you going to do with *that* if you leave?' " He spent many hours walking on the beach that winter, kicking the sand and watching the waves. He had seen his friends leave, one after another. Perhaps more telling was the toll exacted on those who stayed. Men he had been close to, whom he had looked up to, had come to grief because of drugs or alcohol. The level of despair within the order seemed very high. Of course, all of Catholicism was in turmoil; it wasn't just the Dominicans. Fox personally believed that the men who left, and those who remained but were miserable, did not have enough grounding in mysticism and spirituality to sustain them in this lonely calling. "The decision was made by the ocean," he says. "The ocean taught me to stay on my own terms. I realized I had to create a lifestyle and to create work for myself. The ocean taught me that life is not either-or. I would stay and give it a try."

Fox and Doyle had developed an offbeat stage show, which they called "concert commentaries," that they took around to high schools. Doyle would sing some of his liturgical compositions and Fox, in the tradition of Aquinas, would provide a commentary about what the words meant. Eventually they started an underground church, trying out new forms of ritual on Saturday nights in an Oddfellows' hall. Fox was writing *On Becoming a Musical, Mystical Bear*, his book about prayer, in which he was just beginning to announce the themes of what he then called "today's spiritualities," which were drawn from the Hebraic, rather than the Greek, tradition. Already Fox was concentrating on the goodness of creation rather than the theme of the fall from grace and man's need for redemption. He employed a term that would later become a critical feature of his thinking, "panentheism"—that is, God in all things: not God as a distant, separate entity "up there," the machine operator in a mechanical universe (the theistic idea), nor God in nature (the pantheistic, pagan idea), but God as being both a part of and beyond all created matter. The difference between pantheism and panentheism, he later explained, was that "pantheism says that everything is God and God is everything, and that leaves out the transcendence, beyondness of God. It limits God too much." Panentheism, on the other hand, says that "everything is in God and God is in everything." The relationship between God and creation was the same as "fish in water and water in fish." In this analogy, prayer was "swimming."

He was discovering himself not only as a priest but as a writer and as a theologian. The vow he had made to create his own vocation within the order was paying off, although his own existence was meager to the point of being squalid. At Christmas, he urged his underground parishioners to give food to the poor, which they did—a huge basket of groceries to their pastor.

With the publication of *Bear* in 1972, Fox's life began to jell. He received an offer to head the religion department at another women's institution, Barat College in Lake Forest, Illinois. The National Conference of Diocesan Directors of Religious Education asked him to undertake a study of the teaching of spirituality in America. Characteristically, Fox used the opportunity to provide a critique of the whole educational system of theological education, and offered his own model. He was astonished when Mundelein College in Chicago offered him the chance to implement his ideas. Thus his Institute in Culture and Creation Spirituality was born.

Fox stayed in Chicago for eight years. But increasingly he felt drawn to the San Francisco region, which was so rich not only in spiritual enthusiasms but in art and especially in science: according to Fox, nearly a fourth of all American scientists lives in the Bay Area. In 1983 he brought ICCS to Holy Names College, a peaceful and attractive school run by the Sisters of the Name Jesus and Mary, which is set among the redwoods on a hillside overlooking Oakland and the bay, with San Francisco in the distance. There was a chapel where Doyle could teach music. At last Fox felt that he was where he belonged. Here, he believed, he could be in the middle of the intellectual stewpot that was spewing out a new cosmic story; here, the old mechanistic Newtonian worldview was collapsing and the new relativistic Einsteinian model was being created. Like all such historic shifts in perspective, this revolutionary paradigm shift would require radical new thoughts about God and man's place in the universe. It was a perfect place for a theologian who was searching impatiently for new constructs about matter and spirit and new ways of understanding creation. He had the idea that science would lead him to a rediscovery of the Western mystical tradition. His move to Oakland preceded by several months the publication of the book that would bring him the acclaim, and the condemnation, that was bound to accompany a challenge to the old cosmology.

The formal investigation into Fox's theology began in 1984, the year after the publication of *Original Blessing*. When the committee of three Dominican theologians convened to examine Fox's work reported no heresy and actually commended him, the unappeased Cardinal Ratzinger coldly responded: "The problems exposed not only render unacceptable any commendation of this author, they make questionable his very capacity to continue in such work." Ratzinger encouraged the order to issue sanctions that would "not only preclude future difficulties but will publicly redress the present scandal of Father Fox's seeming espousal of witchcraft and the harm which his published books and teaching activities have already brought to the faithful." Father Goergen, Fox's provincial, responded to Ratzinger's accusations by defending Fox's theology as well as his right to publish. But in September 1987 Ratzinger announced in a letter to Father Damian Byrne, the master general of the Dominican order in Rome, that his office was undertaking its own review of *Original Blessing*. Along with the letter, Ratzinger enclosed his own synthesis of the major points the book makes:

> The general thesis of the author, namely that the ancient and authentic spirituality of "Original Blessing" has been unfortunately obscured by one based on a recognition of original sin, is an altogether personal, gratuitous and subjective interpretation of Christian spirituality, of its theological foundations and of the history and thought of the spiritual writers he himself mentions.
>
> One notes especially his practically total neglect of the Magisterium [that is, the Church's official teaching] and his manner of citing what he likes in the Bible and interpreting it his own way. . . .
>
> From a purely theological viewpoint, the author denies the existence of original sin and the doctrine of the Church in its regard. . . . He attributes the entire "error" of this approach to Saint Augustine, whom he excoriates throughout.
>
> His treatment of homosexuality . . . is neither inspired by the Scriptures, nor by the doctrine of the Church. . . . Everything converges into a vague positivistic spirituality with several aspects which have to be a cause of

concern . . . especially the figure of God as Mother, Child, and ourselves as mothers of God.

In short, the book has to be considered dangerous and deviant.

Ratzinger went on in his letter to the master general to ask if he would use his offices "to assure that Fr. Fox's present assignment as Director of the Institute for Creation Spirituality [*sic*] at Holy Names College, Oakland, CA, USA, be terminated and that he be instructed to cease from further dissemination of the central thesis of his book. . . . It also appears necessary that he disassociate himself from 'wicca,' the ideology of 'Starhawk,' a self-styled witch."

The cardinal's crackdown happened to coincide with the breakup of Fox's long-standing friendship with Brendan Doyle, and then with the failing health of Fox's father. George Fox had followed his son's career and the approaching collision with the Vatican with increasing dismay. "My father never understood my brother and his theology," says Michael Fox. "It was a bone of contention and a strain on them both. My father was always thinking that a priest was someone in the parish hall or the dormitory wearing the collar and a robe. Tim never expected to be that." George had gone to Atlanta in 1987 for treatment for headaches. The doctors discovered a brain tumor that was too advanced for surgery. Matt flew to his father's deathbed and sat with him during his last lucid hour. In those final moments both men were desperately trying to bridge the space that separated them. "I'll bet you wish I'd just been an ordinary parish priest, don't you?" Matt asked. His father squeezed his hand very hard. "Yes, I do," he said earnestly, "yes, I do." He still had a lot of power, even at the end.

"Well, Dad," Matt said tearfully, "I couldn't have been the kind of priest I am without the courage you taught me."

After that moment his father slipped into delirium. Later a nurse came to get him to put him in a wheelchair. "I hear you're going to a wonderful place today," the nurse said, meaning the hospice where George was being taken to die.

"Yes, I am," he said quite clearly, then fell dead out of the chair with a massive brain hemorrhage.

"It was a beautiful death," his son remembers.

✦

"I got a letter from Matt in nineteen eighty-two saying he wanted me to teach at his institute," said Starhawk, the dark-haired, brown-eyed former Miriam Simos, as she sat in her backyard in the Mission District of San Francisco, munching on the yellow blossoms of sour grass growing around her lawn chair. "At first I was confused. I thought 'creation spirituality' was probably some fundamentalist group." What she found at ICCS, however, was a staff so eclectic that she seemed to fit right in. Buck Ghosthorse, a Lakota medicine man, was conducting sweat lodges down by the soccer field. Behind the library there was a group of students splayed out on the grass doing dream work. Onye Onyemaechi, a Nigerian drummer, was leading workshops on rituals and trance healing in the old girls' gym. Up in the chapel, Theodore Feldman was teaching Hildegard's twelfth-century chants. This was an exotic blend even by Bay Area standards. And the students—well, Fox had modeled his application for admission on a form he had seen for clown school. There were worn-out social workers, refugees from the military-industrial complex, recovering addicts, Vietnam vets, lesbian theologians, disaffected priests and nuns —all of them seeking answers to the questions their lives had posed but that the conventional religions they had grown up in didn't seem capable of addressing. What they had in common was a moment of discovery, having picked up one of Fox's books or heard him lecture, and deciding that this might be the place for them. In the midst of all this diversity, a wiccan priestess teaching a course on making ritual seemed like a natural addition. "The first time I went out there, I decided to light a cauldron," Starhawk recalled. "Suddenly there were all these nuns jumping over the cauldron on the convent lawn. They had a wonderful time."

He goes too far: that's the accepted line on Matthew Fox. He might have gotten away with everything except the witch. That was something his enemies could fasten on.

The campaign against Fox was launched on two fronts. First came the organized protests at his lectures. He had made a presentation to Dignity, the Catholic gay rights group, in Seattle in 1983. "Just the fact that I stood up and said that homosexuals have a spiritual life at all was bound to get me in trouble," says Fox. The following March he returned to the St. James Cathedral parish in Seattle to talk about the work of Hildegard of Bingen. He was met by a protest group that called itself CUFF—Catholics United for the Faith—the same group that had been hounding the liberal archbishop of Seattle, Raymond Hunthausen, to the point that they had prompted a Vatican investigation of his ministry. (Hunthausen was not removed, but he did suffer a heart attack during the investigation and eventually resigned after the tribunal concluded its probe.) It seemed crazily inappropriate, since Fox was speaking about a medieval mystic few Catholics have ever heard of. He went outside to reason with the protesters, but he was completely unprepared for the fury he saw in their faces. Someone spat on him. Later, he began getting death threats in the mail. One letter, signed by "a Good Christian," said he should be burned at the stake with Starhawk. He held a series of "cosmic Masses" in the gym at Holy Names that were also disrupted by angry protesters. "It was very volatile. They came and pounded on the door, some of them even slipped inside to take notes, which they sent to the Vatican. People were screaming and chanting the rosary at us. Fortunately, we had some big Native Americans there who kept them from doing violence. Afterwards, one of the Indians told me, 'I never knew people who would want to violate another person's worship.' "

It was CUFF that wrote to Ratzinger requesting that his office review Fox's work. That investigation and the subsequent silencing of Fox were not unique. Liberal Catholic theologians such as Charles Curran and Hans Küng were also being disciplined. So in 1988 when Cardinal Ratzinger demanded that the master general of the Dominican order take immediate action, the blow could not have been too much of a surprise.

Fox agreed to go silent for a year, beginning on December 15, 1988. But in characteristic fashion, in the few months before his sentence began he left nothing unsaid. First he wrote "Is the Catholic Church Today a Dysfunctional Family? A Pastoral Letter to Cardinal Ratzinger and the Whole Church," in which he turned the argument around, saying that it was the church, and Ratzinger in particular, who needed instruction. "Ours are times—because of the unprecedented crises of Mother Earth, of our youth, of the spiritual vacuity of institutional Christianity in Europe, of the boredom that most worship instills in persons—for holy impatience, disobedience, and discontinuity," Fox argued. "What will happen to theology in the future if today's theologians simply remain silent in order to appease the Inquisitor of our day? Or in order to keep their jobs or safeguard their pristine reputations in a church that may, in fact, be quite unwell? I believe that for years I have been protecting you from the consequences of your behavior by remaining silent. To continue to do so would be sinful, for your behavior is becoming increasingly scandalous." He went on to outline various ways in which the church was dysfunctional, fascistic, and in need of repentance. "It concerns me deeply that today's Catholic church seems to reward authoritarian personalities who are clearly ill, violent, sexually obsessed, and unable to remember the past." After this salvo he held a press conference. "I believe that Cardinal Ratzinger's theological objections to my work are unbelievably thin," he said. "For example, he complains that I refer to God as 'Mother' in my *Original Blessing* book. Yet the Scriptures, the medieval mystics, and even Pope John Paul I all used motherly images for God. The inability of the Vatican to deal with God as Mother tells us more about the sin of patriarchy than it does about the Godhead. The Congregation says that I deny the doctrine of original sin, which I do not. I do, however, decry the exaggerated importance given that doctrine in the Western church. . . . The Congregation complains that I am a 'fervent feminist.' Jesus was a feminist; Meister Eckhart was a feminist. I do not understand how any follower of Jesus could be so deaf to the suffering of women in recent Western history that she or he would not be a feminist. . . .

"If I could have my way, I would recommend that the headlines for this event ought not to read 'American Theologian Silenced' but rather 'Is the Catholic Church Going Deaf?' "

Responding to questions about his plans for his year of silence, Fox said he intended to travel to Europe and Africa and Latin America to speak to other theologians. He mentioned Father Leonardo Boff, the Brazilian priest and liberation theologian who had also recently been silenced. "Maybe Father Boff and I will have a party at which no one speaks."

A videotape of the press conference circulated among Fox's brothers and sisters. "I remember my sister Terry saying how much Tim reminded her of our father, the way he looked and spoke," says Fox's eldest brother, Tom. "What struck me was the actual line of his jaw, which was set just like my father's. I'll never forget that, the line of his jaw—and the anger underneath."

The second assault on Fox's reputation came the following spring, during his silence. In a special edition of *Listening*, a Dominican magazine that was, ironically, started by Fox while he was a student in Dubuque, a half-dozen academics tore into Fox's oeuvre. Some of their points were telling. Fox was attacked for being a careless, sentimental, and in some respects unscrupulous scholar. "Fox's representations of historical figures and movements tend to be caricatures. His use of polarities, such as that between the fall/redemption tradition and the creation-centered tradition, is too simplistic to be taken seriously by scholars," one wrote. "My criticism of Fox for lack of care as a scholar and thinker can best be cast in terms of Fox's own categories. Fox argues for compassion as an overarching spiritual value, but he himself is lacking in compassion and sensitivity to the sources that he attempts to use. He argues for a need for dialectical consciousness, and yet he draws black and white contrasts between historical figures who do and don't exemplify creation-centered theology. Fox . . . finds it tactically and rhetorically useful to sweep complexities under the rug." Another criticized Fox for being a consumer-oriented theologian whose rhetoric about social justice doesn't have much bite:

> Far from being counter-cultural, any movement which extols eroticism, sensuality, enjoyment of the physical world, the individual over against institutions . . . is highly susceptible to being coopted by a culture which extols these values. . . . Against the intent of Matthew Fox, his writings will serve the interests of what Leonardo Boff calls a "permissive, consumer society." His work will be but one more technique to be purchased by bored middle-class consumers in their ongoing search for meaning and self-fulfillment, without any threat to their lifestyle. Indeed their physical comfort can now be complemented by an interior, psychic comfort. Spirituality then becomes a commodity to be marketed in order to satisy a need.

On the subject of original sin, Fox was accused of misunderstanding the Augustinian tradition, which has no monopoly on contempt for the human body. "Fox is wrong in claiming that these views of human personhood, which have caused so much pain and suffering, are an inevitable consequence of the teaching of original sin." Moreover, in the opinion of this critic, Fox's assertion that this teaching contradicts the goodness of creation is inaccurate. "Fox may want to show that, despite its intended function, the doctrine of original sin is always misapplied in practice. Or, he may want to claim that the concept of original sin is faulty in that, despite the intentions of its creators, it does not succeed in preserving the concept of the goodness of created human nature. That he doesn't do either of these things and instead claims that the doctrine of original sin directly contradicts the goodness of created human nature is a serious flaw in his work."

This attack was followed by another a few months later in the *Catholic World* by Rosemary Radford Ruether, a highly esteemed professor of theology at Garrett Evangelical Seminary in Evanston, Illinois, and also a writer Fox admires and has often cited in his books. As it happens, Ruether is the person who recommended that Starhawk teach at Fox's institute. Now Ruether sneeringly labeled Fox's work "superficial and lacking in historical and spiritual depth." Creation-centered spirituality, she acknowledged, is a valuable tradition with a vast appeal; that's why it's time for "better scholars and theologians" to vindicate this ancient philosophy. "Creation spirituality," Ruether concluded, "is too important to be identified only with the work of Matthew Fox."

This theme—of rescuing creation spirituality from the careless hands of Matthew Fox—is one that was picked up by his provincial, Father Goergen, when I spoke to him. Interestingly, Goergen himself had been a cause célèbre some years before, when he published a book titled *The Sexual Celibate*. Since his election to the provincial office, by the largest margin in the history of his province, Goergen had been a steady defender of Fox's work, both publicly and within the church. It was easy to understand Goergen's dilemma; he was caught between the monarchical fury of Rome, on the one hand—which had made it clear that it wanted Fox out of the order, out of ICCS, and preferably out of the church altogether—and, on the other hand, by the democratic principles of free speech, the immense popular appeal that Fox's work had generated, and the credit that such a widely known theologian brought to his order. Obviously, that load of contradictions had become heavier of late. "The first thing I say to people is that we need to distinguish between creation spirituality and Matt's own theology," Goergen told me. "My sense is that a significant number of people in the church clearly respect and value what they understand by creation spirituality, but there is also a significant number of people in the church—theologians and others—who may be critical of Matt's theology." Goergen cited several thinkers whom he held up as being better exemplars of this tradition: the agrarian writer Thomas Berry, some women writers and ecologists, although none of them were in the clergy or even Catholic. When pressed to give a Catholic example, Goergen pointed to Teilhard de Chardin, who he acknowledged had been disciplined and even despised by the official church. Teilhard died in 1955. When asked for a living example of a creation-centered theologian, other than Fox, Goergen mentioned Rosemary Ruether and himself.

"I'm in an ambiguous role as Matt's superior. In a sense I prefer not to voice those concerns," he said, when I asked why the order seemed bent on a showdown. "I would not want Matt to feel that I was not supportive of his work." Goergen went on to outline many of the complaints that had been voiced by Ruether and others.

"But these are all just academic arguments," I said. "Why is the church so angry at him? Where is the heat coming from?"

"You mean, what might the church—the official church—find to be of such serious concern? Let me think for a second. I'm not sure." Goergen paused. "I think Matt opens himself to challenge because of his direct frontal attacks, such as his attack on Augustine, which is a cause of concern to some academicians. His open letter to Cardinal Ratzinger—clearly, the master of the order felt concern about that. Plus, Matt brings together a variety of issues that by themselves are not threatening, but when put together become a greater threat."

Such as?

"Feminism, coupled with what he has to say about liberation, coupled with Native American religions. I think that may be one of the Vatican's concerns. Is his theology too eclectic? Is he weaving together too many things at a superficial level [so] that he is watering down the Catholic identity or almost creating a New Age–type religion with the appearance of Catholic language? He's so ecumenical that he sees Catholicism as being only one religion among many others.

"However, when it comes to Matt's theology or his freedom to write and speak, I would be supportive of Matt, even if I were critical."

Then what's the problem? Why was Fox being driven out of the order if the provincial supported his right to say and think what he does?

"It probably would have more to do with his personality than his theology," Goergen admitted.

Fox would agree that the problem is one of personality—but not *his* personality. "Aquinas says envy is the mother of hatred," he says. "A lot of the problem with the Catholic church is tied up with envy. If I were an alcoholic priest, I would fit right in, no problem—but because I write books that people actually read, it stirs up envy."

Fox's old friend Brother David, a Benedictine monk at the monastery in Big Sur and a well-known lecturer himself, had watched this conflict develop and saw both sides at fault. "I do not think the Dominicans can possibly kick him out for any doctrinal reasons," Brother David told me. "People think that what Matthew Fox teaches is not acceptable to Catholic thinking. On the contrary, it's quite orthodox. The problem is how he presents it. If he were in any way conciliatory, if he would make the slightest gesture . . . But he never does. It's a shame, because his teaching is extremely important to the church. He's a prophet. However, the moment he gets out of the church, he's a perfectly un-interesting person."

That's the great risk for Fox. He has made a career of struggling against the implacable institution; it's this struggle that has made him famous and has also given form and meaning to his life. If he takes the hint and quits the church, then he becomes just another unanchored New Age spiritual guru; he's no longer a celebrated rebel. On the other hand, in order to stay, he will have to find some way of backing down, which he seems to be constitutionally unable to do.

"Big deal," Fox once told Starhawk when she asked what would happen if the Vatican kicked him out of the priesthood. "What are they going to do—ask me to give back my vow of celibacy?"

◆

The snoring drunk in the aisle seat suddenly lurched onto Fox's shoulder. Fox laughed, then wrinkled his nose. The smell really was quite astonishing. The next two hours on the flight from London to Aberdeen, Scotland, were going to be truly uncomfortable.

"Do you want me to call a stewardess?" I asked. "Maybe we could move."

"That's all right," said Fox. "I've got a shoulder."

There is a darkness under Fox's deep-set blue eyes that testifies to his constant state of exhaustion from his frenetic workload and the lingering background pain of an automobile accident in 1976, which nearly crippled him. He wears a brace at all times, and when he travels and is forced to sit for long spells, such as now, he wears a corset around his shirt and puts a small pillow behind his back. He has endured two operations and hundreds of hours in doctors' offices, traipsing from one specialist to another. The experience eventually led him to a homeopath. Now he is a "complete convert to soft medicine." He also takes acidophilus pills and something called bioplasma, which are tiny white pills that cannot be touched—he has to dispense them into a napkin and pick them out with his tongue, like a Eucharist wafer. He says they give him energy.

He rarely talks about his pain, except to say that it has helped him enter into the pain of others. The fact that he guards it so closely has led some of his friends to wonder if he is not a secret penitent, bearing his pain as a reminder of Christ's suffering. Father Morrissey remembers an occasion a few years ago when Fox came to give an all-day workshop in New Jersey. At the end of the day, Fox was white-faced and obviously physically drained. He rushed into another room to take off his shirt, and Morrissey saw that his back brace had cut into the flesh and was soaked in blood.

When he had his first operation on his neck, which had been damaged in the accident, Fox experienced "the most transcendent dream I ever had." It was shortly after he had discovered the work of Meister Eckhart, his fellow Dominican, in whose writing Fox finds so many echoes of his own thoughts. "In the dream Eckhart came to me and walked with me on the beach." It was evidence, in Fox's opinion, of the communion of saints, which means the fellowship of all believers, living and dead, and which in Catholic doctrine includes the intercession of saints on behalf of true believers. The more I got to know Fox, through reading his work and traveling with him, the more I realized that the communion of saints is at the heart not only of his theology but of the very way he practices theology. He enters into a sort of gnostic dialogue with the saints; indeed, his latest book on Aquinas, which was then still in manuscript, purports to be a conversation between two Dominican brothers, Fox and Aquinas, in which Aquinas is revealed as being a creation-centered thinker much like his living counterpart. I could already hear the catcalls of the critics.

"The communion of saints is in the Nicene Creed," Fox explained. "To me it means the presence of our ancestors. Like the presence of Eckhart and Hildegard are *realities* to me. But in the West, the communion of saints is really a lost doctrine. I think this is one thing we can learn from native peoples, is how to be aware of our ancestors. You get that feeling in an Indian sweat lodge—that you're not alone, you're surrounded by your ancestors, you have roots. That's the healthy side of saints. The shadow side is how we put them on pedestals and make them perfect."

"What is a saint?" I asked.

"According to the New Testament, all Christians are saints. Of course, the issue of sainthood is a cultural matter, it's not just theological. That's where the teaching of Jesus is so radical—we're *all* sons and daughters of God. Otto Rank, who is my favorite psychologist, says a saint is characterized by his lack of bitterness. Flannery O'Connor says something similar—she talks about the lack of self-pity. I would use the words 'beauty' and 'grace.' Also, I've been very affected by something Aquinas noted about the magnanimity: saints are people who have *large souls*. It doesn't matter if they've been canonized or not."

"Who are your saints?"

"Well, Ralph Nader is a saint for me. Otto Rank. Dorothy Day, the founder of the Catholic Worker movement in New York in the thirties. Thomas Merton. Martin Luther King, Sojourner Truth, and definitely Gandhi. Pope John XXIII certainly was. He could laugh at himself—and at his job. Nelson Mandela. Simón Bolívar, Lincoln, Rilke. Howard Thurman, who was a great black preacher and theologian. And of course Eckhart and Hildegard, Julian of Norwich. Merton says that every non-two-legged creature is a saint, so Tristan is a saint."

"Mother Teresa?" I prompted.

"Anyone *Time* magazine declares to be a saint, I am suspicious of. I don't think her kind of holiness is the archetype we need today. For one thing, her position on birth control is too otherworldly."

I didn't say anything, but I had corresponded with Mother Teresa asking for the opportunity to write about her. She declined. "Look around and see the loneliness and pain—in your own family first—then in your neighborhood," she responded. "I ask Our Lady to be a Mother to you, to give you Her Heart so beautiful, so pure, so full of love and humility that you may receive Jesus in the Bread of Life and love and serve Him in the distressing disguise of the poorest of the poor." When I read that letter, I felt a chill brush of air from the abyss that separates the kind of person I am from the kind of person she is. She was inviting me to *be* a saint, not to observe one.

"You know, it's important to meditate on the shadow side of saints," Fox continued, "because perfection is not human, and the striving for perfection can be part of an addictive process. Take Martin Luther King, for example: he was unfaithful. Gandhi was cruel to his wife. Dorothy Day was a sexist—she didn't like women. So was Thomas Aquinas—he called women 'misbegotten males.' So saints aren't people who are right all the time; they are people who *do their work*. It's really about becoming who we really are, because each of us is genuinely unique, down to our molecular level. Everyone has to find their own reason for being here, their unique greatness, their own calling to holiness. That's different for everyone. You know, Meister Eckhart said, 'If the only prayer you say in your entire life is "Thank you," that would suffice.' "

"When we die, what happens?" I asked.

Fox laughed. "You're asking *me*? What do I know?" His laugh dislodged the drunk on his shoulder, who began a slow slide into Fox's lap. "Well, first of all, I think that Western Christianity puts too many eggs into that basket. I stress how if there's life *before* death, life after death will take care of itself. If there isn't, then we're in trouble and we *wander*. That of course is the classic doctrine of purgatory. So we're here to learn love this time around, and that means to live fully. If we do that, then eternal life after death continues—but in another form. Eckhart puts it this way: 'Being goes on.' Life dies, but *being goes on*. Aquinas has this amazing section where he talks about two resurrections. The first resurrection is our waking up *now*. It's the resurrection of our *consciousness*, if you will —which is very close to what I'm saying about living fully first. And then the second resurrection is that of the personhood afterwards. For me, I do believe in resurrection, but I don't know what form it takes. Apparently I don't want to know. I like mystery. I want to be *surprised*!"

He smiled at this thought and then continued: "I think it's very Einsteinian to say, as Hildegard does, that 'no warmth is lost in the universe.' It gets recycled, energy into matter, matter into energy. Eternal life goes on. The forms it takes are far beyond our puny imaginations to decipher. The communion of saints means that all the energies who ever lived as persons are still with us, interacting with us right now! Space and time mean nothing! The interconnectedness doesn't stop just because the heart stops beating. I don't just believe in the communion of saints. I *know* it exists, I've experienced it."

"You mean in your dream of Eckhart? How is that different from just a regular dream?"

"I don't like that phrase 'just a regular dream,' " said Fox. "Where do dreams come from? They come from the universe like any other revelation. Like Eckhart says, 'When I return to God and to the core, the soil, the ground, the stream and the source of the Godhead, no one asks me where I am coming from or where I have been. For no one misses me in the place where God ceases to become.' This is the essence of dying for me —it is a return to the source. That's why I find dying very beautiful." He laughed again. "I'm glad I'm not a parish priest, because I cry at all funerals—and I don't cry out of sadness but out of beauty. I think there's something so *graceful* about people who have lived fully and who have died beautiful deaths. It's a beautiful death because they lived a beautiful life," Fox concluded, echoing, whether he realized it or not, his father's favorite maxim.

What did all this mean? It was deeply appealing; it was like a bath of mystical insights—one should be able to soak in it and feel consoled. I don't know why I felt so distrustful of it. Perhaps it was my own longing for belief that I was distrusting. And yet I envied the fact that the universe was so full of meaning for Fox.

Part of his appeal, at least to me, was that he fused two powerful traditions that were otherwise at war with each other. One was the intellectualism of the Catholic church. He made the ancient arguments between Augustine and Aquinas seem contemporary and really quite urgent. I realized that I wanted to be intellectually persuaded by him; I wanted to discover God through reason. That was the path I could accept, although the truth is, I did not think that the path of reason led to religious belief. The kind of rationalism that the church sponsored was built on the presumption of faith. The arguments of theology made sense only inside the hermetic environment of a faith already acquired. I saw religious belief as a kind of artificial reality; once one accepted the conceits that faith imposed, then one could appreciate and even love the internal coherence of, for instance, the doctrine of the communion of saints. Therefore, reason was harmless and even entertaining. I could feel engaged without really being affected, as if we were playing chess, as long as we stayed on this level.

The other tradition was the irrational and mystical, which was also part of Catholicism, certainly, and of the New Age as well. It was this part of Fox that I distrusted and, I suppose, feared. He seemed too willing to believe. Perhaps I was too unwilling, but I had surrendered to the irrational before. I no longer wanted to live with beliefs that embarrassed me. And so I put distance between myself and the side of me that had been deluded, beguiled by belief, drawn to hope. My whole adult life, as I saw it now, was a search for the truth through the experiences of other people; I was rummaging through their lives to try to find out what was real and what was counterfeit. I could see now that I was hovering above my own life, afraid to fully enter into it, afraid to become a person who was one way and not another, a person who did not feel threatened by the contradictions between reason and intuition.

I saw the deficiencies of both ways of going at life, through the mind or through the heart. Through the lens of reason, the world was pointless and small—at least that is how it appeared to me—although highly focused and reassuringly real. Through the other lens, however, the lens of irrational faith, life was full of connection and directed energy and value. It was a blur of meaning. What I longed for was to be able to see the world through both lenses. Fox would say that would be having a cosmology, a way of seeing that accommodated both science and mysticism, reason and faith. This was his message, at bottom: that the mind and the heart did not have to be at odds; one could think and believe at the same time. No wonder I found myself falling under his spell. I thought if I could find a way of reconciling this split, I could somehow climb back inside my own being.

As the plane landed in Aberdeen, Fox shook the drunken lump in his lap. "Wake up, fella, we're here," he said, to no avail. "Oh, well. Have a nice day." Fox chortled, a bit naughtily, it seemed to me.

✦

Findhorn, the little New Age community in northern Scotland, discovered itself as a spiritual power center in the late sixties, shortly after Peter Caddy, a former officer in the Royal Air Force, got sacked from his job as the manager of a nearby four-star hotel in Cluny. Caddy, his wife, Eileen, their three children, and a woman named Dorothy Maclean—invariably identified as "our colleague" by the Caddys—loaded up their thirty-foot trailer and took up what they thought would be a temporary residence in a local trailer park. Soon after their arrival, however, Eileen received a divine message that they were to stay put. With no immediate job prospects, Peter went on the dole. To fill up his time, he decided to plant a garden—a few lettuce and radish seeds, peas, beans, and rutabagas. Then Dorothy entered into communion with the Pea Deva, the spirit that lives in peas, who offered to help out in the garden. In no time at all, with the connivance of various plant devas and the Landscape Angel, Findhorn became the site of one of the most famous gardens in Great Britain. There were reports of forty-pound cabbages and rutabagas too heavy to lift. This abundance was all the more mysterious because these plants were growing in what was essentially sterile beach soil. When the news broke that the Findhorn community was being co-managed by vegetable spirits, the pilgrimage began. First, of course, in this common-wealth of fanatical gardeners, came the horticulturalists, to verify the phenomenal produce; then the friends of the fairy folk; and then the crystal gazers and the witches and pagans and latter-day druids. Gradually the trailer village on the Moray Firth expanded and prospered; indeed, the triumphant day came when the Caddys bought out the Cluny Hotel to house their overflow guests.

It was still early spring when Fox and I arrived, on Maundy Thursday, and although the crocuses and daffodils were quite beautiful, the trophies of the main garden were not yet in evidence. Joanna Macy, a California Buddhist and environmental activist, had invited Fox to join her in leading a workshop called "Death and Resurrection of Self, Society, and the World." It seemed to me that Findhorn would be a perfect place to see who Fox really is—Catholic priest or New Age guru. The difference, in my opinion, was that the priest was still interested in philosophy and tradition and still wrestled with nettlesome doctrines he might not agree with, but the guru floated away on a carpet of intuition. Here in Findhorn, one could truly believe anything.

For someone who doesn't see devas and leprechauns, Findhorn presents itself as a glorified trailer park. The Caddys' original trailer is still here, encrusted, like most of the others, with porches and added-on rooms, and surrounded by flowers. There is a charm in the smallness of these cottages, but it looked to me, as we wandered through the shrubbery toward Universal Hall, where Fox was scheduled to give his first sermon, as if we were walking through a settlement of Smurfs.

Why believe one thing and not another? It was the question I had posed to myself at the beginning of this project, but now it raised itself again. Why believe in eternal life but not in fairies? The evidence for one is as great as for the other, and from the point of view of pure reason, any religious creed is superstitious and absurd. Apparently, however, some beliefs were more embarrassing to me than others. I wondered what I might think of myself if I actually did see a Daffodil Deva or ran into Pan on the trail.

Universal Hall has a retractable ceiling—in order to accommodate UFOs, I was told. It was a lovely, five-sided room of fine polished wood, filled with about six hundred people, about half of them Findhorn residents, the remainder Europeans who had come especially for the workshop.

"Easter is a time of springing from tombs," Fox began, staring out at his audience through his pale reading glasses, which made his eyes look huge and vague, like smudges of sky through a dirty window. "My thesis is that our Western civilization is entombed. We are entombed as a species. And the question is, 'Can we spring from *our* tombs?' "

Most of the people in the audience had grown up in Christian or Jewish homes but had long since abandoned their faith and their traditions. What they hoped to find at this gathering was a way to reclaim some part of themselves that they had left behind. For many, it was a difficult and at moments bitter experience. One later characterized this entire Easter workshop as "spiritual tourism." And yet they had been drawn here by a nameless sense of loss, a feeling that there was a hole in their lives that must be filled by *something*. A few had been so injured by their religious upbringing that they could scarcely listen to the words of the sermon. Some of the others, mainly the Europeans, had grown up with no religious traditions at all.

This is the backdrop against which Fox's project must be understood: the old religions are dying; all that's left is to try to salvage what is worthwhile from the various traditions and bring them to life with new forms of liturgy. In this respect, his battle with the Vatican is only a useful distraction—it has made him famous. To spiritually alienated people such as the ones gathered here, Fox was a more credible spokesman for religion precisely because the church was trying to stop him from preaching; on the other hand, just because he was a rebel didn't mean that they were going to accept his message.

Fox listed five "boulders" that he said were entombing us as a people. The first boulder is *acedia*, a medieval term that means depression, but which also encompasses sloth, cynicism, and pessimism. Aquinas defined acedia as "a sluggishness of mind that neglects to begin good." It is marked by a preoccupation with death. Fox pointed to the energy the West put into its war with Iraq. "We get aroused in our civilization for war so easily. What does it take to arouse people for peace? Where is the vitality of our political systems, our economic systems, our educational systems? Depression is not just a personal psychological issue. It's a cultural state into which our civilization has fallen. Acedia. We are deep in it, like quicksand."

A second boulder is *apathy*. " 'Apathy' is two Greek words meaning 'no passion,' " Fox observed. "The antidote to apathy and to acedia is to fall in love. To rediscover our erotic attachment to what is beautiful in the universe. That's where we get our passion. As Hildegard of Bingen put it, 'We shall awaken from our dullness and rise vigorously toward justice.' If we fall in love with creation deeper and deeper, we will respond to its endangerment with passion."

Addiction, said Fox, is the largest boulder imprisoning our culture and keeping us from discovering our freedom. "It keeps us out of touch with our inner selves. For example, while we constitute 4 percent of the world's population in the United States, we are using 64 percent of the world's illicit drugs. Now, is the problem with the drug lords in Colombia? Or is the problem in *our souls*—that we need so many drugs? And we add to that our addictions to alcohol, to television, to shopping, to religion, to work, and we realize that we are capable of turning *anything* into an addiction." Only by becoming aware of the divine element inside us, what Fox calls getting in touch with our mystical natures, can we overcome our addictions.

The fourth boulder is *anthropocentrism*—that is, the bias toward interpreting everything in terms of the human. When we put ourselves at the center of creation, we tend to miss the abundance of unconditional love everywhere in the universe. "The angel that rolls away the boulder of anthropocentrism is cosmology," said Fox. "At this very critical moment in the history of our planet, we are getting a whole new creation story." He referred to recent calculations concerning the rate of expansion of the initial fireball that followed the Big Bang. "If it had expanded at the rate of one millionth of a second faster than it did, there would be no Earth. If the temperature had been one degree hotter or cooler, you and I would not be here today. Story after story like this is tumbling out of the new science. Whenever I hear it I think of Julian of Norwich [a fourteenth-century British mystic], who said, 'We've been loved from before the beginning.' "

The final boulder is *avarice*, or greed. "Aquinas says, 'The greed for gain knows no limit and tends to infinity,' " said Fox. "He puts his finger on it when he uses the word 'infinity.' Avarice and greed are a *spiritual quest*. That is the issue. People are looking for the infinite because as a species we have something inside us that needs satisfaction."

It was a passionate performance, the best sermon I had seen Fox deliver; but instead of applauding, the Findhornians wiggled their hands in the air, signifying approval, however tepid. When Fox asked for questions, a bearded German stood and said that he had had a hard time paying attention because of some lingering "shadows" from the day before, "ven ve vere sitting in a monastery togedder, feeling varm vit' one anudder, *and Kevin said it vas cold*!" The German suddenly began to sob. "And Joanna," he said, gulping for air as he addressed the co-leader, Joanna Macy, "I haff already presented my apologies for being a man—*but you didn't give me a hug*!" Finally he sat down, crying, "I am not the Vatican! I am not the Vatican!"

There was a clucking noise that seemed to represent sympathy. Fox took off his glasses and held his head in his hands. Had they heard him at all? And that business about the Vatican—was that the only reason he had been invited, as a certified victim of Catholic repression? It looked like it was going to be a long weekend.

"Do you believe in devas?" I asked him when we returned to our trailer. We were sharing a glass of the excellent local scotch whisky as Fox decompressed. He smiled at the question—he has a quirky, one-sided grin, so that half of his face appears amused and the other half unmoved—and began to tell me about the Indian vision quest he underwent during his year of silence. After Fox had fasted for three days, his friend Buck Ghosthorse left him in a redwood forest, where he sat and prayed alone for twenty-four hours. "I experienced the presence of spirits very powerfully all night long," Fox related. Some of these spirits were menacing, but Fox felt that others, especially the animal spirits, were watching over him. After many hours, he began to discern these friendly spirits in the shadows and patterns of nature. Ghosthorse later explained that being a spiritual leader is a lonely process, and the creatures who lived on the land long before man were encouraging him. "The message was that support doesn't have to come only from *humans*," Fox told me. "Creation itself supports this work."

"So, does that mean you believe in devas?"

"You're always trying to pin things down!" Fox protested. He poured me another scotch whisky, leaving his own glass empty. "Now, *angels*— that's a different matter. I don't believe in angels. I *know* they exist." While he was working on his book on Hildegard, who often communicated with angels, Fox himself became aware of the presence of other beings. Sometimes he felt that they interceded for him. Once, at another workshop, a woman came up to him and said, "The entire time you were speaking there was an angel standing beside you, a big fellow ten feet tall wearing a white tie and tails. I asked him what he was doing there and he said, 'Oh, I've been protecting this fellow since he was twelve years old.' "

"You do believe in devas," I surmised.

"Tell you the truth, I'd never even heard of devas before I got here. What are they, like elves or leprechauns? Anyway, you have to want to see them, and I don't think you really do."

"That's not true," I said defensively. "If such things exist—angels, elves, devas—if they exist, I want to see them."

"Why?" Fox asked suspiciously. "Oh, I know—you want to *interview* them!" He pointed an accusing finger at me. "You'll *never* see them! They protect themselves against people like you!"

Laughing to himself, he went off to bed.

◆

That night I had a vivid dream. I was sitting at the head of a long table. It seemed to be a dinner party held in my honor. My family was there, and my close friends. Then the table seemed to extend and I saw many others—people I work with, others I enjoy seeing. My daughter's cello teacher was there, and our neighbors. The table began changing shapes like a kaleidoscope; it became round, and then heart-shaped. I saw my relatives on both sides of the family, and then my ancestors extending on and on.

"Are you *kidding*?" Fox exclaimed at breakfast. "That's a wonderful dream! And do you realize what yesterday *was*? Saint Parsifal's day! It was the day of his feast, when he receives a heart! And of course it was at a round table! Oh, I can't believe that dream! I had a dream, too, but it really doesn't compare."

"What was your dream?"

"You and I were walking along and we ran into Prince Charles. He had broken his arm. He wanted us to help."

"Did we?"

"Ha! I guess not. At least I don't remember."

Good Friday was more successful, in Fox's opinion. He had come up with a ritual in which the Catholic celebration of the stations of the cross would be re-enacted using the crucifixion of Mother Earth in place of Jesus. I could imagine how the Vatican would respond to that. We formed a train of shivering pilgrims walking through the gorse-covered dunes, singing a Kyrie. At one station, we were invited to say the names of friends who had died of AIDS-related diseases or were infected with HIV, a solemn and eventually appalling procedure that went on and on. At another, victims of childhood abuse symbolically threw off their shackles of shame. Chernobyl and Hiroshima were stops on the tour. The endangered animals of the world mourned the destruction of their habitat. By the end, many of the participants were openly crying.

"Now *that's* a ritual!" Fox said proudly as he stood atop a dune watching the somber parade. He wanted to know what I thought of it. I said I had mixed feelings.

"Oh, your feelings are always mixed," he said dismissively, but I could tell that it got under his skin.

In a moment he caught up with me as I was walking back to the trailer. "So, Larry didn't like it, did he?" Fox teased. There was anger in his voice. "What was it—too passionate for you? Too meaningful?"

"Excessive emotion makes me uncomfortable," I admitted.

"But there are so many weak and wounded people. You shouldn't let them take the experience away from you," he said, fidgeting anxiously with his scarf.

"Anyway, it's too much like religion for me," I said. "All that emotion and showy belief—it strikes me as shallow and phony."

Fox interrupted to talk about prayer being a way to heal those wounded people, and how being a part of group ritual can lead to breakthroughs. I found myself growing very impatient with him. "Are you going to listen to me?" I finally said. "It's religion I can't handle. I just can't surrender, I can't give up my integrity even if it is possible to have a larger experience. It's just not me. I can't make a leap of faith."

Fox stopped and looked at me. I think it was the first time he really saw who I was. He simply nodded. I walked on.

◆

For the first time in years, Fox was serving his priestly functions, however idiosyncratically. He presided over a combination Passover seder–Last Supper on Thursday, and offered Communion. He preached sermons on Good Friday and now on Holy Saturday. It had an odd effect on him. He could sense that his audience was turning against him—there was a lot of grumbling about his sermonizing. Fox seemed to gain energy from their disaffection. He began to chide them indirectly by criticizing the New Age for its lack of roots and for the absence of any understanding of evil. "That's what Easter is all about," he said. "Good Friday was an experience of suffering and pain and letting go, and the emptiness that comes from that. But Holy Saturday is a day of silence and darkness and thinking, a day of letting be. In the Christian tradition it is the day Christ descended into the nether world, into the dark night of the soul. For us Europeans and ex-Europeans, what we are most afraid of is darkness itself, which for us is the irrational, right-brain side of ourselves—and what we are doing is *very* irrational. Holy Saturday is a day of holy obscurity and holy waiting. It is the day the holy seed is planted in the ground, as it must be, because the seed only grows in the dark. Eckhart says, 'If you want the kernel, you must break the shell.' On Holy Saturday, our shells do break open, our hearts break open, and that's okay. We, like Jesus, can survive the descent into the underworld, because he precedes us and shows us the way."

Some of us were going to enter a sweat lodge that night. "This too is a journey into the womb, into the pit, and there is power there." Fox related his own initial experience in a sweat lodge, with a group of Indians in Minnesota. "For the first twenty minutes I thought I was going to *die* in there! After that, I realized that there was no fire exit, and no fire extinguisher, so I yielded to the experience. I said, 'Yes, I am going to die'—and it's precisely in that act of surrender that the prayer started to happen."

That evening after sunset about twenty of us gathered around a bonfire behind the main garden. There was a low tent—actually, it was a blue plastic tarp stretched over bent branches and weighed down on the perimeter with large stones. A shred of light lingered in the sky as the Australian who was leading the sweat told us what to expect. The fire was studded with big rounded rocks gathered from the beach. They were already glowing red, as if the fire had passed from the logs through the stones and they were burning now inside. The air was frigid and the fire was welcome. I noticed that there was a trench leading from the fire into the lodge. The leader told us that there would be four rounds of prayer with one brief break. If we felt faint, we could ask to leave; but whenever we left we must retrace our steps by crawling out the same way we entered.

I looked around. More than half of the participants were women, including a pair of elderly English schoolteachers who were asking whether they should take their inhalers. It seemed to me that if the sweat was as arduous as Fox had warned us it would be, these two couldn't last long. There was a muscular Scotsman with a deep and jovial voice, a pretty Irish woman with dark brows and arresting brown eyes, a blond Swedish couple who held hands and looked apprehensive. Before we went into the lodge, we were each given a length of red thread to tie around our wrist. The final prayer, we were told, would be accompanied by a vow we made to ourselves, and this slender bracelet would serve as a reminder of our pledge.

Now we stripped off our clothes and laid them in neat piles behind the lodge. This part of the ceremony had caught Fox off guard. He had stressed that I needed to bring a bathing suit if I wanted to do the sweat, and I had the sense that he felt compromised. We lined up like a group of army recruits headed for our physicals. As we approached the lodge we knelt down on all fours to crawl inside. Passing through the small opening to this dark chamber, we each uttered "All my ancestors," as we had been instructed. I felt foolish and exposed. The level of absurdity was very high—a bunch of naked white people on the cold coast of northern Scotland pretending to be Plains Indians. We had to crowd together to fit in, so that we were shoulder to shoulder and knee to knee. The ceiling was so low I couldn't straighten out properly, and there was a rough branch against my back. I could only imagine how uncomfortable I would be two hours from now. The earth was spongy and cool under a light coating of straw.

In front of us was a deep, empty pit. As soon as were were all inside and bunched together, the leader called for the stones. One after another, they were flung into the pit with a pitchfork, forming a smoldering pyramid. They kept coming—too many of them, I worried. They were so superheated that they were completely translucent; you could see the veins inside and what seemed to be currents of air billowing through them. Now the pit looked like a lava bed. It had a strange liquid appearance, like simmering spaghetti sauce. The leader sprinkled some sage on the rocks, and then water, and the stones smoked and sizzled. The tent flap closed and we settled in to the dull glow of bodies and the incense of sage and the lung-searing, breath-stealing heat. "The first round of prayer is thankfulness," our leader said in his Aussie drawl.

People quickly introduced themselves through their prayers. Several spoke about their pets, especially their cats, and how thankful they were for them. Fox was grateful for his work. One woman prayed to the spirit that lived in her pansies. I felt self-conscious as I spoke about my love for my family—as if I were more blessed than anyone else. But that little edge of smugness was wearing away rather quickly as the heat in this cauldron began to rise. Sweat was cascading off me, but I couldn't tell what was my sweat and what was Fox's, on one side of me, or the Scotsman's, on the other. I was breathing very shallowly, panting really, hoping that the prayers would be gotten over with quickly.

By the second round, I felt very close to death. I wasn't hearing things very clearly. We were speaking about forgiveness. It seemed to me that Fox forgave his superiors. Those elderly schoolteachers who I thought would be unconscious by now were carrying on as if they had just been served tea; moreover, they had a lot to forgive. I hated them. I wanted to put a gag in their mouths. It was galling to realize that I was going to have to crawl out in disgrace while they babbled on. When one finally did stop speaking, I interrupted the flow of prayer because I didn't think I could last until my turn. "I'm really suffering," said a voice that no longer sounded familiar. My chest was compressed and my lungs were full of pain. It reminded me suddenly of Jesus suffocating on the cross. "I used to believe in him and in his sacrifice," I said. "I no longer do. But I realize how indifferent I've become to the suffering of other people. I ask to be forgiven." Then, under my breath, I said, "Matt, help me."

I felt his hand on my shoulder. "Hit your chest," he said. "It'll give you strength."

Strangely, it did. I was able to endure the next several prayers in the round, and then the flap of the tent opened and a gush of cool air blew in. I gulped it down. We slowly moved out on all fours for a break. People were there with buckets of water, which they ladled out for us. I knew that it must be cold out here, because our helpers were wearing coats and sweaters, but I was inside a scalded shell. I crawled into the grass and collapsed. I thought I might burn the earth.

When the leader called us, I found myself struggling back to my feet to get in line. "You don't have to do this," Fox told me. I didn't know what to say. The truth was, I *did* have to do this, even if it killed me. I really thought I would rather die inside that lodge than put on my clothes and walk back to the trailer by myself.

No one stayed behind. Once again we crushed together. The stones were black now, but fresh, hot new ones were added, so that the pile loomed higher in front of us, and I worried that some of the rocks might tumble off and roll into our laps—or else explode.

The pain came sooner this time; we were all so weak. We prayed about our fears. I heard the voice of the Irish woman, who said she was so afraid of suffocating. She could hardly breathe, and it reminded her of her father; he was a logger, and a tree had fallen on him. He had died of suffocation. I admired her courage and I realized that I was not the only one who was suffering. The big Scotsman was balled up beside me in a whimpering fetal ball. In a moment, I could feel that Fox too was curled up and clawing at the earth for a cool bubble of air. Somehow I had become detached from the heat. There was a flap of blistered skin on the ball of my foot, which I peeled off. I thought: this is my body. It was as if the part of me observing that was a very long way away from my pain-ridden flesh, although suddenly I would get scared and feel overwhelmed again. But somehow that little flap of skin helped me stand outside the fear and, it seemed, my own mortality.

The final round was our pledge to ourselves. Fox passed. I knew what I was going to say, however. "I vow to seek love and not to betray it," I said, tossing that bit of skin into the stones to seal the promise.

I worried about Fox. I knew he was in pain; I could hear him gasping and striking his chest. I wondered what it was about this approximation of hell that called to him. Much of his life, it seemed to me, had been spent in trying to escape from his own tomb, to break free of the deadness of the hospital, the seminary, celibacy, the moral and intellectual confinements of the church. His whole life was a struggle for freedom to express himself; and yet hadn't he chosen the very restrictions he now fought against? Hadn't he crawled into a tomb of his own making?

We were about to leave the tent when Fox spoke his vow. "More joy," he said in a dry, cracking voice.

Outside, a drum was beating. When the flap opened and we crawled through it, I was too weak to stand. A light rain was falling. It felt like a benediction. I lay in the grass and listened to the drum—*ba-bum, babumph!*—and let the rain cool me down. Gradually, my heartbeat slowed, and the most fantastic thing happened. My heartbeat and the drumbeat synchronized. In that moment of resonance, the earth itself began to pulse. I felt like a baby riding my mother's breast; her powerful heart was drumming its rhythm through my body; her heart and mine had become a single organ, inseparable and eternal.

Gradually I was pulled back into my consciousness. I looked around at the other ghostly forms in the rain. We were all becoming aware again of our sexuality, along with the excitement and self-consciousness that comes with that. I rolled over onto my back and closed my eyes.

Suddenly I remembered the premonition of this experience; it was the fantasy I had been having for months before I came: a dark room filled with naked people praying. I had been haunted by it. The only difference between the fantasy and what I had just been through was the heat—I had never imagined the heat—but I knew with certainty that this was an experience I had been waiting to have.

At daybreak the next morning, we stood on a dune watching a storm brewing in the North Sea. "Christ is risen!" Fox declared to the several dozen people who had awakened for this early ceremony. Then we built a fire out of oak staves and danced around the flames. Afterwards, Fox was going back to offer Mass. Something had changed him, I could tell. "I've rediscovered my own Christianity," he admitted as we stood on the dunes. "I guess I had to come to someplace so far out that it made me seem normal!"

It was Easter again, whatever that meant. The sun was rising. When it reached California, Walker Railey would stand again in a pulpit to resurrect his preaching career. That was the kind of ironic counterpoint I had come to expect in life. It was Easter, four years before, that Railey preached his sermon in a bulletproof vest and the tragedy that awakened my search for faith began. Now here I was standing in the dawn feeling full and grateful for the life that was mine to enjoy. After this long and, I suppose, eccentric examination of the varieties of religious belief, I couldn't say that I believed any differently than when I started. But I *was* different. I had not experienced a spiritual transformation, but something had touched me. I felt new. I didn't know how long this feeling might last, or what it might lead to.

After the service, I went down to the shore. There was an old concrete pylon from a sea wall that had long since been pummeled into shards. The North Sea lay in front of me, cold and gray and brooding like the heavy morning sky. I stripped off my clothes and ran into the frigid waves. I had never been so cold. I thought my heart would stop, but I kept running until the surf knocked me down.

"Thank you," I said.

Notes

xii *In France . . . about 12 percent:* Figures are drawn from Fox, *Creation Spirituality,* p. 74 note.

WALKER RAILEY'S DEMON

5 *as had Methodism:* According to pollster George Gallup, Jr., Methodists are the most likely to stray from their faith: one out of three Methodists leaves the denomination. Catholics are second, with one out of ten leaving the faith. (Interview with George Gallup, Jr.)

17 *The bishop of Houston, a secret homosexual:* See Emily Yoffe's insightful and revealing portrait, "The Double Life of Finis Crutchfield," *Texas Monthly,* October 1987.

18 *divorce rate among ministers: Newsweek,* August 28, 1989.

28 *detectives who reviewed the tape:* Dallas *Morning News,* March 22, 1992.

34 *Doug Mulder, a ferocious former prosecutor:* Mulder was the prosecutor who put an innocent man, Randall Dale Adams, on death row. Adams was later pardoned after the case received international attention through the documentary film *The Thin Blue Line.*

39 *Ryan had been partially strangled:* Dallas *Morning News,* March 22, 1992.

JIMMY SWAGGART: FALSE MESSIAH

47 *the impulse toward progress and modernity . . . and a yearning for the restoration:* Cf. Richard T. Hughes, ed., *The American Quest for the Primitive Church* (Champaign, Ill.: University of Illinois Press, 1988), who makes the interesting case that primitivism and modernism are both expressions of an antihistorical urge—that both encourage the belief, so common in America, that one can escape the consequences of history either through lunging toward the past or by leaping into the future. Hughes writes (p. 12):

To understand primitivism and modernity as fundamentally connected in this way goes far toward explaining many of the seeming anachronisms of our age that puzzle many observers. It helps explain, for example, how it is that many members of traditions with deeply restorationist roots—fundamentalist, Churches of Christ, Baptist, Mormon, and pentecostal, for example—can embrace the modern world with religious zeal and perceive in that embrace no paradox, no irony, and no contradiction at all. The space-age cathedrals with which fundamentalists and evangelicals of various stripes have dotted the urban landscape across America stand as mute testimony to that embrace, and perhaps symbolize the ironic primitivist/modernist perspective that forms, for many, the substance of their theology.

50 The figures cited here come from the Jimmy Swaggart Ministries 1986 Financial Stewardship Report; Baton Rouge *State Times*, February 22, 1988; *New York Times*, February 22, 1988; and the *Evangelist* (a monthly publication of Jimmy Swaggart Ministries), April 1988.

51 *"Monday morning"*: *Evangelist*, April 1988, and "Camp Meeting," Swaggart's Thanksgiving sermon of 1987.

"monstrosity of heresy" and *"complete contradiction"*: George Cornell, "Swaggart Oddly Belittling Himself Before His Fall," Associated Press report, March 4, 1988. Swaggart has also said, "The Catholic practice of confessing sins to a priest is a doctrine of devils" (Austin *American-Statesman*, March 24, 1987).

dancing is sinful: Swaggart, *Questions and Answers* (Baton Rouge: Jimmy Swaggart Ministries, 1985), pp. 16, 22.

"AIDS can be contracted": Austin *American-Statesman*, March 24, 1987.

"all rock music.": Swaggart, *Music: The New Pornography* (Baton Rouge: Jimmy Swaggart Ministries, 1984), p. 15.

"The main problem": Swaggart, *Armageddon: The Future of Planet Earth* (Jimmy Swaggart Ministries, 1987), p. 8. Similarly, Swaggart believes that "all this talk about the problems facing us today because of our wayward children could be solved by the revival of the old-fashioned razor-strop, coupled with lots of love" (*Armageddon*, pp. 11–12).

"the worst sin": Swaggart, *Homosexuality: Its Cause and Its Cure* (Baton Rouge: Jimmy Swaggart Ministries, 1982), p. 19.

52 "pervert, queer *or* faggot": Swaggart, *Armageddon*, p. 10. Swaggart also makes the case that homosexuals should be called "dogs":

> In Deuteronomy 23:18 God said, *"Thou shalt not bring the hire of a whore, or the price of a dog, into the house of the Lord thy God for any vow."* Now, the term "dog" here has no reference to the canine variety. It speaks of the male prostitute, the homosexual, the sodomite.
>
> In Revelation 22:15, our Lord said the same thing. *"For without are dogs, and sorcerers, and whoremongers, and murderers, and idolators, and whosoever loveth and maketh a lie."* Here He is again speaking of homosexuals.
>
> So we can see from this that God's terminology for those who would give themselves over to a reprobate mind (resulting in the terrible degeneracy of homosexuality) would be to refer to them as "dogs."

Swaggart goes on to assert that God believes that not only "the homosexual [is] worthy of death, but (perhaps) also those who *approve* of homosexuality" (Swaggart, *Homosexuality*, pp. 20–21; emphasis in original).

"institutions damned by God" and *"a system of atheistic socialism": Current Biography*, 1987, p. 51.

"pitiful pukish pulp": David Snyder, "Jimmy Lee Swaggart: King of the Hell-Fire Evangelists," *Dixie,* January 27, 1985, p. 11.

"I speak in tongues": "The Evangelist," John Camp's 1983 documentary, WBRZ-TV, Baton Rouge, Louisiana.

"He's got a style": Houston *Chronicle,* February 28, 1988.

Fifty thousand letters: Baton Rouge *Morning Advocate,* May 1, 1987. According to *U.S. News,* April 6, 1987, Swaggart's mail averaged only forty thousand letters per week. "In contrast, scholars estimate that Jesus, in his lifetime, preached to no more than 30,000."

55 *"If you can imagine a bull's eye":* Interview with the Reverend Andy Harris. On Frances Swaggart's behavior: "They intimidate the hell out of people," says John Camp, former WBRZ-TV reporter. Professor Stephen Winzenburg of Florida Southern College, author of a content-analysis study of television preachers (he monitored their broadcasts for eight years), had several run-ins with Frances Swaggart. "Frances called me when I put in my study that I felt that Jimmy made outlandish statements," says Winzenburg. "She had a fit. I quoted Jimmy that 'heaven is a literal planet.' Now that's certainly outlandish. Frances said, 'No, that's the truth. Jimmy has the truth.' " The study showed that in March 1988, Swaggart spent 40 percent of his air time on music, 44 percent on fund-raising, and only 3 percent on his spiritual message. Says Winzenburg: "Frances tried to get me to change my results" (Interview with Stephen Winzenburg).

56 *"vile, vulgar, profane old man":* Nick Tosches, *Hellfire: The Jerry Lee Lewis Story* (New York: Delacorte Press, 1982), p. 207.

"He never seemed to have the problems": Jimmy Swaggart with Robert Paul Lamb, *To Cross a River* (Jimmy Swaggart Ministries, 1984), pp. 12–13.

57 *"Who's she?":* Ibid., pp. 11–12.

On the Pentecostal revival: cf. Catherine L. Albanese, *America, Religions & Religion* (Belmont, Calif.: Wadsworth Publishing Co., 1981), p. 105; H. Newton Malony and A. Adams Lovekin, *Glossolalia: Behavioral Science Perspectives on Speaking in Tongues* (Oxford: Oxford University Press, 1985), pp. 6–7, 24; and J. L. Sherrill, *They Speak with Other Tongues* (New York: McGraw-Hill, 1964), pp. 37–38.

58 *Tibetan monks who quoted Shakespeare:* Malony and Lovekin, op. cit., p. 24.

Plutarch and Virgil: John P. Kildahl, *The Psychology of Speaking in Tongues* (New York: Harper & Row, 1972), p. 11.

speak and write in Martian: Malony and Lovekin, op. cit., p. 14. The "Martian" language was shown to be a distortion of French.

On Parham and the early Pentecostals: "Without a trace of self-consciousness—or self-criticism, one might add—pentecostals recurringly identified themselves with Christ and their revival with the Holy Spirit. Parham casually pointed out, for example, that the day he received the baptism he had waited upon the Lord from 9 A.M. until 3 P.M., the very hours that Christ had hung upon the cross" (Grant Wacker, "Playing for Keeps: The Primitivist Impulse in Early Pentecostalism," in Hughes, op. cit., p. 202).

59 *no personality differences between glossolalics and nonglossolalics:* Malony and Lovekin, op. cit., p. 5.

"bridge-burning experience": "In a society where highly expressive religious practices are considered deviant, a new convert's ecstatic uttering of streams of unintelligible

syllables and his demonstration of joyous enthusiasm and enraptured faith in the Glory and Power of God are enough to burn a great many bridges" (Luther P. Gerlach, "Pentecostalism: Revolution or Counter-Revolution?" in Irvin I. Zaretsky and Mark P. Leone, eds., *Religious Movements in Contemporary America* [Princeton, N.J.: Princeton University Press, 1974]).

60 *"David and Goliath were my favorite"*: Swaggart and Lamb, op. cit., p. 20.
"an entreating voice": Ibid., p. 21.

61 *"A dread swept over"*: Ibid., pp. 31–32.
"The last night": Ibid., pp. 33–34.

63 *"my family started rock and roll"*: Interview with Stephen Winzenburg.

64 *"We'd go down there and sell newspapers"*: Jerry Lee Lewis interview with WSMV-TV, Nashville, Tennessee, in "Jerry Lee Lewis: I Am What I Am" (Hallway Productions, 1988).
"Lord, I want you to give me": Swaggart and Lamb, op. cit., p. 35; Myra Gale Lewis with Murray Silver, *Great Balls of Fire: The Uncensored Story of Jerry Lee Lewis* (New York: Morrow, 1982), p. 3.
in German and Japanese: Steve Chapple, "Whole Lotta Savin' Goin' On," *Mother Jones*, July/August 1986.

65 *"I didn't know what was happening"*: Swaggart and Lamb, op. cit., pp. 44–45.
"It was a lark": Ibid., p. 47.
"I no longer considered": Ibid., p. 48.

66 *"A strange feeling"*: Ibid., pp. 53–54.
"the meanest, lowest-down": "Jerry Lee Lewis: I Am What I Am."
"For years after that": Swaggart and Lamb, op. cit., p. 61.

67 *"He wouldn't put on a bathing suit"*: *New York Times*, February 28, 1988.
"I would not open my eyes": Swaggart and Lamb, op. cit., p. 60.
"in the wee, still hours": Swaggart, *Armageddon*, p. 45.
"When I was a boy": Ibid., p. 32.
"More than once": Ibid., p. 45.

68 *"She was fifteen"*: John Camp interview with Swaggart, WBRZ-TV "Eyewitness News Closeup," April 13, 1988.
"the only woman I ever kissed": Ibid.
"just like Billy Graham": Irene Gilley in John Camp's documentary "Give Me That Big Time Religion," 1983.

69 *"one hit record"*: Lewis and Silver, op. cit., p. 49.
two more record-pressing plants: Roy Orbison interview in "Jerry Lee Lewis: I Am What I Am."
"How can the devil save souls?": Ibid.
"I preached that morning": Ibid. Myra Lewis has a contrary account; she says it was Sun Swaggart who preached and Myra who cried. "Jerry was deeply moved, not by what Sun had said, but by Myra's display of emotion" (Lewis and Silver, op. cit., pp. 98–99).
"I said, 'Yes, Jerry' ": "Jerry Lee Lewis: I Am What I Am"; also Swaggart and Lamb, op. cit., p. 90.

70 *still believed in Santa Claus:* Lewis and Silver, op. cit., p. 130.
He had posters made up: Interview with David Beatty, first cousin of Lewis and Swaggart. Incidentally, Beatty claims that the car Jerry Lee gave Jimmy was actually meant for him: "Jerry said, 'No, David, if I sell a million records, I'm going to buy you a car.' I made a fatal error. I told Jimmy about it."
"I have sold more long-play albums": Camp's "The Evangelist."

71 *Shawn, who was found dead:* For an account of Shawn Lewis's death and Jerry Lee's history with women, see "The Strange and Mysterious Death of Mrs. Jerry Lee Lewis," by Richard Ben Cramer in *Rolling Stone*, March 1, 1984.

73 *"A man can't serve two masters":* Tosches, op. cit., pp. 225–27.
    "Whosoever among you": Interviews with David Beatty and J. W. Whitten; also Lewis and Silver, op. cit., p. 311.
    Their paths would cross again: There are differing versions of this episode. Andy Harris told me it occurred in Dayton, which is confirmed by Swaggart in an interview with WSMV-TV. Jerry Lee Lewis, who may not be a reliable source on this matter, says it was in Baton Rouge. J. W. Whitten, Lewis's longtime manager, told me it took place in Columbus, Ohio.
    "Jerry Lee's my cousin": WSMV-TV interview.

74 *"He got power next to God":* Tosches, op. cit., p. 245.
    "If you fail": New Orleans *Times-Picayune*, April 13, 1987.
    "I must do it": Swaggart's message in his 1986 Annual Report of Jimmy Swaggart Ministries. To underline this point, Swaggart sent a printed announcement to his ministerial peers and his television competitors, which said, "God told me He would anoint only this ministry to save the world for Christ." On the other side of this declaration was a solicitation for funds (Interview with Richard Dortch, former president of the PTL Club).

76 *She would later fail a lie-detector test:* Baton Rouge *State Times*, March 17, 1988.
    "I was in the washroom": Peggy Carriere interview with Marvin McGraw, WBRZ-TV.
    slave of sexual perversion: Interviews with the Reverend James Hammill (retired) and Andy Harris. Hammill, who was present at the meeting in Springfield, surmised from Swaggart's confession that he may have been abused as a child.

77 *"Once the individual indulges":* Jimmy Swaggart, *Pornography, America's Dark Stain* (Baton Rouge: Jimmy Swaggart Ministries, 1985), pp. 11–12.
    "This is always the first mark": Swaggart, *Questions and Answers*, p. 76.
    "God is going to call me home": "Followers Come Through for Roberts," Cox News Service, March 23, 1987. Swaggart's exchange with Roberts: Camp, 1988. Swaggart's attacks on fellow preachers in his own denomination became so heated that some members of the Assemblies of God were speaking of a "Pentecostal Inquisition." In 1987, Swaggart's co-pastor of the Family Worship Center, Jim Rentz, filed charges of "doctrinal deviation" against Karl Strader, pastor of the 7,400-member Carpenter's Home Church in Lakeland, Florida, the most significant church in the AG denomination. "The reason we did it is this," Swaggart told the *Washington Post* (April 8, 1987). "Pentecostals and charismatics are two different worlds." Thus he opened a schism no one else had ever observed. "Charismatic," according to Swaggart, "can imply undue preoccupation with the gifts of the Spirit [speaking in tongues, specifically], rather than the total life-style suggested by the word 'Pentecostal.' " (*Charisma*, June 1987).

78 *Swaggart handed his Bible:* Interview with Andy Harris.
    "Rebuke before all": Baton Rouge *Morning Advocate*, March 2, 1988.
    Gorman's $90 million defamation suit: On September 13, 1991, a New Orleans jury found that Jimmy Swaggart, Jimmy Swaggart Ministries, and co-defendant Reverend Michael Indest had defamed Marvin Gorman. Gorman was awarded $1 million in personal damages and $9 million for his bankrupt ministry.
    Bakker was the darling: Andy Harris interview. On the longing for status, Richard Dortch explained it thus: "When you're raised in a church on the wrong side of

the tracks, raised to believe you're a dummy, your self-esteem is zero. A lot of AG kids were raised that way. We felt we were a bunch of dumb Holy Rollers. We were marked. We were all just scarred kids trying to find our way home." Dortch went to prison for his part in the PTL scandal (Interview with Richard Dortch.)

79   *"I don't fit in":* Jimmy Swaggart sermon, "Rebellion, Retribution, and Redemption," 1983.

  rumors that Bakker was bisexual: Andy Harris interview and CBS "Face the Nation," April 26, 1987.

  "all the corrupt preachers": New Orleans *Times-Picayune*, April 13, 1987.

80   *"Sometimes I would see him":* Debra Murphree interview with Joe Giardina, WVUE-TV, New Orleans, February 24, 1988.

  "A lot of people tell me that": Art Harris and Jason Berry, "Jimmy Swaggart's Secret Sex Life," *Penthouse*, July 1988.

  a sum reported to be in six figures: U.S. *News*, April 11, 1988.

81   *Penthouse alone was losing $1.6 million:* Savvy, November 1986.

  Pornography and Christianity are necessary opposites. This particular correspondence is touched on by the French philosopher Georges Bataille:

> Common prostitution as an institution complements the world of Christianity.
>
> Christianity has created a sacred world from which everything horrible or impure has been excluded. In its turn, low prostitution has created the contemporary profane world where men have slumped into hopeless indifference before the unclean and from which the lucid precision of the working world has been shut out.
>
> It is difficult to distinguish the workings of Christianity from the much vaster process exploited and given a coherent form by Christianity.

  (Bataille, *Erotism: Death and Sensuality*, translated by Mary Dalwood [San Francisco: City Lights Books, 1986], pp. 135–36.)

  Swaggart visited her twenty or twenty-five times: Harris and Berry, op. cit.

  "He was so cheap": Ibid.

82   *"He'd always try to talk me into":* Ibid.

  "I was on my knees, doggie-style": Ibid. Swaggart maintains he never had actual intercourse.

83   *Randy . . . had spent some time with Debra:* Ibid.

  "What do you want, Marvin?": Baton Rouge *State Times*, March 8, 1988.

84   *"poor, pitiful preacher":* Stephen Winzenburg interview.

  Let me tell you this": Swaggart sermon, "Camp Meeting."

  "cruising, looking for ladies": WBRZ-TV interview.

MADALYN O'HAIR AND GOD ALMIGHTY

90   *"false light":* Although journalists are often cautioned about the intricacies of defamation and libel, "false light portrayal" is a rather obscure feature of invasion-of-privacy law. Unlike libel, false light portrayal does not have to be defamatory, merely highly offensive, so that a reasonable person would have a right to feel injured. Examples given in standard tort law are: Person A, who is a famous poet, discovers that Person B has published a really awful poem and signed A's name to it; or a

war hero whose life becomes the subject of a movie discovers that he is shown having a romance that never happened. In both cases, the aggrieved subjects have been portrayed in a false light, although not defamed.

In the case of public figures, false light portrayal is subject to the same restrictions as libel and defamation: that is, malice and a reckless disregard for the truth must be established.

Because O'Hair did not specify any particular statements that defamed her or cast her in a false light, the defense attorneys did not take this charge very seriously.

92 *"most hated woman in America"*: *Current Biography*, January 1977, says that these are her own words, although the title was first awarded to Madalyn Murray by Ralph Ginzberg, publisher of *Fact*, in 1962. An article with the same title by Jane Howard in *Life*, July 19, 1964, made the association stick in the public mind. Six years later, Madalyn had upgraded her status to "the most hated woman in the world" (Austin *American-Statesman*, August 27, 1968).

assaulting five Baltimore policemen: The original police department records have been purged. The lowest number of policemen that Madalyn claims she assaulted—ten —comes from her October 1965 *Playboy* interview. Other figures come from the 1970 film *Madalyn* by Bob Elkins and from *Austin People Today*, December 1975. In an unpublished letter to the editor of *Texas Monthly*, dated December 24, 1988, Madalyn asserts that "I was charged with 'assault' against twelve police *as* police and with 'assault' against individual persons as the twelve police were individually named, a total of twenty-four counts of assault." According to the Baltimore *Sun* (June 21, 1964), police came to Mrs. Murray's home to retrieve a seventeen-year-old girl named Susan Abramovitz. Mrs. Murray, her elder son, William, and her mother were charged with assaulting five policemen.

refuge in a Unitarian church: Playboy interview.

ex–FBI informer: Richard O'Hair testified at a House Un-American Activities Committee investigation of communism in Detroit that in his capacity as an FBI informant he had fingered dozens of party members. He then moved to Johnson City, New York, to spy on workers in a plant that made shoes and uniforms for the Army (Austin *American-Statesman*, March 14, 1978). According to Madalyn, her former husband "was employed to break and enter into Communist and other left-wing organizations throughout New York State. He later performed the same duties for the CIA" (Letter to editor of *Texas Monthly*).

"I love a good fight": Robert Liston, "Mrs. Murray's War on God," *Saturday Evening Post*, July 11, 1964.

"I am a walking, talking personification": Austin *American-Statesman*, July 27, 1985.

"more than a million pieces of mail": Austin *American-Statesman*, July 13, 1975, and Dallas *Morning News*, August 7, 1969. See also "After 8 Years, the Madalyn O'Hair Rumor Is Strong—and Still Wrong," *Christianity Today*, January 21, 1983.

93 *"more mail than we have ever received"*: Dallas *Morning News*, January 25, 1986.

"more than just an Atheist": Madalyn O'Hair, *Why I Am An Atheist* (Austin: American Atheist Press, 1980), p. 1.

"Madalyn Murray has brought more discord": Vitali Negri, *American Rationalist*, November 1964.

petty, jealous little ex-bureaucrat: G. Richard Bozarth, "Madalyn Murray O'Hair and a Mouth That Roars," *American Rationalist*, January–February 1983.

96 *Twenty-three schools and eleven colleges: Central Texan*, September 17–30, 1970.

"Compared to most cud-chewing": Quoted in *Life*, July 19, 1964.

96 *"My degrees are primarily":* Jon Murray and Madalyn O'Hair, *All the Questions You Ever Wanted to Ask American Atheists, With All the Answers* (Austin: American Atheist Press, 1986), p. 185.

an "alphabet of degrees": Insider's Newsletter, June 1980.

"more hours in college": Bynum Shaw, "God Probably Loves Mrs. Murray," *Esquire,* October 1964.

"There is no woman": Insider's Newsletter, June 1980.

Minnesota Institute of Philosophy: Jane Conrad, *Mad Madalyn* (self-published, 1983), p. 3, and *Current Biography,* January 1977. See also *Daily Texan,* March 31, 1976, which asserts that Madalyn has "a Ph.D. in religion, a law degree and several bachelor's degrees."

never been admitted to the practice of law: "I was not been [*sic*] permitted to take the bar examination in Texas because I refused to complete that part of an application which called upon me to reaffirm a belief in a Supreme Being," Madalyn writes (Letter to editor of *Texas Monthly*).

97 *Massachusetts colony:* Liston, op. cit.

date as 1611: Insider's Newsletter, June 1980, and "About the Author" in *Why I Am An Atheist.*

Reverend Mays: According to the librarian of the Daughters of the American Revolution, a Reverend William Mays was a minister in the Jamestown colony.

"Even Madalyn's birth": William J. Murray, *My Life Without God* (Nashville: Thomas Nelson Publishers, 1982), p. 9.

her father was a wealthy contractor: According to Ann M. Loyd, librarian in the Pennsylvania department of the Carnegie Library of Pittsburgh, while the name John I. Mays does appear in the city directory, no such name appears in the Pittsburgh Blue Book or the Pittsburgh Social Register, nor is there a listing for the Pittsburgh Steel Erection Company in the city industrial directories.

"always been affluent": Insider's Newsletter, June 1980.

"The chauffeur of our Rolls-Royce": Madalyn Murray O'Hair, *An Atheist Epic: Bill Murray, the Bible, and the Baltimore Board of Education* (Austin: American Atheist Press, 1970), p. vii.

Pup opened a roadhouse: Murray, op. cit., pp. 10–11.

98 *"My father knew only steel": Poland* magazine, quoted in Shaw, op. cit.

"Nazi and a rayshist": Ibid.

"He was the only construction man": Insider's Newsletter, June 5, 1983.

"drop dead": O'Hair, *An Atheist Epic,* p. 284.

"cowed, whipped dog": Insider's Newsletter, June 5, 1983.

"I do think I have resolved": Elkins, op. cit. According to Gloria Tholen, a former employee of the American Atheist Center, Madalyn actually had a suit pending against her mother when she died.

Madalyn Mays was baptized: Murray, op. cit., p. 10.

"I was totally, completely appalled": Murray and O'Hair, op. cit., p. 82.

99 *"This means that every . . . veteran":* Ibid., p. 55.

still a virgin: O'Hair, *An Atheist Epic,* p. ix.

eloped with a steelworker: According to the Allegany (Maryland) County Clerk, Madalyn Evalyn Mays and John Henry Roths were married by George Baughman, a Methodist minister, on October 9, 1941.

served as a cryptographer: Playboy interview.

"In letters home": Murray, op. cit., p. 12.

"Mother always relished": Ibid., p. 12. Madalyn related a similar story to the Austin *American-Statesman*, September 11, 1987. "O'Hair says she learned about the wealth of the Vatican first-hand when she was in the Women's Army Corps under Gen. Dwight Eisenhower. She said a Vatican employee took her to see the wealth and personal belongings not normally seen by the visitors.

" 'The Crown of Ferdinand and Isabella was in a case, and I asked if I could try it on. The guy said no, but I said, 'Come on, let me try it on.' I tried it on and my god, my knees buckled.' "

In her 1988 unpublished letter to the editor of *Texas Monthly*, O'Hair says, "I was never stationed in Rome."

100 *"They became intimate"*: Murray, op. cit., p. 12.

"She soon learned": Ibid., p. 13.

"By this time Mother's antagonism": Ibid., p. 14.

she began calling herself Madalyn Murray: In her correspondence to the editor of *Texas Monthly*, Madalyn makes the bizarre claim "During my life, as an ardent feminist, I have always used my maiden name," although in fact she has not gone by the name Mays since 1941.

"It pleased their grandparents": Murray, op. cit., p. 20.

101 *various jobs: Playboy* interview.

ploy to persuade the Soviets: Rick Abrams, "Not in His Mother's Image," *Dallas Life*, March 13, 1983. Later, Murray told me the suit was concocted to divert attention from the fact that his brother was about to enter public school in the fall, and his birth certificate would show that he was illegitimate.

102 *"The Supreme Court has made God"* and *"This is another step"*: Quoted in "The Making of a Modern Myth," Robert E. Nordlander's speech before the eleventh annual Freedom from Religion Foundation convention, October 8, 1988.

"We find the Bible": Quoted in Murray, op. cit., p. 87.

court would have made the same decision: "Actually her case was very weak," says Ed Schempp. "She was a minor part of the case. It irritates us agnostics that she is taking full credit for the decision as an atheist" (Interview with Ed Schempp). See also William E. Collie, *"Schempp* Reconsidered: The Relation Between Religion and Public Education," *Phi Delta Kappan*, September 1983.

103 *"When we had first moved"*: O'Hair, *An Atheist Epic*, pp. 146–47.

"I just want a man": Playboy interview. Madalyn comments: "No man in the nation, at that time, held himself qualified enough to answer" (Letter to editor of *Texas Monthly*).

"both cruelty and love": Quoted in Conrad, op. cit., p. 13.

aggravated assault: Murray, op. cit., p. 193; and Abrams, op. cit.

"my mother's maniacal compaign": William J. Murray with Al Janssen, *The Church Is Not for Perfect People* (Eugene, Ore.: Harvest House, 1987), p. 36.

104 *clerical collar:* Cf. Elkins, op. cit.

prophesied by Jesus: Murray and O'Hair, op. cit., p. 48.

"Atheists do not have a 'belief system' ": Ibid., p. 134.

105 *"Everything traced has been found"*: O'Hair, *Why I Am an Atheist*, p. 38.

108 *skyrocketing rise in crimes:* According to FBI Uniform Crime Reports, the per capita incidence of murder and rape (to take two examples) has risen 97 percent and 177.8 percent, respectively, since the 1963 court decision. Violent crime and robbery had actually been declining as the sixties began, and overall crime was keeping steady with the rate of population growth. The rate of increase in these categories, plus

property crime, begins to rise in 1961, but the dramatic turn upward begins in 1963. Cf. Hugh Davis Graham and Ted Robert Gurr, *Violence in American Historical and Comparative Perspectives* (New York: Bantam Books, 1969), p. 503.

110   *"Bill simply got fed up"*: *Insider's Newsletter*, June 1980.

    "My son is disturbed": Abrams, op. cit.

111   *"He was pummeled"*: O'Hair, *An Atheist Epic*, p. 117.

    "the part I played": Austin *American-Statesman*, May 11, 1980.

    "Why do you keep calling me 'Madalyn'?": Murray, op. cit., p. 18.

112   *attempted capital murder:* Murray had fired a rifle through the door of his house when a policeman knocked. The charge was later reduced to aggravated assault. Murray pleaded guilty and received five years' probation.

    A great winged angel: Whether he knew it or not, Murray's dream replicates the famous vision of Constantine the Great as he stood on the banks of the Tiber in A.D. 312. He saw a burning cross in the sky, with the legend "In hoc signo vinces" —In this sign you will conquer. The following morning Constantine's army defeated the pagan forces defending Rome, and Christianity became the official religion of the empire.

113   *preventing . . . Buzz Aldrin from taking . . . Communion:* Interview with retired Colonel Edwin E. "Buzz" Aldrin.

    On the suit against the pope: *Daily Texan*, October 4, 1979, and interview with Bryan Lynch, former treasurer of American Atheist Center. Not all of Madalyn's suits have been in the public interest; frequently they have been launched on her own behalf or to protect her image. She sued *Screw* magazine for $6 million because it featured a nude photograph of a young woman identified as Madalyn Murray (Austin *Citizen*, July 26, 1976). A suit against Brigadier General William D. McCain and his organization, Americans United for a Sound Foreign Policy, claimed that the general violated her trademark by using her name. He had said, "If Madalyn Murray had been at Normandy, she wouldn't have let our brave boys have the comfort of a chaplain" (Pittsburgh *Press*, October 16, 1983). A similar slander suit against Billy Graham was dismissed (Murray, op. cit., p. 243). On the other hand, Madalyn has been ordered to pay $50,000 and $45,000 in two separate slander suits brought against her in Austin (*Daily Texan*, December 12, 1978).

    100,000 members: Austin *American-Statesman*, November 27, 1981.

114   *Sixty thousand or seventy thousand families:* Austin *People Today*, December 1975, and Dallas *Morning News*, May 18, 1978.

    "If I headed the atheist movement": *Texas Methodist*, August 2, 1980.

    actual membership is 2,400: The figure is confirmed by Cloe Sofikitis, a former employee of American Atheist Center: "She does not have fifty thousand members. She has twenty-two hundred to twenty-four hundred. I handled the mailing list."

    "In a continuing way": *Insider's Newsletter*, March 1984.

    "not an atheist activist": Bozarth, op. cit.

116   *"of Neapolitan extraction"*: *American Atheist*, June 1988.

    "democracy kills": Ibid.

    "I work full-time": Murray and O'Hair, op. cit., p. 136.

117   *"My most exciting victory"*: Austin *Citizen*, July 26, 1976.

    "The moment we mix politics": *Daily Texan*, April 19, 1979.

    calling herself an anarchist: Elkins, op. cit.

    contemplated a race for governor: *Daily Texan*, April 19, 1979.

    6 percent of the vote: *Insider's Newsletter*, June 1979.

considered running for president: Daily Texan, April 15, 1980.
"every cotton-picking thing": Insider's Newsletter, March 15, 1984.
119 *"what the hell":* O'Hair, An Atheist Epic, p. xi.

ANTON LAVEY: SYMPATHY FOR THE DEVIL

122 *His book* The Satanic Bible: Much of this work seems to have been plagiarized from
an obscure nineteenth-century work called *Might Is Right* by Ragnar Redbeard, a.k.a.
Arthur Desmond.
"I've never presented myself": Eugene Robinson, interview with Anton LaVey, *Birth
of Tragedy*, November 1986–January 1987.
rumors of human sacrifice: In the burgeoning literature concerning satanic activity,
see Larry Kahaner, *Cults That Kill* (New York: Warner Books, 1988); Lauren Stra-
ford, *Satan's Underground* (Eugene, Ore.: Harvest House, 1988); Judith Spencer,
Suffer the Child (New York: Pocket Books, 1989); Arthur Lyons, *Satan Wants You:
The Cult of Devil Worship in America* (New York: Mysterious Press, 1988); Carl A.
Raschke, *Painted Black: From Drug Killings to Heavy Metal—The Alarming True
Story of How Satanism Is Terrorizing Our Communities* (San Francisco: Harper &
Row, 1990); Jeffrey S. Victor, "The Spread of Satanic-Cult Rumors," *Skeptical In-
quirer*, Spring 1990; a two-part series by Robert D. Hicks, "Police Pursuit of Satanic
Crime," *Skeptical Inquirer*, Spring 1990, Summer 1990.
survivors of ritual abuse: Walter C. Young, Roberta G. Sachs, and Bennett G. Braun,
"A New Clinical Syndrome: Patients Reporting Ritual Abuse in Childhood by
Satanic Cults" *Child Abuse & Neglect* 15, no. 3 (1991); Los Angeles County Commission for Women, *Ritual Abuse: Report of the Ritual Abuse Task Force*, September
15, 1989; Sally Hill and Jean Goodwin, "Satanism: Similarities Between Patient Accounts and Pre-Inquisition Historical Sources," *Dissociation*, March 1989; and Susan
C. Van Benschoten, "Multiple Personality Disorder and Satanic Ritual Abuse: The
Issue of Credibility," *Dissociation*, March 1990.
123 Anton Szandor LaVey, *The Satanic Witch* (Los Angeles: Feral House, 1989), p. 106.
126 *"Had tail removed":* Blanche Barton, *The Secret Life of a Satanist* (Los Angeles: Feral
House, 1990), p. 22.
127 *makes no mention of a tail:* "[LaVey's mother] could not know he was a devil baby.
He had no claws, tail, horn stumps, or yellow eyes" (Burton H. Wolfe, *The Devil's
Avenger* [New York: Pyramid Books, 1974], p. 24).
came home with malaria: Barton, op. cit., p. 4.
128 *"Erotic Crystallization Inertia":* Also called "Emotional Crystallization Inertia"—the
difference, says LaVey, is that "one is more Freudian."
"Tony made sure": Barton, op. cit., p. 28.
129 *"After a short time":* Ibid., p. 29.
"You have just one defense": Wolfe, op. cit., p. 35.
"Anton would subsequently perform": Barton, op. cit., p. 33.
130 *"I knew then":* From Burton H. Wolfe's introduction to LaVey's *The Satanic Bible*
(New York: Avon Books, 1969).
131 *"whole West Adams section":* There is no West Adams section in Los Angeles, although
there is an Adams Boulevard.
"There is no God": Barton, op. cit., pp. 59–60.
134 *"According to the court hearings":* Raschke, op. cit., p. 70.

Notes

134 *"after carefully studying Anton LaVey's* Satanic Bible": Ibid., p. 60.
   Patricia Hall . . . arrested for flogging: Lyons, op. cit., p. 96.

135 *"some or a lot of faith" in satanism: Seventeen,* July 1990.

136 *later her husband:* Hicks, *Skeptical Inquirer,* op. cit., Summer 1990.
   the phenomenon of cult survivors began: Ibid.; cf. also Van Benschoten, op. cit., and Kenneth V. Lanning, "Ritual Abuse: A Law Enforcement View or Perspective," *Child Abuse & Neglect* 15, no. 3 (1991), pp. 171–73.
   In a study of thirty-seven patients: Young, Sachs, and Braun, op. cit., pp. 180–90.
   "It can't be just a coincidence": Peter Carroll, "Cult Crimes: A City Policewoman Probes the Underworld of Satanic Worship," *San Francisco* magazine, August 1987.
   about 50 percent of the MPD patients: Figures from various sources range from 20 percent to 85 percent (Carroll, op. cit.; interview with Dr. John Fleming, medical director of Cedar Springs Psychiatric Hospital in Colorado Springs).

137 *"ideological bonding mechanism":* Kahaner, op. cit., p. 249.
   "far more powerful": Raschke, op. cit., p. 39.
   "We are the new establishment": Ibid., pp. 130–31.

138 *Donald Werby, one of the wealthiest:* In 1990, Werby pleaded guilty to having sex with underage prostitutes; he was sentenced to nine months of community service and was fined $300,000.

139 *Togare was taken to the city zoo:* According to Edward M. Webber, a.k.a. Veet Mano, a publicist associated with LaVey's founding of the Church of Satan, LaVey's lion was a part of a court settlement in which Webber attached Togare after LaVey failed to pay for the publicity work Webber had performed ("Interview with the Founder of the Church of Satan," *Scroll of Set* [newsletter of the Temple of Set] 17, no. 3).

140 *The knickknacks they were contending:* Wall Street Journal, September 14, 1988.
   LaVey has often alluded to having property: "In addition to the two huge homes he maintains for his personal use in Sonoma County wine country and the hills of Hollywood in California, Anton and the Church have access to estates in Santa Barbara, California; Las Vegas, Nevada; Long Island, New York; Salzburg, Austria; Switzerland; and Bavaria" (Wolfe, op. cit., pp. 212–13). See also Fred Harden, "Anton LaVey: Disciple of the Devil," *Hustler,* December 1979; Dick Russell, "Anton LaVey: The Satanist Who Wants to Rule the World," *Argosy,* June 1975 ("the converted convent in Italy, the mansion in Bavaria, the three ocean-going salvage ships at his disposal in Belfast, and a devoted Sicilian driver . . ."); and Walt Harrington, "The Devil in Anton LaVey," *Washington Post Magazine* ("several luxurious homes and a 185-foot yacht at his disposal"—subsequently when LaVey described his yacht to me, it was only 85 feet long). After losing the palimony suit to Diane, LaVey filed personal bankruptcy to avoid losing his house. According to deed records filed in the bankruptcy proceedings, the house was actually purchased by LaVey's parents, then signed over to Anton and Diane in 1971, giving each a half-interest.

141 *"The forbidden industry":* Anton Szandor LaVey, "Pentagonal Revisionism," *The Cloven Hoof* (newsletter of the Church of Satan) 21, no. 2 (1988).
   "Like an old Duesenberg": Arthur Lyons, *The Second Coming: Satanism in America* (New York: Dodd, Mead, 1970), pp. 182–83.

142 *"It is a popular misconception":* LaVey, *The Satanic Bible,* p. 40.

143 *"When all religious faith":* Ibid., p. 45.

144 *"The villain becomes the hero":* Robinson, op. cit.
   "The best way to deal with temptation": Ibid.
   "Satanism does not advocate": LaVey, *The Satanic Bible,* p. 70.

146 *"But Sharon":* Susan Atkins with Bob Slosser, *Child of Satan, Child of God* (Jacksonville, Fla.: Logos International, 1977), p. 70.

"He did not speak of this pact": Michael A. Aquino, *The Church of Satan* (privately printed, 1983), p. 13.

"Ninth Solstice Message": Quoted and "transcribed" by Aquino, op. cit., p. A-345.

147 *"an essential, intelligent entity":* Ibid., p. A-343.

151 *a satanic wedding:* The marriage itself lasted three years and ended amicably, according to John Raymond.

"the best paid commercial": Lyons, *The Second Coming*, p. 198–99.

152 *"Kahlil Gibran with balls":* Wolfe, op. cit., p. 179.

"Mr. LaVey was furious": May Mann, *Jayne Mansfield* (New York: Pocket Books, 1974), p. 197.

156 *"I don't want to give anyone the satisfaction":* Barton, op. cit., p. 226.

WILL CAMPBELL: A PROPHET IN HIS OWN COUNTRY

158 *"In all these years":* Marshall Frady, *Billy Graham: A Parable of American Righteousness* (Boston: Little, Brown, 1979).

159 *"I have seen and known":* Will D. Campbell, *Race and the Renewal of the Church* (Philadelphia: Westminster Press, 1962), pp. 24–25.

167 *"is inhumanity, by advancing the illusion":* Marshall Frady, *Southerners* (New York: New American Library, 1980), p. 392.

170 *"But what's your actual* business?*":* Ibid., p. 377.

"Well, tough shit": Thomas L. Connelly, *Will Campbell and the Soul of the South* (New York: Continuum, 1982), p. 145.

172 *"Suddenly everything became clear":* Will D. Campbell, *Brother to a Dragonfly* (New York: Seabury Press, 1977), p. 222.

"at twenty years of a ministry": Ibid., p. 222.

Jonathan can never have died": Frye Gaillard, *Race, Rock & Religion* (Charlotte, N.C.: East Woods Press, 1982), p. 52.

"A whole bunch of my civil rights friends": Ibid., p. 52.

174 *"I think I was already beginning":* Dr. Orley B. Caudill, interviewer, *An Oral History with Will Davis Campbell, Christian Preacher*, Mississippi Oral History Program of the University of Southern Mississippi, vol. 157, 1980, p. 29.

176 *"Sure, I wanted to be a country singer":* Connelly, op. cit., p. 93.

184 *"It was a holy position":* Campbell, *Brother to a Dragonfly*, p. 76.

190 *"Joe explained":* Ibid., p. 27.

196 *"Painfully, Smith, Campbell, and the other adults":* Taylor Branch, *Parting the Waters: America in the King Years, 1954–63* (New York: Simon and Schuster, 1988), p. 394.

"We will continue our journey": Ibid., p. 450.

200 *"I believe in God":* John Egerton, *A Mind to Stay Here: Profiles from the South* (New York: Macmillan, 1970), p. 22.

MATTHEW FOX ROLLS AWAY THE STONE

204 *"In religion we have been operating":* Matthew Fox, *Original Blessing* (Santa Fe: Bear & Co., 1983), p. 26.

Notes

205 *"Matt Fox in historical costume"*: Kenneth C. Russell, "Matthew Fox's *Illuminations of Hildegard of Bingen*," in *Listening: Journal of Religion and Culture*, Spring 1989.
"hard work and creativity": Quoted as preface to Matthew Fox, "Is the Catholic Church Today a Dysfunctional Family? A Pastoral Letter to Cardinal Ratzinger and the Whole Church," *Creation*, November/December 1988.
"the more basic question": Ibid.

208 *"Even though I had the credentials"*: Mark Matousek, "Toward a Spiritual Renaissance," interview with Matthew Fox, *Common Boundary*, July–August 1990.
"How seriously can we take": Russell, op. cit.
drained of priests and nuns: These figures come from P. J. Kennedy & Sons, publishers of *The Official Catholic Directory*.

209 *"The churches have tried"*: Matousek, op. cit.

210 *"and preachers are concerned"*: Matthew Fox, "Creation Spirituality: A Personal Retrospective," *Listening: Journal of Religion and Culture*, Spring 1989.

211 *Christianity has always had a conflict*: Cf. Elaine Pagels, *Adam, Eve, and the Serpent* (New York: Random House, 1988).

212 *"I was tossed and spilled"*: St. Augustine, *Confessions*, translated by R. S. Pine-Coffin (New York: Penguin Books, 1961), book Z, chapter 2.
"a hissing cauldron of lust": Ibid., book 3, chapter 1.

214 *"If I were asked to name"*: Matthew Fox, *The Coming of the Cosmic Christ* (New York: Harper & Row, 1988), p. 163.
"Lust is a great, awesome, and wonderful beast": Ibid., p. 178.

215 *"I try. Most of the time"*: Matousek, op. cit.

216 *"One cannot speak"*: Fox, "Creation Spirituality."

217 *"blew my soul wide open"*: Ibid.
"At various times I shared": Ibid.

219 *"filled with gratitude"*: Matthew Fox, *Creation Spirituality* (HarperSanFrancisco, 1991), p. 95.

221 *"Mystical experiences abounded"*: Fox, "Creation Spirituality."

224 *"It was because of him"*: Ibid.
"We have been talking": Ibid.

227 *"pantheism says that everything is God"*: Matthew Fox interview on *Video Edition*, October 1985, produced by *Catholic Voice*, the Oakland diocesan newspaper.
"fish in water": Fox, "Creation Spirituality." Reprinted in Matthew Fox, "Is the Church Today a Dysfunctional Family? A Pastoral Letter to Cardinal Ratzinger and the Whole Church." *Creation Spirituality*, November/December 1988, p. 25.

231 *Hunthausen was not removed*: For an account of this affair, see Penny Lernoux, *People of God: The Struggle for World Catholicism* (New York: Penguin Books, 1989).

232 *"Fox's representations of historical figures"*: Tiina Allik, "Matthew Fox: On the Goodness of Creation and Finitude," *Listening: Journal of Religion and Culture*, Spring 1989.

233 *"Far from being counter-cultural"*: Roberto S. Goizueta, "Liberating Creation Spirituality," *Listening*, op. cit.
"Fox is wrong in claiming": Allik, op. cit.
"Fox may want to show": Ibid.

234 *"superficial and lacking"*: Rosemary Radford Ruether, "Matthew Fox and Creation Spirituality: Strengths and Weaknesses," *Catholic World*, July/August 1990.

Photographic Credits

ALSO BY

LAWRENCE WRIGHT

Remembering Satan

"The most powerful and disturbing true crime narrative to appear since Truman Capote's *In Cold Blood*."

—*Time*

At once a true psychological detective story, a family tragedy, and a mordant comedy about what happens when modern psychiatry succumbs to hysterias as old as Salem, *Remembering Satan* is an inquest into the controversial case of Paul Ingram, a sheriff's deputy in Olympia, Washington, whose grown daughters suddenly accused him of having molested them in the course of demonic rites. As Lawrence Wright traces the tale of this shattered family, he raises profound questions about the phenomenon of "recovered memory."

Nonfiction/0-679-75582-9

Available at your local bookstore, or call toll-free:
1-800-793-2665 (credit cards only).

Printed in the United States
by Baker & Taylor Publisher Services